TEXAS A&M UNIVERSITY PRESS College Station

Dan K. Utley & Cynthia J. Beeman

Foreword by Truett Latimer

History Ahead

Stories beyond the Texas Roadside Markers

LIBRARY OF CONGRESS CATALOGING-IN-PUBLICATION DATA

Utley, Dan K.
    History ahead : stories beyond the Texas roadside markers / Dan K. Utley
and Cynthia J. Beeman ; foreword by Truett Latimer. — 1st ed.
      p. cm.
    Includes bibliographical references and index.
    ISBN-13: 978-1-60344-151-3 (flexbound with flaps : alk. paper)
    ISBN-10: 1-60344-151-4 (flexbound with flaps : alk. paper)
    1. Historical markers—Texas.   2. Texas—History.   3. Texas—History—
Anecdotes.   4. Texas—Description and travel.   5. Texas—Biography.
6. Geographical perception—Texas.   I. Beeman, Cynthia J.   II. Title.
F387.U85   2010
976.4—dc22
2009023264

"My spirit soars over vast distances and through eons of time."

Dedicated to our friend and mentor,
CURTIS D. TUNNELL (1934–2001), *a tireless time traveler who freely shared his boundless love of history with us. He sought the stories where they existed.*

Contents

Foreword

I n 1932, Texans approved a constitutional amendment creating the Texas Centennial Commission. Among other things, it provided that every county in the state would receive a historical marker indicating its date of establishment and the source of its name. The simple markers placed under the program were made of Texas pink granite from Marble Falls with a descriptive brass plaque on top. Other granite markers approved as part of the centennial provided basic information on myriad historical topics related to Texas independence.

In 1953, the Texas Legislature, through passage of Senate Concurrent Resolution 55, created the Texas State Historical Survey Committee. The resolution charged the committee with a wide range of tasks to accomplish, but they provided no state appropriation whatsoever to help them do so. The first organizational meeting occurred in Austin on November 17, 1953, and the commissioners selected James E. Wheat of Woodville as chairman. Eighteen prominent Texans who each possessed their own set of credentials in Texas history had been appointed by then Governor Allan Shivers, who addressed the organizational meeting. Among the members was Dr. Rupert N. Richardson of Abilene, known as the "Dean of Texas historians" and the author of such works as *Texas: The Lone Star State; The Comanche Barrier to South Plains Settlement;* and *Colonel Edward M. House: The Texas Years.* He was also my history professor at Hardin-Simmons College and someone whose sense of Texas history I greatly respected.

It was not until the early 1960s that the committee received authorization to "prescribe, approve and erect historical markers," thus ending an extended void when no Texas markers were placed. It was about this time that a gentleman from Odessa was appointed to the committee. He was John Ben Shepperd, a native of Gladewater who had served as president of the United States Junior Chamber of Commerce and later as attorney general of the state. At the time of his appointment as a commissioner, he was serving as general counsel to Noel and Rodman in Odessa and had a lot of time and resources available. Shepperd soon became chairman of the committee, and the marker program began to progress at a much faster pace. He came up with a plan that he called RAMPS, for the Recordation, Appreciation, Marking, Preservation, and Survey of Texas History. Among other ambitious portions of the plan, it called for the placing of five thousand Official Texas Historical Markers in five years. The aggressiveness of this goal was not without its detractors, who worried that placing almost three markers a day would lead to inaccuracies in the text of the markers. Nevertheless, General Shepperd prevailed, and according to his count, the committee soon met its early marker goals. From that point on, Texas was in the lead nationally. Now Texas has more than thirteen thousand markers, far more than any other state. The Texas program is the most successful in the nation with one hundred to two hundred markers placed each year.

It is appropriate, though, that the program has achieved a certain maturity through its relatively brief history. From the beginning, it was the thought and indeed the thrust of the program that this was what Dr. Richardson often called "the people's history." Unlike programs in other states, the marker program of Texas begins at the local level as county historical commissions work in partnership with the state to record and mark important aspects of their local history. Importantly, Official Texas Historical Markers interpret history, help preserve sites, and serve as focal points for heritage tourism in each of our 254 counties.

Historians Dan K. Utley and Cynthia J. Beeman are uniquely qualified to tell the stories behind our historical markers as they have both served as researchers, writers, and directors of the state marker program. Between the two of them they represent a continuum of the program that reaches from 1979 to 2007. In order to write this book, the authors began with the basic marker texts and then conducted their own research to verify the information, expand the stories, and then analyze them within broader historical contexts and themes. The purpose of the book is to explore the diverse history of Texas as told through its state markers—

"the people's history." Topics include important aspects of cultural, social, architectural, military, business, gender, and political history.

Texas history will be served well—and understood better—through the publication of this book, and we are indebted to the authors for their tremendous effort in bringing this unique historical approach to reality.

TRUETT LATIMER, *Houston*
Executive Director, Texas Historical Commission, 1965–81

Acknowledgments

We both enjoy hiking, and it has long been an important part of our friendship. Together, and with others, we have traveled countless trails of Texas from the mountains of West Texas and the canyons of the Edwards Plateau to the Piney Woods of deep East Texas. The time we have spent on those trails has always been productive, and we welcomed the opportunities to escape the pressures of our shared work in public history to think, plan, and unwind. No time on the trail, it seemed, was ever wasted, and we always returned to the tasks ahead with new resolve. To us, this project has been a bit like a through-hike on a meandering, braided trail, complete with hills—lots of hills—a few valleys, some confusing side trails, interesting fellow hikers, and yes, even a few critters along the way.

As befits the analogy, we began planning this book in earnest at Bastrop State Park in early December 2007. Sitting beneath tall pine trees at the edge of the park's small lake, we mapped out where our journey would take us, as well as those who might join us by reading the stories we had to tell. For the most part we have managed to stay on course and on schedule, thanks in large part to our esteemed guide, Dr. Mary Lenn Dixon at Texas A&M University Press. We could not imagine setting out on this or any similar journey without such friendly, professional, and persuasive guidance. She would be quick to note, however—and we would certainly concur—that she is part of a larger team effort that has long supported writers and promoted new scholarship, and so we duly acknowledge the excellent work of the entire press staff. They are without equal.

The nature of our journey caused us to focus our initial research efforts on files and photos associated with the Texas Historical Commission (THC), the state agency charged with administering the Official Texas Historical Marker Program. As a result, we have many staff members to thank individually, including: Bratten Thomason, Bob Brinkman, Greg Smith, Charles Sadnick, and William McWhorter of the History Programs Division, which we used to call home; Roland Pantermuehl of the Archeology Division; Brett Cruse of the Historic Sites Division; and Stan Graves of the Division of Architecture. Special thanks go to the THC's indefatigable Kimberly Gamble, who oversees the marker files, among her many other tasks, and answers all inquiries with great humor, enthusiasm, and shared interest.

Those outside the THC who provided particularly noteworthy research assistance include: Sherrie Kline Smith of the Kansas City Public Library; Dorothy Schoenhals of Follett, Texas, who is associated with both the Lipscomb County Historical Commission and the Wolf Creek Heritage Museum; Tom Scott of the Fannin County Historical Museum in Bonham, Texas; Dr. Char Miller of Trinity University, San Antonio; Mildred and W. F. Bohlmann of Schulenburg, Texas; Archie Scott of Austin; Nancy Dunn of the Artesia Historical Museum and Art Center, Artesia, New Mexico; Nan Marie Lawler, University of Arkansas Library, Fayetteville; Larry N. Jones, former curator for the Smithsonian Institution who now enjoys retirement near Waynesboro, Pennsylvania; Karen Fort of the McAllen Heritage Center, McAllen, Texas; James Hull, recently retired from the Texas Forestry Service in College Station; Jonathan Gerland, director of the History Center, Diboll; and last but not least, our friend and fellow rock-and-roller forever, Dr. Archie P. McDonald.

For photos and images we relied on a number of people to help us find our way through the thicket of formats that ranged from historic black and white copies to the electronic world of tiffs and jpegs. Our guides included: Elizabeth Heath, Ward County Historical Commission and Million Barrel Museum, Monahans, Texas (she also provided research assistance); Fred Collins, Kleb Woods Nature Preserve, Tomball; Lauren Ham, Museum of the Gulf Coast, Port Arthur, Texas; Rita Patteson, Armstrong Browning Library, Baylor University; Ari Wilkins, Dallas Public Library; Patrick Lemelle, University of Texas at San Antonio Institute of Texan Cultures; Cynthia Ostroff, Yale University Library; Ray Gouldsberry of Schulenburg, Texas; Ginger Trotter of the Texas Forestry Museum, Lufkin; and

Linda Russell, director, Burton Cotton Gin Museum, Burton, Texas. Special thanks to John Anderson, archivist extraordinaire of the Texas State Library and Archives Commission, and to Carolyn Kozo Cole, of the Los Angeles Public Library in California, who set a high standard through her kind assistance. And finally—and sadly—we recognize the generous assistance of our friend and colleague, the late Bill Stein, former director of the Nesbitt Memorial Library, Columbus, Texas.

This book is a positive reflection of good times we enjoyed in the employ of the Texas Historical Commission. We were blessed to have worked there during what we truly believe were "golden years." Part of what made that association so memorable, and also what led us to believe others might be interested in the stories behind the marker stories, were our longtime friends and fellow historians who toiled with us in the finely focused field of interpretation known as the Official Texas Historical Marker Program. We would not have made it this far without the support of our valued teammates, particularly Frances A. Rickard, who used her editorial eagle eye in reviewing the manuscript; James W. Steely, always the go-to guy on matters of Texas history; and Claire Williams Martindale, who took over the program at a pivotal point in its evolution.

As with all books, we feel certain, there are a number of "spiritual guides"—individuals who provided those intangibles of understanding, insight, encouragement, inspiration, and moral support. First and foremost in that regard are our families, who through generations of living in Texas have instilled in us a strong sense of place and a curiosity about what makes its past so special. Thanks to Peggy Rose Dyer Beeman, who conveyed her love of history to her children, and George Edward Beeman (1919–2003), who stopped the car countless times on family vacations to read historical markers. And thanks to Mabel Prater Utley (1913–89), who valued family history, and Festus John Utley Jr. (1912–71), who believed, as Rudyard Kipling once noted, "If history were taught in the form of stories, it would never be forgotten." And no mention of family support would be complete without recognition of Debby Davis Utley—friend to Cynthia and wife to Dan. She was the first to provide valued encouragement and personal space, and in the early morning hours when she no doubt preferred to sleep, also the first to hear many of the stories included herein.

And finally, our sincerest thanks to the county historical commissions of Texas, both past and present. With little political or financial support and often even less public recognition, they nevertheless work tirelessly to preserve the rich and diverse history of the state for future generations. They serve as the foundation for the Texas marker program, providing the frontline analysis and review that allows the state staff to turn their history into marker text. The county historical commissions, in effect, blaze the trails for others to follow, and those who enjoy reading the roadside markers of Texas owe them a debt of gratitude for their unselfish work. Their efforts made this book possible, but more importantly, they provided direction for our collective understanding of how we move *History Ahead* on that ever-moving continuum of time. We rest today at the end of this particular trail in the shade of trees they planted long ago. Thanks.

Introduction

istorical markers are iconic elements of the modern American cultural landscape, and perhaps nowhere is that statement more evident than in Texas, a state that truly values its unique history. Official Texas Historical Markers can be found in each county of the state, where they serve to preserve and interpret a unique and diverse heritage. Texas boasts more state-approved markers than any other state, and taken in their totality they represent one of the largest and most far-reaching public collections of a people's history in the nation. Included within their brief inscriptions are the defining components of cultures and societies, as well as their successes and failures, hopes and follies, and ability to endure. As with all history, there are also the unmistakable lessons from the past, subject of course to individual interpretation. And if done right, the inscriptions offer more than simple stories simply told. Reaching beyond the realm of trivia, a well-written marker should speak to relevance, purpose, and significance, and should challenge readers to experience the past in context or to reconsider oft-told tales through new frames of reference. Contrary to what some might believe, history is not static; it is dynamic, renewable, and ever-changing.

The Official Texas Historical Marker Program, like the history it serves to preserve and record, is also evolutionary. That is perhaps to be expected with such a public process that by its nature continually changes to meet new societal needs and interests, as well as government objectives. At the frontline of the process are the local historians, marker sponsors, and county historical commissions who conduct the basic research and gather the supporting documentation required for marker application. Once they have reviewed and possibly debated the merits of the proposed topics, the commissions pass approved applications along to the Texas Historical Commission. There, public historians and governor-appointed commissioners evaluate the work within pre-scribed guidelines, verify the accuracy and local analysis as best they can, and determine the overarching significance of proposed topics within broader statewide objectives. The state and county are partners in the process, even sharing financial support for the program, and if all goes well—and it most often does—they eventually concur on the matter of eligibility. At that point, state historians draft the marker inscriptions by condensing multiple-page narratives down to only a few sentences that hopefully convey relevance, diversity, integrity, and context, as well as a good story, to the general public. It is a complex process with many layers of involvement and review but one that plays out successfully hundreds of times a year in all regions of the state. And it has worked successfully for almost half a century, with no end in sight. In Texas, history remains in good supply.

The purpose of this book is to offer readers, in effect, a reversal of the standard marker process. That is, we began our journey with the marker texts and then worked backward, applying new sources and perspectives to enlarge the stories and then connect them to other aspects of history. The criteria for the stories we have included here are relatively simple. The marker stories had to be, first and foremost, compelling in nature, providing interesting areas worthy of exploration by authors and readers alike. They also had to be documented with fresh resources—part of that ever-changing aspect of the past that continually draws historians and history enthusiasts. The topics we chose allowed us to share some of the lesser-known, but not less significant, stories that speak to the seemingly limitless diversity of culture and geography that makes our state so unique historically. Ultimately, though, we had to follow Shakespeare's lead and be true to ourselves. So, these stories reflect our own interests and inquisitiveness. We had fun exploring these topics, and we hope that shows in the final product. We wrote these stories for ourselves, at least initially, but we also wrote them for the countless travelers who have stopped to read the many markers of Texas and wondered if there was more to the story. There is; there always is. We hope you agree.

PART ONE
A TEXAS SENSE OF PLACE

A Texas Sense of Place

🌐 CHAPTER

✳ Sidebar

Map by Molly O'Hallovan

1

SAVING ELMER'S WOODS

A reclusive man who lived in the woods, Elmer never bothered anyone. All he wanted was to be left alone with nature, but progress and the growing suburban sprawl near Houston intruded on his simple life. His story might have been just one of many in a long string of cautionary tales relating the loss of once-pristine wilderness to suburban development. Instead, it is the story of the simple wishes of a quiet man who loved trees and animals and of the unlikely alliance of environmentalists, lawyers, and government agents that ultimately saved his island of wilderness on the outskirts of one of the largest cities in the United States.

Elmer Kleb, who spoke with the inflection of his German ancestors, lived his entire life in a small house in the woods northwest of Houston. His great-grandfather, Conrad Kleb, brought his family to Texas in 1846. Sailing from Wehrda, Germany, they arrived at the Port of Galveston on October 29 of that year, having immigrated under the auspices of the Adelsverein (*Verein zum Schutze deutscher Einwanderer in Texas*, or Society for the Protection of German Immigrants in Texas). Conrad's wife, Elisabeth Bolender Kleb, along with two young daughters, died either during the voyage or shortly after the family reached Texas. By 1850, Conrad, his new wife, Elisabeth Glass Kleb, and four sons were living near Rose Hill (Spring Creek), a community of German immigrants near present Tomball in northwest Harris County. In 1854, for $125, Conrad Kleb purchased 107 acres out of the Abraham Roberts Survey and established a family farm. Edward Kleb, son of Conrad's oldest son, Andrew, and a first-generation Texan, married Minnie Willmann, and the couple made a living off the farm Edward inherited, growing vegetables and cotton and raising chickens, cattle, and sheep.

They built a small frame house about 1896, and in 1903 they purchased additional acreage to enlarge their farm. Edward and Minnie Kleb had two children: a son, Elmer, born September 20, 1907, and a daughter, Myrtle, who was born in 1913 and died at age 23 in 1936.[1]

According to family sources, Elmer Kleb, nicknamed "Lumpy," attended school in nearby Rose Hill, but he never fit in with the other students and dropped out after either the fourth or seventh grade (family sources differ on the year). Even at a young age, he preferred to remain close to home and reportedly rarely left the family land. Embracing the nature that surrounded him, he half-heartedly helped his parents with farming chores, but he spent most of his time roaming the woods, communing with the birds and wild animals that populated the Kleb farm. Edward Kleb died in 1951, and Elmer, by then in his forties, assisted his mother with the farm until her death in 1967. The sole heir to the family estate, Elmer Kleb ceased farming operations and instead began to plant more trees to shelter his beloved birds and animals. Gradually becoming more and more reclusive, he lived simply in the house in which he was born. Having no income, he stopped paying utility bills and taxes, and by the early 1980s he was living in a house with no electricity or running water—the well had run dry years before—on land heavily encumbered by delinquent taxes.[2]

Contentedly planting trees and tending to the birds and animals on his land—including a wounded vulture that he nursed back to health and that lived in the house with him—Elmer Kleb took little notice of the lack of utilities or the growing tax bill. Relatives—who pointedly described him as a recluse, not a hermit, saying he was happy to speak with anyone who visited—occasionally provided him with food, water, and money. They tried to convince him to sell a portion of the land to pay the overdue taxes, but he steadfastly refused, saying he wanted to donate all the land to the Houston chapter of the Audubon Society for a wildlife refuge. With an outstanding tax bill, however, he could not legally donate the property.[3]

As several taxing entities—Harris County as well as two local school districts—attempted to collect payment, Kleb's plight and

Elmer Kleb, 1913. Nicknamed "Lumpy," Elmer Kleb never fit in at school and preferred to roam the woods of his family's land. Taken the same year his younger sister was born, this formal portrait contrasts sharply with the backwoods life he later led. Courtesy Kleb Woods Nature Center

living situation gradually gained the attention of environmental activists and the media, including local newspapers, the *New York Times,* and the British television network ITV, which sent a film crew to Houston to produce a half-hour documentary about him entitled "Preserving Elmer." Describing Kleb as "a small, spry man with tangled gray hair and a long gray beard" and calling him "a fading American archetype of the rural eccentric," reporters wrote sympathetic stories about him and his frustrated relatives' efforts to prevent foreclosure of his land. "He's so in love with the birds and the bees and the buzzards that he won't sell an acre of land to pay his taxes so he can keep the rest of it," a cousin told the *New York Times.* "How do you explain someone like that?"[4] Finally, the courts stepped in, declared Kleb incompetent to handle his own affairs, and appointed an attorney to represent his interests. While Kleb still wanted his land to go to the Audubon Society, and society members launched a fundraising campaign to help pay off the back taxes, it soon became clear that course of action was not feasible. As plans to sell a portion of the land progressed, a survey crew used clear-cutting methods while plotting the property boundaries, angering the quiet man of the woods. "They cut my grapevine," he told a reporter. "They didn't have to do that."[5]

Responding to numerous public inquiries and pleas to find a way to preserve the land, Kleb's attorney worked with the Harris County commissioner in whose district the property was located, as well as representatives of the Trust for Public Lands and officials with the Texas Parks and Wildlife Department (TPWD) to explore options. In 1991, with a grant from TPWD, Harris County purchased the land, paid the $737,500 tax bill, and set up a trust fund to take care of Elmer Kleb for the remainder of his life. According to the terms of the sale, he could continue living in his house in the woods, and while plans to turn the property into a nature preserve would begin, they would not infringe on the land immediately surrounding the cottage. The first phase of the Kleb Woods Nature Preserve opened to the public in 1994, with picnic areas and group camping facilities. Elmer Kleb continued to live peaceably on the land until July 5, 1999, when he died at age 91. His obituary in the *Houston Chronicle* detailed his colorful life and the efforts to pre-

Elmer Kleb, circa 1988. Surrounded by rusting farm equipment, a tumble-down house, and his beloved trees and animals, Elmer Kleb attracted worldwide media attention when he refused to sell his land to satisfy delinquent taxes. Courtesy Kleb Woods Nature Center.

serve his woods and noted his burial in a family plot at the historic Roberts Cemetery (about two miles west of the farm).[6]

After Kleb's death, the county began transforming the remaining acreage into a nature preserve and county park and hired Houston architect Graham B. Luhn to draw up plans to restore the four-room family house. A fairly unremarkable structure in terms of architectural style according to Luhn, it nevertheless stands as a good example of a nineteenth-century vernacular farmhouse that retains its original form, design, and materials. In addition, it possesses historical significance as the home of a family associated with German immigration to Texas and in the fact that it remained in the same family for more than a century. Luhn deter-

*Kleb Family Home, 2008. Carefully restored following Elmer Kleb's death,
the house now serves as a visitor center and museum at the Kleb Woods
Nature Center. The Texas Historical Commission designated it a Recorded
Texas Historic Landmark in 2006. Photograph by Cynthia J. Beeman*

mined the house was in good structural condition, with minimal
changes over the years for wiring and plumbing. (The only interior
plumbing fixture was a cold-water faucet in the kitchen that connected to a pipe running to the well.) Carefully documented with
regard to construction materials and interior finishes, the simple
frame house underwent a complete restoration and now serves as
an element of the park's living history farm. In 2006, the Texas Historical Commission designated the Kleb Family House a Recorded
Texas Historic Landmark and placed a historical marker at the site
to convey the property's unique history.[7]

The Kleb Woods Nature Preserve offers the public an opportunity to experience nature in Elmer's woods. With hiking trails, picnic areas, camping facilities, a demonstration garden based on Kleb family letters and documents, and artifacts from the time of the Kleb family occupation on display in the visitor center, the nature preserve has become a popular destination for families, birding enthusiasts, and groups such as the Master Naturalists organization.[8]

At times seemingly oblivious to the frenetic activity of the environmentalists, attorneys, relatives, and government officials that ultimately decided the fate of his land, the reclusive Elmer Kleb nevertheless managed to retain his home and his woods, and the nature preserve he envisioned became a reality. An attorney who represented him in his competency hearing told a newspaper reporter, "He had these clear, clear blue eyes. Everybody thought he was a crazy old man, and he wasn't."[9]

MARKER LOCATION: 20301 Mueschke Road, Tomball

ROBERTS CEMETERY

The final resting place of Elmer Kleb and his family, the Roberts Cemetery has a storied history of its own. Located about two miles west of Kleb Woods Nature Preserve, the cemetery is on land once owned by Abraham (Abram) Roberts (1773–1850), a member of Stephen F. Austin's "Old Three Hundred" colony who brought his family to Texas in the 1820s, and from whom members of the Kleb family later purchased land. The small settlement of New Kentucky that grew up around Roberts's homestead attracted numerous German immigrant families in the 1840s, at which time the name changed to Spring Creek; it later became Rose Hill or Rosehill, named for P. W. Rose, another pioneer settler. Burials in the cemetery, which began as a family graveyard, date to the 1850s and include those of Roberts family members, German pioneers, and members of the Montgomery family, who operated a large plantation in the area prior to the Civil War. Also known as the "Old Roberts Burial Ground," the original two-acre site and an additional acre officially became a community cemetery in 1919. A separate African American cemetery noted as Roberts Cemetery in some records is located nearby on land Abraham Roberts provided for slaves on the Montgomery plantation. The Texas Historical Commission placed an Official Texas Historical Marker at the Roberts Cemetery in 1997.

MARKER LOCATION

Roberts Cemetery Road, 0.4 mi. N of FM 2920, Tomball

Sources: Roberts Cemetery Official Texas Historical Marker file, Texas Historical Commission, Austin (hereafter cited as THC marker files); Claudia Hazlewood, "Rose Hill, Texas," *The New Handbook of Texas*, vol. 5, ed. Ron Tyler (Austin: Texas State Historical Association, 1996), p. 680 (hereafter cited as *New Handbook of Texas*).

2 "WHILE YOU ARE HESITATING OTHERS ARE BUYING – ACT TO-DAY!"

The American dream of home ownership and prosperity brought thousands of immigrants to Texas in the late nineteenth and early twentieth centuries. The expansion of the country's railroad system following the Civil War opened up vast territories for settlement, and railroad company promotional efforts resulted in a new wave of real estate development and population shifts as families relocated from the cold winters of the North and Midwest to the more temperate environs of the Southwest. Settlement inevitably followed the railroads, and whole towns sprang up along the rail lines and farm belts as land promoters offered the prospect of new and exciting homes, and latter-day pioneers struck out to find their fortunes and sink their roots in fertile soil. As one historian has noted, "For the railroads Texas became an object to be advertised. . . . Texas was the 'Empire State,' the 'Winter Garden,' the land of the Homestead Exemption, and the 'Eldorado' for farmers, according to the railroad brochures produced in abundance."[1] With such superlatives luring potential land buyers, it is not surprising that, along with reputable companies and legitimate real estate ventures, unscrupulous and self-serving salesmen also got on board the immigration train. South Texas, including the grassland prairies not far inland along the Gulf Coast, appealed to a number of land promoters, and several towns in rural Colorado County trace their beginnings to the hopeful dreams of settlers from the Midwest.

Chesterville, in southeastern Colorado County near the Wharton County line, dates to 1894, when a Chicago land developer named John Linderholm bought up 60,000 acres and, as was the case with most of these land promotion schemes, transported potential customers from the Midwest to the South Texas coastal plains on special excursion trains. Advertisements boasted "40 Acres a Living; 80 Acres Comfort; 160 Acres Wealth" and featured photographs of local farming results as well as testimonials from successful farmers.[2] The new town soon boasted a post office, about twenty businesses including the *Chesterville News* newspaper, a school, and several churches. The surrounding land, however, was not the miraculous farmland the promoters advertised, and the town remained small, with many families returning to their former homes up north. Even the Linderholms sold out and returned to Chicago.

Promoters touted Rock Island, founded in 1896 in the southwest portion of Colorado County on the Texas and New Orleans Railroad line, as "a lush tropical paradise." With initial settlement by about three dozen families, the town's population peaked at five hundred in the 1920s. Primary businesses that supported area farmers included a creamery and a fig canning and preserving plant.[3] To the consternation of many citizens in the early twentieth century, the Rock Island Improvement Company, a group of businessmen in the town, moved several buildings to nearby Garwood. Settled in the 1890s, Garwood had an economy based largely on rice farming and boasted a school, post office, churches, and a hotel by the turn of the twentieth century. It, too, attracted land promoters, and in 1906, literature claiming outstanding crops of oranges and other fruits brought in buyers who purchased land sight unseen. However, the new settlers soon realized the claims were fraudulent, with the photographs taken elsewhere, and most left to return to their former homes or try their luck elsewhere. The rice economy and the town's location on the Gulf, Colorado, and Santa Fe Railway enabled it to survive, if not flourish, and today Garwood remains a viable small town in the county.

Founded in the late 1880s, the town of Cheetham was not platted until 1896. Its location on the San Antonio and Aransas Pass Railway line supported the primary local product of cordwood, which was shipped to market by rail. Although also promoted to midwestern farmers about 1906, the town did not see any appreciable changes from those efforts and essentially disappeared by the mid-twentieth century.[4] The nearby community of Sheridan, on the other hand, enjoyed a more prosperous history. The town began when its namesake, early settler Hugh Sheridan, sold thousands of acres in 1908 to the San Antonio Loan and Securities Company, which in turn joined with the San Antonio and Aransas Pass Railway to divide the land into small farms and market it through midwestern advertising and excursion trains. Farmers in the Sheridan area, unlike those near other promotional towns in Colorado County, were moderately successful in their endeavors, with figs, potatoes, strawberries, cucumbers, and melons the primary crops. The Sheridan Fig Preserving Company shipped goods by rail to markets throughout the country, and by 1914 the town included numerous businesses, a post office, a hotel, a park, a newspaper, and a population of 150.[5] The Sheridan oil and gas field, discovered in the 1940s, assured the area's economic survival, although the farms that started the community gave way to mineral production.

Most promotional towns in Colorado County survived with at least a modicum of stability. Perhaps the most intriguing story, though, concerns one that lasted only a few years—Provident City—the site of which was commemorated with an Official Texas Historical Marker in 1986. Compared to the mythical Scottish town of Brigadoon by a local writer, Provident City had a colorful, if brief, history.[6] The Provident Land Company of Kansas City, Missouri, developed the town in an area of southwest Colorado County known as the Goldenrod Prairie. According to local citizens, however, the whole Provident City endeavor was nothing more than a well-organized real estate scam.

A profile of the development company in a 1911 Kansas City business directory featured a photograph showing a field of fig trees in Texas and the following description of the company's activities:

> A large per cent of the development which is being made in the Southwest is directed from Kansas City and one of the leading companies is the Provident Land Company. . . . This company is interested in colonization lands in Southwestern Texas, where there is a greater diversity of soils and a more

equable climate than any other part of the world. With forty thousand acres in the most productive section of this country, they offer tracts for colonization purposes in suitable sizes, and their proposition should open the eyes of capital to the brilliant opportunities that are offered in this—the most rapidly developing part of the United States. It is a well known fact that one good investment is worth a lifetime of labor, and this statement supplemented by the fact that land is the basis of wealth, should be sufficient incentive to the man who earns a modest income to invest a portion of his earnings in lands, and there is no better opportunity than offered by Texas lands, and the fact that this company owns the cream of the holdings now unsettled, together with the fact that they are a reliable, old established and highly rated firm whose officers are noted for their personal integrity and reliability renders their offices a most desirable medium through which to get acquainted with conditions in the Gulf Coast Country of Texas.[7]

Local sources maintain the company bought up the land purely to take advantage of gullible and unsuspecting land purchasers and that land agents used high pressure and dishonest sales tactics to lure customers who, upon arriving from out-of-state to claim the land they had bought sight unseen, found "some of the poorest farm land in the state." The Provident Land Company purchased the Goldenrod Prairie property in 1909, and by 1910 the town was surveyed and a plat map filed in the county clerk's office.[8] The company built a hotel in nearby Ganado—the closest railroad town approximately twenty miles away in neighboring Jackson County—to house potential land buyers, and sales agents transported them in festive surreys to view the Provident City land offerings. The sellers assured prospective settlers that a rail line under construction would soon offer passenger and freight service at Provident City on a route that would link to the Santa Fe line at Glen Flora in Wharton County. The line was surveyed and a portion of the roadbed built, but the project was never completed, leaving Provident City without a vital transportation route. Nevertheless, scores of families succumbed to the sales pitches and bought land

Provident Land Company office, circa 1910. Company agents transported potential customers from the rail station in nearby Ganado to its property on Goldenrod Prairie in Colorado County. Families from the Midwest traveled to Texas on special excursion trains to view and purchase land touted by the company as the "finest place ever seen." Crane postcard view, courtesy Texas State Library and Archives Commission

to establish farms, and the enterprise showed early signs of success. The company also built a hotel in Provident City to house its customers, and within a few years the town thrived and exhibited all the hallmarks of a burgeoning community.

Among the local businesses were grocery and general stores, a bank, blacksmith, harness shop, feed store, lumber company, furniture store and undertaker, meat market, restaurant, drugstore, jewelry store, the *Provident City Times* newspaper, and the Blue Goose Saloon. A post office, sawmill, canning factory, and broom factory also served the area, and the Baptists and Methodists built churches. Miss Edna Barnes and Miss Zou Urguhart taught pupils in a two-story, four-room schoolhouse. The Provident City Commercial Club promoted local businesses, and a Woodmen of the World fraternal lodge provided community service. The town even

Provident City Hotel, circa 1911. Built to impress and house potential land buyers, this hotel operated by the Provident Land Company served as the center of operations for the promotional town. A wide wraparound porch supported by Doric columns and carved balusters provided a pleasant gathering place for guests. Crane postcard view, courtesy Texas State Library and Archives Commission

fielded a baseball team that played other towns in a South Texas amateur league.[9] At its peak, Provident City's population reached 500.

The Homefinder, a monthly magazine published in Kansas City by the Provident Land Company "devoted to the interests of the farmer, fruit grower, truck gardener and investor, with especial reference to the Provident Tract—Gulf Coast Country of Texas" continued to sing the praises of the development and did not let up on the hard sell approach that enticed families to move to Texas. The September 1911 issue featured photographs of fruit orchards, rice fields, sugar cane, corn, and other vegetable fields, as

Provident City Brand Tomatoes. During its brief history, the town of Provident City supported several local businesses and industries, including a canning factory. This can of tomatoes became a souvenir of the town, passed down through several generations of one local family. Courtesy Nesbitt Memorial Library, Columbus.

well as images of Provident City homes. Headlines touted claims such as "Finest Place Ever Seen—Everybody Satisfied," "Land and Climate Excellent," "Big Cotton Crop Means Era of Prosperity," and "Corn Yields from 70 to 100 Bushels per Acre in the Coast Country of Texas."

But while a few farmers seemed to be making a go of it, many others were discovering the farmland was not as productive as they expected, and their modest spreads could not support their families. Just two years into the venture, *The Homefinder* revealed doubts rising in Provident City. The company's magazine began to sound a bit desperate. A message "To the Prospective Buyer" included a plea: "If there is anything we can do to make the matter plainer to you, we will do it. Tell us what your objections are and we will try to clear up your doubts. We want to hear from you; in fact, we need your co-operation in this, for it might be possible that several things of vital importance to you were not properly explained in our literature or by our representative. Give us this one chance to defend ourselves and give you what is your right to have—the facts in the case." At the same time, in large print in a box on another page, an ad spoke to the company's desperation to sell its land; it practically screamed, "While You are Hesitating Others are Buying—Act To-Day!"[10]

Dissatisfaction and financial troubles took their toll on Provident City. Farm families began leaving in droves. The bank went into receivership. And despite a big public event celebrating the commencement of the grading of land, the promised railroad spur never materialized, so the struggling farmers could not get the few crops they managed to grow to market. Local newspapers had reported in May 1911 "the rapid growth of the community is still progressing," but a scant two years later the dream was over. In July 1913, under the headline "Provident City 'Boom,'" a writer for the *Hallettsville New Era* relayed a conversation with H. M. Crabb, a leading citizen of the nearby community of Seclusion:

> A reporter asked him of the status of Provident City and he says that this boom city is now practically a dream city. Everybody that was financially able to leave has shook its dust from his or her feet, while the few that still remain are there only because they are as yet not able to get away. Tar and feathers would be too good for the real estate sharks that were responsible for this wholesale robbery of poor fellows from Kansas, Missouri, and Oklahoma and other states who bought this land "sight unseen" on the flattering representations of the sharks aforesaid. One victim told the writer only a few weeks ago that he had been "roped in" by the land agents, after seeing some moving pictures of the wonderful Provident City country at a moving picture show in a Kansas town, the smooth agents having of course "doctored" these pictures and arranged with the proprietor to show them to the suckers. In these pictures, by the way, there were great orange trees and groves, the building of the Provident City "railway," etc.[11]

Despite such rising opposition and derision appearing in the local press, the company continued to market its colony to unsuspecting midwesterners. In 1915, area newspapers still received news from residents of Seclusion. In a story titled "*Hallettsville New*

Era Tells of Land Sharks at Provident City," the *Eagle Lake Headlight* recounted R. J. Clark's testimony to the Hallettsville reporter:

He says that the Kansas City land sharks are still "bumping suckers" in Provident City. Lately a man came down all the way from Wichita, Kansas, to inspect a tract of 40 acres adjoining Provident City that he had bought from the company at the rate of $40 per acre, and what was more, he had paid for it all. On arriving at this wonderful "city" he found that his tract was part of a large block of land that had been sold under sheriff's sale by the Provident company at the rate of $4 per acre some months back. The land company thereupon agreed to give him any 40 acre tract he wished to take.

Mr. Clark happened to talk to the man about this time, and at once advised him in this wise: "Don't take any of their land. Ask for your money back, instead. Be satisfied if you get just half your money back, but don't take any of their land, as it is worth but a small part of what you paid for it. You can't possibly make a living on forty acres of it."

The story continued to blast the "land grafters" for duping poor, unfortunate would-be settlers into buying "crawfish" land and relayed information regarding an ongoing battle between the company and local citizens who tried to warn the prospective land purchasers they met:

The land sharks know that our people know that the land is almost worthless and are the kind of folks that would not hesitate to tell the poor northerners the truth about it. So the land sharks craftily fill their victims full of tales about how the cattlemen and ranchmen of that part of the county are opposed to settlement, how they will try all they can to keep settlers out even to the point of cutting fences, etc., stories that of course sound ridiculous. . . . However the poor fellows believe what is told them at least long enough for them to be tied up hard and fast with nearly valueless land on their hands.

"Why," said Mr. Clark, "one good lady on whom was unloaded some of this land, was made to believe that on a certain large tree near the colony the ranchmen had hung eight settlers in past years. She believed it so strong that just before returning to her northern home she took a Kodak picture of the tree as a souvenir of Texas toughness to show her people. Of course, we all took it as a joke, but it was darned serious when you think of it."

Wrapping up the story, the editor added a notation saying "Marked copies of this article will be sent to the various leading newspapers in Kansas, Missouri and other states from where the poor fellows come from [sic] that are cheated in this respect. We are going to do what we can to stop this infernal robbery."[12]

By 1920, little remained of once-promising Provident City. Area newspaper stories and state business directories of the time show a steady decline as businesses, townspeople, and surrounding farmers decamped. *El Campo Citizen* columnist Ruby Ethel Tardiff, writing about it in 1966, remembered, "The town started breaking up between the years of 1915 and 1920, with the families drifting away, mostly back to the north from which they came. When I saw the town for the first time in the late 1920s all that remained of the business district was the stately old hotel, a grocery store, a schoolhouse, and a deserted bank."[13] James G. Hopkins of Garwood, the Colorado County Historical Commission member who initiated and prepared the state marker application for Provident City, wrote, "The decline was rapid, most people stayed a year or so; but a number lived there for many years. I lived there as a small child, played in the broom factory, used the broom-sticks for stick horses. My older brother and cousin kept trying to open the safe in the abandoned bank."[14]

Eventually the town site and most of the land surrounding it became part of the Goldenrod Ranch operated by the R. H. Hancock family. The post office remained open until 1953 serving scattered rural dwellings, and the schoolhouse, rebuilt as a one-story structure, continued in use for children of ranch workers into the 1960s. The business district, streets, houses, churches, and people are all gone now, replaced by the native grasslands that preceded them. The only vestige of the town still remaining is the former Provident

Provident City Hotel, 2008. Converted for use as the headquarters building of a private ranch, the hotel is the last remaining structure at the former site of Provident City. Situated just off a gravel county road on the grassland prairie, it is a well-maintained reminder of the short-lived town. Photograph by Cynthia J. Beeman.

City Hotel, converted for use as the ranch headquarters. Visible through a field of prairie grass from the gravel road that is now County Road 17, it is located, as Mr. Hopkins wrote a bit tongue-in-cheek, at the corner of 10 Street and Avenue B.

MARKER LOCATION: (from Columbus) SH 71 S 16 mi. to US 90 at Altair; 13.5 mi. W on US 90 to Sheridan; 18 mi. S on FM 2437 to FM 530; 2 mi. E on Co. Rd. 17 to Co. Rd. 248.

Transom detail, Provident City Hotel, 2008. This etched-glass window reveals an elegant feature above the double-door corner entry of the hotel building, which retains its historic architectural appearance. Photograph by Cynthia J. Beeman.

GEORGE H. PAUL, SOUTH TEXAS LAND PROMOTER

One of the most successful land promoters in early twentieth-century Texas, George H. Paul (1877–1965) is responsible, at least in part, for the development of numerous communities in San Patricio and Nueces counties. Born on a farm in Iowa, Paul began his career working for a land company in that state selling property in Canada to American settlers. By 1907, he was in Corpus Christi doing business as the George H. Paul Land Company, organizing excursion trains to transport potential land buyers from the Midwest to South Texas. That year, he worked with Robert Driscoll to subdivide part of the Driscoll Ranch into cotton farms and promote the town of Robstown in Nueces County. The George H. Paul Building, a two-story red brick structure, served as the company's Robstown headquarters and also housed a general store, school, and bank. The community flourished as farmers grew cotton and winter vegetable crops.

Riding the success of his venture in Robstown, Paul entered into a contract with the Coleman-Fulton Pasture Company in 1908 to purchase 56,000 acres in San Patricio County for development. He hired crews of Mexican migrant workers to clear the land of dense brush and, once again targeting his sales pitches to midwesterners, brought trainloads of potential buyers to the area and developed two more towns. Sodville, located south of Sinton and west of Taft along present FM 1074, attracted settlers from the Midwest as well as from other parts of Texas and within a few short years boasted a school, a general store, two churches, and two cotton gins. But despite early positive farming results, Sodville declined in the years following the Second World War, and little remains of the town today. West Portland, the second town formed out of the Coleman-Fulton Pasture Company land, located on the San Antonio and Aransas Pass Railway in the southern part of San Patricio County, attracted settlers primarily from Kansas. They arrived weekly by train beginning in 1908, and within a year they established an active community with a school, churches, and

homes. Area cotton farmers built the West Portland Gin Cooperative in 1922, and it became the center of the community.

In 1910, Paul found another willing partner in John H. Shary. The
two purchased about 70,000 acres from the John J. Welder Ranch
in the Sinton vicinity and developed the towns of St. Paul and
West Sinton. Paul platted the town of St. Paul (reportedly named
in his honor by the residents) about six miles north of Sinton,
and the Shary Land Company promoted its settlement through a
network of land agents working in the Midwest. (Shary later relocated to the Rio Grande Valley, developed vast areas there, as well,
and became a major force in the burgeoning Texas citrus farming
industry.) Excursion trains from Kansas City brought prospective
buyers to St. Paul twice a month, and settlers streamed in, establishing farms and building homes. The three-story Shary Hotel
served as headquarters for land sales, and the town also included
stores, churches, schools, a post office, a telephone exchange, a
bank, and a busy railroad depot. The George H. Paul Company also
operated a large company farm and a farm store, which together
employed more than three hundred people. Several gins served
area cotton farmers, and the community continued to thrive until
shortly after World War II, when many families relocated to nearby
cities.

West Sinton, about twelve miles west of its namesake town,
also rose from former J. J. Welder Ranch lands and attracted both
Midwest and Texas settlers. A family named Adams, who moved
to the area from Guadalupe County in 1913, set aside land for a
school the following year. The schoolhouse also served as a church
and gathering place, and the community became known as both
West Sinton and Adams School. Settlement continued to increase
despite hardships caused by the devastating influenza epidemic
of 1918–19 and a fierce hurricane in 1919. A community cotton gin
served area farmers until the 1980s.

Although directly involved in the sale and development of an
estimated half-million acres in South Texas, George H. Paul did

not retain any land or mineral rights for himself. He outlived both his wife and son, and in his later years lived alone in a basement apartment in Nebraska. He died there in relative poverty at age 88. The Texas Historical Commission placed Official Texas Historical Markers at a number of sites that commemorate his work promoting the early twentieth-century development of the region:

Site of George H. Paul Building, northwest corner of 5th and
    Main, Robstown, Nueces County
St. Paul, US 181, six mi. N of Sinton, San Patricio County
Sodville Community, intersection of FM 1944 and FM 1074,
    about five mi. S of Sinton, San Patricio County
Site of West Portland, intersection of FM 893 and FM 1074,
    seven mi. W of Portland, San Patricio County
West Sinton Community, intersection of FM 630 and FM 796,
    twelve mi. W of Sinton, San Patricio County

Sources: Keith Guthrie, *The History of San Patricio County* (Austin: Nortex Press/ Eakin Press, 1986); THC marker files (listed above); George O. Coalson, "George H. Paul," *New Handbook of Texas*, vol. 5, pp. 96–97; Christopher Long, "Robstown, Texas," *New Handbook of Texas*, vol. 5, p. 630; Mark Odintz, "Sodville, Texas," *New Handbook of Texas*, vol. 5, p. 1134; Keith Guthrie, "West Portland, Texas," *New Handbook of Texas*, vol. 6, p. 901; Weldon Hart, "John Harry Shary," *New Handbook of Texas*, vol. 5, p. 998.

A CROP OF SUCKERS

In the Texas Panhandle, about twenty-five miles southwest of Muleshoe near the New Mexico border, is the site of the ghost town of Virginia City, platted in 1909 by Matthew C. Vaughan and Samuel D. McCloud on behalf of the Vaughan Land Company of Waterloo, Iowa. Company officials, who purchased former ranchland for development (most of present Bailey County consisted of divisions of the famed XIT Ranch prior to 1901), told prospective land buyers Virginia City would become the county seat of the soon-to-be-organized county. With a town plat showing a block of land set aside for a courthouse square, as well as sites designated for schools, parks, churches, and residential neighborhoods, the company began marketing the development through real estate agents in the Midwest. Sparsely settled prior to the turn of the twentieth century—the federal census recorded only four people living there in 1900—Bailey County would not be formally organized, with Muleshoe as its county seat, until 1919. By then, few traces of Virginia City remained.

As was the case with many land promotion schemes of the time, the Vaughan Land Company advertised the availability of fertile farmland at rock-bottom prices, laid out a town, built a few structures—including a hotel to house prospective buyers—and brought eager homesteaders to Texas on excursion trains. From 1907 to 1909, thanks to an unusual period of abundant rainfall, the area around the town appeared green and fertile, with shallow lakes (playas) in the region filled with water. Lured by photographs in promotional literature showing lush vegetation, clients disembarked from trains at the nearest station in Portales, New Mexico, where company sales agents met them and drove them to the Virginia City site in buggies, wagons, or automobiles. The company paid all expenses from the buyers' point of origin to Texas, including accommodations at the company-owned hotel. Land agents escorted prospective buyers around the town, showed them land for sale, as well as construction of a roadbed for a coming railroad line (never constructed), and then drove them back to Portales just in time to catch a train returning north. Never without their company escorts, the clients had few if any opportunities to speak with area residents and so could not ask questions of anyone other than company agents. Reportedly, however, at least one prospective land buyer managed to speak to a local cowboy; asked what the principal crops of the area were, the cowboy is said to have replied, "Suckers." Although a number of families moved to Virginia City and attempted to establish farms out of the former ranchlands, a severe drought that began in 1910 sent them back to their former homes in droves. Within a few short years, the last of the residents abandoned Virginia City, leaving only the company hotel building to mark the site. The Texas State Historical Survey Committee (now Texas Historical Commission) placed an Official Texas Historical Marker at the site of the short-lived community in 1968.

MARKER LOCATION

From Muleshoe, 13.5 mi. S on SH 214; 11.1 mi. W on FM 298; 2 mi. S on FM 1731.

Sources: Site of Virginia City, Bailey County, THC marker files; Martha Flores, "Land Companies," in *Early Bailey County History*, ed. LaVonne McKillip (Muleshoe, Texas: Bob Stovall Printing, 1978); Charles G. Davis, "Virginia City, Texas," *New Handbook of Texas*, vol. 6, p. 760; William R. Hunt and John Leffler, "Bailey County," *New Handbook of Texas*, vol. 1, p. 338.

3

A PLAN FOR THE COMING SEASON

At the London gravesite of the renowned English architect and scientist Sir Christopher Wren (1632–1723) in St. Paul's Cathedral, the expansive and opulent early eighteenth-century baroque structure he designed, is a tablet bearing his epitaph. It ends with the oft-repeated Latin phrase, *Si monumentum requiris, circumspice.* (If you seek his monument, look about.) In a sense, the same maxim might apply to the memory of King Cotton in Texas. While extant vestiges of the state's early cotton culture fail to reflect Wren's stylistic exuberance, representing instead a more utilitarian expression of architectural design, they nonetheless speak to the hopes and aspirations of a particular era and culture. Although cotton production remains a viable and nationally significant industry in much of Texas, its evolutionary and transgenerational sweep across the state from east to west left behind many unique and significant but outdated elements of the built environment.

The cultural utilization of cotton in Texas dates to its earliest inhabitants, who, as Spaniard Álvar Nuñez Cabeza de Vaca observed on his journeys across the region in the 1500s, wove the fiber for clothing and blankets. Spanish missionaries who came later relied on Native American labor for the systematic cultivation of the plant. When Anglo-American settlement began under Mexican authority in the 1820s, the first colonists made cotton the preferred crop of choice, and new residents brought with them the cotton culture of the Old South, complete with the institution of slavery, inexorably tied to crop production for decades. The settlers also introduced the relatively new technology of ginning—mechanically separating the cotton fibers from the seeds—and the earliest gin operations appeared in Stephen F. Austin's colony and farther east around San Augustine. Texas proved to be an ideal location for cotton production, and it thrived even during the revolution, the republic era, and subsequent statehood. As a result, well before the U.S. Civil War, Texas was among the top cotton-producing states in the nation. Production understandably declined during the war, although the commodity remained in sufficient supply to be the object of both Union and Confederate military strategies. Afterward, cotton farming once again served as the underpinning of economic development in the state and with the advent of railroads moved steadily from fertile valleys to the uplands and farther inland.[1]

As King Cotton increased its reign, it served as an early determinant of communities; gins, along with schools, churches, and mercantiles, marked the centers of dispersed agricultural settlements, resulting in a commercial and social focus. Rail lines chased the commodity, and with improved transportation and mechanization, as well as redefined settlement patterns, cotton farming reached out well beyond the Gulf Coast and East Texas regions. In both cities and rural crossroad communities along the way there appeared the distinctive cotton gin complexes, with their easily recognized gin houses and associated seed houses, burr burners, water systems, and warehouses. In other areas there were also the related cottonseed oil mills, compresses, freight depots, machine shops, factories, supply houses, equipment showrooms, and, in some cases, even worker housing. Farther afield from the central gins were transportation-related structures of railroad hubs and seaports and also the brokerage centers in the larger cities. Adding in farmhouses and tenant houses, barns, sheds, and other structures directly related to cotton production, the cultural inventory of the built environment as it relates to that one industry is staggering. A comprehensive architectural and archeological survey of cotton-related structures in Texas would be an undertaking of the highest order, approaching the realm of impossibility. And, as cotton continues as a viable crop and the state remains a national production leader, the numbers will only increase, despite some losses along the way.

The number of cotton gins in Texas provides a central, albeit limited, focus for analysis. By 1860, there were approximately 2,000 operational gins in the state. By 1912, that number increased to more than 4,600, but by 1925 it fell below 4,000, although that reflected a slight increase from the figures only three years earlier. But essentially by the 1920s, and certainly by the 1930s, the total number of operational gins indicated a downward trend.[2] That number taken out of context, though, is misleading. By the 1930s, there was also a trend away from smaller operations toward larger and more efficient complexes. Also not reflected in the total number is the regional movement of cotton, tracking roughly westward to the plains as new lands opened for cultivation and construction of rail lines reached new markets. With improved methods of mechanization and farming techniques, increased production costs, and the decline of small family farms, it became advantageous, despite often unstable commodity prices, to farm cotton on a larger scale. With that gradual evolution, small one- and two-stand gins gave way to larger operations, mule power yielded to tractor horsepower, crossroad cotton settlements disappeared, and former cotton fields changed over to pasturage.

With those changes, the impact on the cultural landscape also shifted, and some of King Cotton's early monuments started to fade away. In many areas of the state, generations with different economic directions and life experiences came to inherit the remnants of a bygone era and dealt with them as challenges for town planning, historic preservation, heritage tourism, and even public safety. Responses varied from demolition and neglect to adaptive reuse and creative interpretation. As a result, some surviving cotton-era structures now serve other purposes, providing space for, among other things, a restaurant (Fredericksburg), a winery (Sisterdale), machine shops, storage facilities, and barns. Others, like the sizable cotton gin complex at the center of Pflugerville, an old German agricultural settlement in northern Travis County—now rapidly evolving as a suburb of Austin—serve as stark historical backdrops for more modern development. Not far away, in the Williamson County communities of Walburg and Theon, old gins remain virtually intact, in a sort of mothballed state of preservation, as if they could return to action if cotton should somehow make a miraculous economic recovery. And in one community along the blacklands of western Washington County, a gin uniquely serves as a museum of the cotton culture and the focal point of heritage tourism and celebration.

Burton, an incorporated town of 400 people located thirteen miles west of Brenham along U.S. 290, represents one of the best preserved and most intact examples of a small cotton town in the state. Established in 1862 and named for pioneer settler John M. Burton, the settlement showed early promise as an agricultural center due to its location on the Houston and Texas Central Railway line that ran through Brenham and on to Austin. It grew steadily through the latter part of the nineteenth century and by 1910 had a population close to 600. Cotton and corn were agricultural mainstays of that era, and Burton boasted two gins (Wendt and Knipstein).[3]

Cotton production levels from farms in western Washington County during the early twentieth century were sufficient enough to warrant establishment of a third gin at Burton, and in December 1913, local farmers and businessmen met to form the Burton Farmers Gin Association, a cooperative venture that offered $50 shares toward $10,000 in operational capital. A constitution guided the work of the association.[4]

The Burton area, as well as much of western Washington County, attracted German American farmers who favored the region's blackland soils, and the German influence is evident in the names of several association officers: Dallmeyer, Boehnemann, Klanke, Oevermann, Hopmann, Stolz, and Felder. A. S. Whitener Jr. served as the first president.[5] In January 1914, the association acquired a building site covering several acres and encompassing multiple town lots in two blocks. Construction soon began on a simple, rectilinear two-story galvanized gin house with a gabled roof, a configuration sufficient for the initial equipment and also representational of other Texas gins. The ceiling height allowed for overhead conveyance of the cotton and eventually the separated seeds, with the primary or ginning floor space for operation of the stands and the baling box press. Underneath, a line shaft eighty feet long with multiple pulleys provided power to belts that ran the machinery.

An early photograph of the Burton Farmers Gin shows cotton wagons queued up to offload raw cotton via the sucker tube to second-floor gin stands. As the cooperative association introduced new mechanical equipment over the years, the gin house grew with additions, roof dormers, and extensions, as well as a seed house that now stands to the forefront of this view. Courtesy Burton Cotton Gin Museum.

A western framing system of heavy timbers served as the skeleton of the gin house, and galvanized metal cladding allowed for expediency and durability but also a measure of fire protection; gin fires were commonplace. A wood-burning steam engine, converted for coal within a few years, provided the initial power.[6]

The building evolved over time, as did most thriving gin operations, with the addition of new equipment to meet increased demand. When the gin opened in 1914, it handled only the so-called "clean" cotton, handpicked clean from the surrounding boll, a time-consuming method of harvesting the crop but one that required less equipment to process. New technology, though, in the form of a stick machine, allowed workers to "snap" or "pull" the cotton, boll and all, which shortened field time. Since the separation process then occurred in the gin, workers could move faster through the fields. More efficient blowers and dryers added new interior space to the overall system, and so the outside of the gin grew as well with new gabled additions on the roofline to accommodate reworked interior space.

The most significant change, though, came in 1925 with the

addition of a dual cylinder, twin-flywheel, diesel-powered, Bessemer Type IV 125-horsepower engine purchased from the Lummus Gin Sales Company of Dallas. The company provided the association with plans for a concrete support platform, and soon after its completion the engine arrived, partially assembled, at Burton by rail. Association members worked together to build a wooden spur line to the gin and then spent the better part of two days, using jacks and crowbars, slowly inching the almost five-ton piece of equipment roughly 200 feet to its new business location. The dimensions proved accurate, and the farmers had the engine in place and running in short order.[7]

The new engine necessitated further substantial alterations to the original gin structure, including a water cooling tower, a shed addition for the engine, and underground mufflers made from old boilers for the exhaust pipes located some distance away to prevent back-fumes. Despite the effort to minimize the noise from the powerful engine, though, its deep-throated roar and the unmistakable hit-and-miss popping of the exhaust could be heard for miles. Like a pervasive rolling thunder, the engine mercilessly shook and rattled every part of the gin structure, threatening to tear it from its mooring, but it somehow managed to survive. Over time, members enclosed the engine shed addition and built a small office above. There, despite the almost deafening engine noise, the continual structural shaking, and the rattling of the windows, the gin manager oversaw the operation, and his assistant managed to process the requisite paperwork of crop receipts, bills, payroll, and safety reports. From 1923 to 1961, Henry Wehring Sr. served as manager, and for a time his teenage daughter handled the books. Years later, Ora Nell Wehring Moseley recalled, "Oh, it was terribly noisy—very, very noisy. And the office was right above that big diesel engine down there. . . . You'd almost have to have earplugs. . . . You just have no idea how noisy. But it was so much activity, and it's just kind of exciting for a young person like me at fourteen to be able to be up there and have, I felt like, a big responsibility, which it was."[8]

Not only was the engine noisy, but it ran long hours as well, often ten to twelve hours a day and sometimes longer as the demand dictated. Town residents adapted to the inconvenience during gin-ning season and even managed to sleep while the engine ran, only to be awakened abruptly by the immediate quiet when workers finally shut it down for the evening.

The Lady B, as gin workers called the Bessemer engine, remained in prime running order from 1925 to the early 1960s, when a tem-porary breakdown resulted in the association's decision to replace it with an Allis-Chalmers electric motor that also generated 125 horsepower. The Bessemer remained in place, though, and upon overhaul continued to provide backup power as needed.[9]

When cotton was ready for ginning in the fall of the year, the operation began early in the morning. Farmers lined up their overflowing wagons and either left them there and headed back to the farm for other chores, if they lived nearby, or remained in the gin yard, sleeping underneath their wagons or visiting with others as they waited. Once it was their turn, all attention turned to the process, which began with a powerful telescoping suction tube that emptied the wagon and conveyed the cotton overhead where machines dried, separated, and cleaned it before it fell into the five Lummus gin stands, the heart of the operation. In each stand, circular saws rotating at high speeds separated the lint from the seeds, and conveyors transferred the latter to the adja-cent seed house, from where farmers could sell them back to the gin or reclaim them for the next year's crop or for use as cattle feed. The cotton lint continued on inside the gin and made its way into the baling box, where a hydraulic ram pressed it into a bale that workers covered in cloth, bound with metal bands, and then rolled out onto the gin floor. The Burton gin had a two-box operation, so as one filled the finished bale could be released from the other and then tagged with a unique number for identification purposes. The speed of the process changed over time with new equipment, but an output of seven bales an hour was standard in the Burton gin; in a long day, the gin might produce one hundred bales.[10]

While the size of bales fluctuated, they were generally in the range of 500–550 pounds, requiring a gross input of roughly 1,400 pounds of picked cotton (more for pulled). Workers moved the fin-ished bales to the loading area and cut samples for the farmers,

A recent photo of an iron-wheeled wooden cotton wagon at the Burton Cotton Gin Museum. Located near the sucker tube operation, the wagon is beneath the shed addition that covers conveyance mechanisms between the original gin house (right) *and the later seed house* (left). Courtesy Texas Department of Transportation. Photograph by Stan A. Williams.

who then presented them to local brokers and buyers for grading and price estimates. If the farmer approved of the estimates, the sale often ended at the gin after he settled up with the association on the gin fee. If prices were low or fluctuating, the farmer had the option to store bales at the nearby warehouse, for an additional fee, or take them home in hopes prices would eventually rise and make the payout more profitable. The process, from seed to bale, was a gambler's trade, and all parties—farmer, gin operator, and buyer—understandably vied for the highest profit they could achieve. The seasonal ebb and flow of the market, coupled with year-long, crop-dependent credit lines provided by local merchants, though, meant some farmers realized only limited payouts in years of poor crop yields or low prices. Ginning season was the money season, and farmers, tenants, bankers, merchants, gin workers, and others depended heavily on strong yields for their livelihoods.

At the end of each ginning season, when the last of the cotton had been "scrapped" from the fields and processed, workers and association members shut down the operation and prepared for the following season. They completed and filed paperwork, reworked the engine, cleaned the various pieces of equipment, relaxed the belts, and, in effect, mothballed the entire complex for the ensuing months. For many years in Burton, the closing of the gin came with the implied hope of a better crop the following year. The only gin in town by the late 1940s—the Wendt gin closed earlier, and the association purchased the Knipstein complex to rework for milling functions—the Farmers Association operation continued providing a revenue stream for its investors. By the 1960s, though, a steady decline in acreage under cultivation presaged a major change for the local cotton culture, and the end finally came in the 1970s despite all hope and optimism. Although it had processed thousands of bales annually in its early years of operation, the Burton Farmers Gin handled only eighteen in 1973 and sixteen the following year—the final bale, although no one realized it at the time, rolled out of the baling box on November 13, 1974. In the days that followed, as at the end of all previous seasons, the workers once again readied the operation for the next year. This time, however, there was no following season; the Burton Farmers Association Gin had run its historic course, remaining in operation for sixty years.[11]

From the 1970s to the 1980s, the old gin house remained silent and almost forgotten, although residents talked from time to time of either dismantling it or offering the land to another industrial enterprise. Meanwhile, former cotton fields in the surrounding area turned to pasturage as farming gave way to ranching around Burton. Local businesses declined and several closed for good; others managed to remain open on a limited basis. The population of Burton declined as a result, settling at around 300 in the 1980s.

But, as is often the case, the lack of local revenue also served to preserve important elements of the community's historic fabric, and what might have been a negative became a positive as local residents began to view their significant past as an asset to the quality of life they enjoyed. So, in the 1980s, a group of concerned citizens initiated a survey of the town's historical resources in order to promote a measure of direction for the development that was sure to come with the county's continued growth. As an integral part of the survey to determine which sites within the town qualified for listing in the National Register of Historic Places, the gin once again became the focal point of activity. Few at the time, though, realized the survey would lead to the resurrection of the gin, providing that hoped-for new season, one more economically promising and lasting than those in earlier years.

As work on the National Register nomination proceeded, local residents established a preservation group known as Operation Restoration, which purchased the gin property in 1986. Its early mission was to restore the gin and preserve the associated records, which remained undisturbed inside the gin, but also to promote the historic resources of Burton. The organization started small, with only a few volunteers, but it grew quickly as others shared the vision. Early on, members contacted the Smithsonian Institution in Washington, D.C., which sent museum specialist Larry N. Jones to Washington County to participate in initial planning discussions with other advisors. His findings confirmed the historical integrity of the resource and helped place it in a national context; a gin of that vintage, with its mechanical system intact and its records complete, made it unique and worthy of broader preservation and interpretive efforts. Soon, members recruited an advisory board, and participants included representatives of the Texas Historical Commission (THC), Texas A&M University, Baylor University, and the National Trust for Historic Preservation. Early efforts focused on resource protection and funding, so as Operation Restoration solicited grants and planned for a community festival, it also secured the National Register listing and obtained an Official Texas Historical Marker that provided the protective Recorded Texas Historic Landmark designation. The latter meant the THC, the state agency for historic preservation, would have input on all plans. Several years later, the American Society of Mechanical

Engineers also recognized the gin as its 175th National Historic Mechanical Engineering Landmark.[12]

In 1990, Operation Restoration kicked off its first Cotton Gin Festival, and it has since continued as an annual spring event, increasing in scope and programming and attracting more than 10,000 visitors in recent years. Against the backdrop of the historic gin, they come for food, crafts, music, exhibits, auctions, and other special events but also for guided tours through King Cotton's monument. Some experience it for the first time, others are return visitors, and still others come to recall the unmistakable sights, sounds, and smells of their own cotton culture background.

Over the years, Operation Restoration became Burton Cotton Gin Museum, Inc., and acquired additional property, including a warehouse, a mechanic's shop, the Wehring leather shop, and other related sites. Members, some of them descendants of original gin association officers and stockholders, helped restore Lady B to run at the annual festival and other special events. Utilizing advice and direction from Texas A&M University engineers and other machinery experts, and relying on a supply of West Texas cotton, members eventually succeeded in once again ginning cotton in Burton, albeit for demonstration purposes.

In the early 1990s, as a complement to the physical restoration of the cotton complex in Burton, the Baylor University Institute for Oral History embarked on a systematic program to record memories of those who grew up in the twentieth-century cotton culture of Washington County. The connection is not only appropriate but also historical, given that the university began in 1845 at the nearby Washington County town of Independence. In a sense, through its participation with the preservation project in Burton, Baylor returned to its roots. Under the early leadership of the institute's director, Dr. Thomas L. Charlton, Baylor oral historians cast a wide net, interviewing former gin workers, cotton pickers, merchants, buyers, bankers, and others, including individuals long active in the restoration effort. The processed interviews are now part of the Texas Collection at Baylor University, where they are available for students and other researchers who have "mined" them for a number of theses, books, and articles.

Grover Williams (center, wearing red cap), *who grew up on a cotton farm in the Burton area, leads a tour of the gin complex. The gin house in the background provides visual evidence of the evolutionary nature of such structures.* Courtesy Texas Department of Transportation. Photograph by Stan A. Williams.

The memories of two local men with rich experiences of picking cotton that made its way to the Burton Farmers Gin provide special insights into the quality and depth of the oral histories. Eddie Wegner, a descendant of German Texan farmers, remembered that despite the adversities and uncertainties of the gambler's trade, cotton seemed to prevail. As he remembered, "We made some money if we had surplus pigs or hogs or chickens, fryers, eggs . . . but that was all small cash. The cotton is what we depended on for the main cash flow. And the quantity and the quality of the cotton crop, and the price, of course, that was in effect at the time you sold your cotton, that was the determining factor of how well or how bad the little farmer lived. Because you had to have clothes. You had to have gasoline and oil for the old jalopy."[13]

And Grover Williams, an African American farmer originally from the Flat Prairie community near Burton, described the pain and field discipline associated with the stoop labor of picking cotton. Speaking of his parents, he told, "If they did catch us on our knees, we'd get up and say, 'Mama, my back's hurting.' You know what they'd say, don't you? They'd say, 'Boy, you don't have a back, you've just got a gristle.'"[14]

Stories associated with the Burton Farmers Gin are at the same time universal and unique, given the pervasive presence of King Cotton in Texas history and the diversity of the human experience. Such is also the nature of the gin itself. Typical of a vernacular building type once common across the state, it now functions as a one-of-a-kind living museum, an innovative example of industrial preservation and heritage education. Almost a century after local farmers first gathered to sell stock and plan its construction, the gin now returns dividends in the form of community pride and action—historical vindication for those workers who, decades ago, routinely, but with cautious optimism, planned once again for the coming season.

MARKER LOCATION: South side, 300 block of Main St., Burton.

GEORGE SESSIONS PERRY

A native of Rockdale in Milam County, George Sessions Perry (1910–56) grew up surrounded by the cotton culture of Central Texas. The strong sense of place he developed there never left him, and he drew on it regularly for inspiration in his career as a writer. Perry authored many articles and books and also served as a World War II correspondent, but his works on rural lifeways in Texas proved particularly popular. His most memorable book is *Hold Autumn in Your Hand* (1941), a fictionalized account of tenant farmer Sam Tucker that won Perry the National Book Award, the first Texas book to receive that honor. The story opens with one of the most dramatic literary entrances in Texas fiction: "The Texas January day was all blue and gold and barely crisp. Only the absence of leaves and sap, the presence of straggling bands of awkward crows, the gray-yellow flutter of field larks, and the broad, matter-of-fact hibernation of the earth said it was winter as Sam Tucker walked along the road, his long legs functioning automatically, farmerly. His body had about it the look of country dogs at the end of winter, when they are all ribs and leg muscles and jaw muscles and teeth. His eyes were bright and dark and small, with no more evil or softness in them than a hawk's. His hands were knotty with big knuckles and were gloved with protective calluses" (p. 7). Perry's sensitive portrayal of Tucker's personal struggles within the tenancy system is compelling, replete with the vagaries of cotton production, like heavy rains and rising water, that made it a gambler's trade: "When the river had receded, there was a silence in the bottoms that had not been there before. Shapes were suspended awkwardly in new, as yet unassimilated, death. The felt sound and motion of growing cotton, which had until now gone unnoticed, were no longer there. The substance of thousands of shirts and trousers, of sheets and jumpers and socks, of warm knit drawers that might have been worn against the cold, had gone down the river or was rotting in mud" (p. 11). An Official Texas Historical Marker in Rockdale, appropriately sited on the grounds of the local library, commemorates the life and literary influence of George Sessions Perry. Nearby, a marker for the Matinee Musical Club also mentions Perry, who served as the 1916 mascot for the woman's club founded by his aunt, Mary Ann Coffield Perry.

MARKER LOCATION
Matinee Musical Club, 305 E. Davilla Ave.; George Sessions Perry, 201 Ackerman, in courtyard of Lucy Hill Patterson Memorial Library, Rockdale.

Source: George Sessions Perry, *Hold Autumn in Your Hand* (Albuquerque: University of New Mexico Press, 1969).

ROBERT S. MUNGER

A pioneer inventor and innovator in the cotton gin industry, Fayette County native Robert Sylvester Munger (1854–1923) learned the basics of the process while working in the family gin operation in Mexia, Limestone County. A keen observer of mechanical systems with a talent for combining operations for efficiency, he developed the concept of system ginning still in use today. Munger relied on interconnected machinery fed by a central pneumatic flue system that moved the cotton steadily through the ginning process. Many of his innovations, including the double baling box, saw cleaners, and an improved suction system for unloading cotton wagons, are evident in the Burton Farmers Gin. Munger and his brother Stephen began manufacturing their own line of cotton gins and machinery at Dallas in the 1880s and followed it with a similar operation in Alabama. In 1900, they merged their interests with the Continental Gin Company. Soon after, Robert Munger embarked on a new career in real estate and started work on the prestigious residential development known as Munger Place in Dallas. The achievements of Robert S. Munger are noted in two Official Texas Historical Markers in Dallas: one for the Continental Gin Company Showroom Building at 232 N. Trunk Avenue, and the other for Swiss Avenue (5500 block of Swiss Avenue), part of the Munger Place addition.

Sources: Continental Gin Company and Swiss Avenue, Dallas County, THC marker files.

4
THE HEALER
OF LOS OLMOS

The practice of faith healing—the evocation of supernatural or divine intervention in the healing process—has been an integral part of medical treatment from ancient times to the present. Evidence of its cultural existence in Texas, viewed broadly, can be found in symbolic shamanistic pictographs in Pecos River rock shelters, in home altars and religious iconography, and in prayer chapels of modern medical centers. Personal beliefs in the healing power of faith are part of a historical continuum that crosses all cultures and regions in the state, encompassing to varying degrees elements of folklore, spiritualism, mysticism, and ritualism. It is nevertheless a little-known and often misunderstood facet of social history that binds together works of shamans, *curanderos,* tent revivalists, herbalists, television evangelists, and many others.

Curanderismo, the specialized faith healing directed by practitioners known as curanderos (male) or *curanderas* (female), has long-standing traditional ties to the Hispanic culture, although other cultures have embraced it as well. Much has been written of the practice, and a wide variety of researchers, from sociologists, historians, and anthropologists to religious scholars, folklorists, and physicians, have tried over the years to codify its various components, to understand its role in the broader context of medical science, and to measure its effectiveness. Despite such scholarship, the true impact of the practice comes down to the meaning and relevance of personal faith, which commonly defies both analytical understanding and scientific definition.

One of the most intriguing and compelling landmarks of curanderismo in Texas can be found a few miles northeast of Falfurrias

in Brooks County at the burial site of Pedro Jaramillo. It is a vener-
ated site, within the boundaries of a small community cemetery,
that attracts visitors daily—some drawn as faith pilgrims to a
familiar shrine and others motivated by curiosity, respect, family
history, desperation, or hope. Most are touched in some measure
by the scene they observe, for the Jaramillo grave is one of the
most unusual in the state. In many ways, its role as the destination
of countless faith journeys transcends the historical significance
of the individual whose burial it commemorates, although the legends surrounding both are forever intertwined.

Little is known of the early years of Pedro Jaramillo (1829–1907).
The child of Tarascan Indian parents, he grew up in the ranch
country near Guadalajara, Jalisco, Mexico. Lacking a formal education, he never learned to read or write, but he developed remarkable abilities that led him to a life of service to others. As a young
man in Mexico, Jaramillo experienced, by means of an accident,
what he believed was the special *don de Dios* (gift of God) that set
his course of healing. While riding a horse through brush country
near his home, he suffered a severe blow to his face that injured
his nose; details differ on whether he was thrown from the horse
or hit by a tree limb. Regardless, the wound caused Jaramillo considerable pain that persisted and intensified over time. Unable to
sleep, he took a walk in the nearby woods and at a low-lying area
where water settled, he laid down and placed his face in the soft
mud to seek relief from the pain. His experiment worked, and after
three days of the special mud treatments in the woods, his injury
healed, although he would bear a noticeable scar across the bridge
of his nose for the rest of his life.

With the cessation of pain, Jaramillo returned to his home,
where he at last began to sleep soundly. As he did, though, a voice
he believed to be that of God awakened him with the revelation
that he had received the gift of healing. The first test of his new
gift was reportedly the healing of his overseer. Later, in a vow of
faith to God as his mother's health declined, he promised to leave
Mexico upon her death. When she passed away, he made good on
his vow and moved to South Texas. Jaramillo knew the area, having earlier accompanied a companion who sold liquors at the Los

Don Pedro Jaramillo, 1894. Evident in the photo is the scar on his nose, caused by an incident he experienced as a young man that led to his lifetime of healing. Courtesy University of Texas at San Antonio Institute of Texan Cultures, #087-0239. Loaned by Estate of James and Scottie Roddie Pirie.

Canales Ranch. In the early 1880s, Jaramillo ventured to the community of Los Olmos (the Elms), then a part of Starr County, where he constructed a small mud and wood hut known as a *jacal* and began his public practice as a curandero.

Jaramillo, who came to be known by local residents as Don Pedro and Don Pedrito, charged nothing for his services, although he accepted meager gifts and donations as he deemed appropriate. He used the funds to expand his service to others and often donated money to the local Catholic church. He claimed no personal curative powers, believing instead that the strong faith of his patients, exhibited through their obedience to his God-given *recetas* (prescriptions), provided the healing. In this approach, he differed from other South Texas curanderos who used more complex procedures involving herbs, incantations, or potions. Jaramillo relied on the spontaneity of his recetas, generally simple procedures accompanied by intense praying. They included, for example, a set number of tepid baths or glasses of water, the ingestion of sugar cubes or raw eggs, and, perhaps as a reflection of his own miraculous cure, the application of mud. Numbers, particularly three and nine, were important elements of the repetitive procedures.[1]

At the time Don Pedrito lived in Los Olmos, it was a dispersed agricultural settlement centered on Los Olmos Creek, which flows eastward to Laguna Salada on Baffin Bay. The community's history reaches back to 1830, and possibly earlier; the settlement is believed to be the oldest in Brooks County, which formed in 1911. Los Olmos community began as part of a land grant from the State of Tamaulipas to Ramón de la Garza, who, with his wife Estanislada (Navarro), moved to the area by the 1830s. Cattle and sheep ranches served as the economic mainstay. By 1880, there were sufficient numbers of settlers in the area to establish a school. A post office under the name Los Olmos operated for a few years but discontinued service in 1882. Another opened in 1884 under the name Paisano and remained in operation until 1905. At its peak, the Los Olmos–Paisano settlement contained only a few hundred residents and a small number of commercial operations, primarily general stores. It declined as the nearby railroad town of Falfurrias, later the county seat, developed in the early twentieth century, and today only the community cemetery and a few scattered houses provide evidence of the historic community.[2]

Early Los Olmos residents had limited access to professional medical treatment, with few doctors in neighboring towns and counties available to provide care. Distance and personal economics led many—Anglos and Hispanics alike—to seek treatment from the village curandero, Don Pedrito. As news of his successful healings spread, hundreds visited his small jacal regularly, and there he dispensed not only his recetas but donated groceries and other supplies as well. As the crowds grew, he employed others, including a cook, to help him provide necessary services and meals. A large portion of the daily mail at the post office came addressed to the faith healer, who answered them with assistance from helpers, and the railroad at Falfurrias brought scores of visitors transported to Los Olmos by wagons that made several trips back and forth daily.

Much in demand throughout the region, Jaramillo soon began to travel outside his community in order to help others who sought his healing practice, and his journeys took him as far away as San Antonio, Laredo, and Corpus Christi. Wearing peasant clothing and traveling on foot or on a donkey, sometimes with a friend or helper, he slowly made his way across the South Texas area, dispensing healing remedies along the way. Upon his return to Los Olmos, he often found hundreds of followers camped near his home awaiting treatments or food. The latter became an increasingly larger part of his public service, especially during drought years of the 1890s.[3]

It was during that era that a young woman living on a nearby ranch first heard about the miracles performed by Don Pedrito. Viola Ruth Dodson (1876–1963), born on the Perdido Ranch in Nueces County and educated there, in a Corpus Christi school for a year, and later at Lagarto College in Live Oak County, spoke Spanish fluently and had a great appreciation for the rich Mexican culture and lore in her part of the state.[4]

Dodson first became aware of the curandero of Los Olmos during the drought of 1893, when her father and brother drove cattle south from their ranch to an area known as the Sands in search of better forage. As she later wrote: "As my father and brother rode along through the thinly populated, drought-stricken, sandy country, finding it in no better condition than the part of the country they had left, they came to a lake now almost dry. In the middle of it, they said, wallowing around in the muddy water was a nude Mexican man. They thought that he was surely a demented person who had wandered away from his home and was not responsible for what he was doing.[5] When they talked to the muddy man and asked about his situation, however, they learned instead he was faithfully following a prescription from Don Pedrito Jaramillo.

After this encounter by her family members, Dodson heard more stories of the faith healer and his miracles, and she carefully listened as others told of their encounters and experiences with him. Then one day in 1907, a Mexican friend of hers, who she identified in her writings as Trinidad, came to her house to tell her Don Pedrito had died. As Dodson noted, "He seemed to imply that there was nothing more to be said for him, that his career was finished."[6] And, indeed, the story might have ended there had it not been for the continuing faith of followers, the transgenerational passage of reminiscences, and the inquisitiveness of Dodson.

Through her interest in regional culture, Dodson came to know the renowned University of Texas folklorist J. Frank Dobie, who directed the Texas Folklore Society as secretary and editor from 1923 to 1943. Dobie encouraged Dodson to write about her life experiences in South Texas, and so in the 1930s she drew on her reminiscences, and those of others, to record stories of the land between the Nueces River and the Rio Grande. When she learned from Dobie that no one had written about Don Pedrito, she decided to focus her research on the legendary curandero. Working with residents who knew him or had knowledge of the stories and traditions handed down since his death, she compiled a book, written in Spanish, entitled *Don Pedrito Jaramillo, "curandero"* (1934). In 1951, the Texas Folklore Society included an updated version in English as part of a publication entitled *The Healer of Los Olmos and other Mexican Lore,* with a foreword by her colleague, Dobie. Containing detailed examples of Jaramillo's remedies and accounts of the miraculous cures they produced, it became a classic of southwestern folklore.[7]

Dodson's work not only preserved details of the faith healer's work, it also provided important insights into his own faith and philosophy. He chose, for example, an almost monastic existence, maintaining a simple and frugal lifestyle, and foregoing the use of donations for personal gain. "He thought that since God had bestowed on him the power to help humanity," she wrote, "he could also take that power away from him if he used it for his own benefit." She further observed, "What the curandero received with one hand, he gave away with the other."[8] Dodson also chronicled other special "gifts" of the healer, including clairvoyance, which he used to discern the sincerity or honesty of those he served.

Additionally, Dodson provided important details about the context of Jaramillo's existence in South Texas, a period of only twenty-five years. She wrote that some residents viewed him with suspicion, believing him to be a *brujo* (wizard) but that at least one local physician, Dr. J. S. Sutherland, acknowledged and valued his spiritual contributions to physical healing. Dodson provided evidence of how Jaramillo fit into broader patterns of faith and religion in South Texas, particularly among traditional Roman Catholics. Although the Church never canonized Jaramillo or officially recognized his miracles, instead reminding parishioners to separate his good deeds—as well as commemorative icons—from accepted spiritual teachings, a tendency for the two lines of faith to merge soon developed. Among his followers, the curandero of Los Olmos remains "saintly," and many faithful have long taken their medicines or ended their prayers "in the name of God and Don Pedrito."[9]

Just as Dodson's seminal folklore work helped pass the story of Jaramillo to future generations, so too did the actions of his followers, who even after his death faithfully visited Los Olmos to walk in the footsteps of a holy man, to seek hope, relevance, and understanding, and to receive cures through answered prayers. As the number of pilgrims grew steadily, followers erected a crude wooden structure to provide shelter for those who worshipped at his grave. The visitors decorated it with evidence of personal pilgrimages and faith: photos, discarded crutches, handwritten notes, rosaries, military medals, printed prayers, lighted candles, and tiny *milagros,* stylized replicas of arms, legs, hearts, and eyes in need of healing. Over the years, the pilgrimages of original followers gave way to tradition as their descendants—some still living locally and others from greater distances—also made the journey to the Los Olmos community cemetery for healing in the name of Don Pedrito. Over a century after his death, the faithful still come.

Viola Ruth Dodson died in 1963 and was buried in her adopted hometown of Mathis in San Patricio County. A few years later, members of the Brooks County Historical Commission familiar with her work prepared an application to the Texas State Historical Survey Committee (TSHSC), forerunner of the Texas Historical Commission (THC), for an Official Texas Historical Marker—with an inscription to be written in both English and Spanish—to commemorate the story of the faith healer of Los Olmos. The state marker program was then in its infancy, and it fell to staff historian Deolece Parmelee to provide the initial analysis, review, and recommendation to state commissioners who would make the final decision on the topic's eligibility.

The dilemma Parmelee faced in her review is one that has long confronted historians—the viability of folklore in historical interpretation. In her initial notes she wrote, "This topic comes closer to being in the realm of folklore than that of history. Personally, I am very much interested and intrigued with it as a marker topic, but I doubt that enough time has passed for a good historical evaluation of the topic." She failed to elaborate on what that time frame should be, but it is worth noting that over sixty years had then passed since Jaramillo's death. Parmelee went on to note, "I dislike to veto the topic, but we would have to treat it as the biography of a man who has been superstitiously regarded but who seems to have had only local significance."[10]

Parmelee, a seemingly tireless researcher who frequently helped local historians gather facts and documentation for their applications, followed up her initial inclination against approval with her own investigations that included a set of questions to members of the Brooks County Historical Survey Committee. In response, chair Florence Schuetz provided additional information but also an admonition borrowed from TSHSC Commissioner John Ben Shepperd.

Lighted prayer candles at the gravesite of Don Pedro Jaramillo, Los Olmos.
Photograph by Randy Mallory.

Writing in promotion of Heritage Appreciation Week in 1967, Shepperd noted: "The preservation of the historical heritage of our counties is of fundamental importance. Life is enriched by history. ...it is the key to a past that lives in our own times. ... This program is concerned with both the places where history was made, and the individuals who made it."[11] Schuetz firmly concluded her argument with "I rest my case."

No notes or papers indicate if Commissioner Shepperd ever discussed the application with historian Parmelee, but a month after her first analysis she drafted the following lines to the reviewers, indicating a slight change of perspective: "Personally, I believe firmly in faith healings, but I do not want to help believers fall into the clutches of wicked exploiters." Just who she thought would exploit the marker is unclear, but she passed the decision on to the reviewers, both commissioners and her supervisors, without a clear recommendation regarding eligibility.

The state committee ultimately approved the marker application, but the responses of two commissioners are worthy of note. Rosine Wilson, a respected preservationist from Beaumont who later co-authored a history of the TSHSC/THC with Parmelee, observed, "I do not think any harm would come from granting this marker. Faith healers, rainmakers, lightening [sic] rod salesmen, mediums and the like were not mere legend—they existed and are part of our history."[12] The noted Texas historian Herbert P. Gambrell, a commissioner from Dallas, provided a lengthier review, noting in part, "Unfortunately, some significant items in 'history' have been based upon oft-repeated and widely accepted legends." Offering both pros and cons relative to eligibility, he concluded his comments without a strong recommendation for either position: "The prudent thing would be to hold fast to the position already taken [i.e., rejection]. But, I lean, being a soft-hearted old Easy Mark, to doing whatever we can to humor those intensely interested Citizens of Brooks County. In other words, as Jim Hogg once said, 'I sit squarely on a telegraph wire, like a sparrow.' You may count my vote either way, and I promise to raise no question."[13] So, with only minimal concern, the TSHSC approved the application, and members of the Brooks County Historical Survey Committee

Visible in this photo of the grave house at Don Pedro Jaramillo's gravesite are a folk art likeness of the healer, as well as flowers, photographs, and other gifts left by devoted followers and worshipers. Photograph by Randy Mallory.

joined with residents of Los Olmos to plan a marker dedication for March 26, 1972. Tragically, just over a week before the ceremony, a fire believed to have started when a wreath came in contact with a prayer candle, spread quickly through the wooden grave house, destroying it and all of the contents, except for a photograph of Don Pedrito. The community quickly rallied, gathering donations and supplies to replace the small chapel.

Despite the momentary setback, the event proceeded as planned, and a crowd estimated at 2,000 attended the dedication ceremony at the small rural cemetery. Special guests included U.S. Congressman Eligio "Kika" de la Garza and the widow and descendants of Severiano Barrera, adopted son of Pedro Jaramillo. In his dedicatory remarks, the congressman noted that while some historical markers commemorated battles, the one at Los Olmos simply honored "a man of good will who brought no evil to anyone."[14]

When the ceremony concluded, local roads clogged by hundreds of cars and trucks caused considerable delays as those present at the event slowly made their way back to the main roads. As they necessarily lingered in the process, though, they noted even more vehicles making their way to the cemetery as scores of other individuals walked toward the faith healer's grave reverently with flowers, wreaths, candles, and other gifts in hand. And the visitors continue to the present—drawn by tradition, faith, and curiosity but also by an appreciation for a compelling story that reflects culture, history, folklore, and an abiding sense of place.

MARKER LOCATIONS
Don Pedro Jaramillo: 1 mi. N of Falfurrias on US 281,
    then 2 mi. ENE on FM 1418 and S on FM 1418 0.5 mi.
Los Olmos: 1 mi. N on US 287, then 2 mi. ENE on FM 1418

DOBIE'S LOS OLMOS

Folklorist J. Frank Dobie (1888–1964), the mentor of Viola Ruth Dodson who encouraged her to chronicle the folklore of the South Texas brush country, had his own Los Olmos connection. His, however, was in his native Live Oak County, more than sixty miles north of the one in Brooks County. Dobie grew up in the brush country southeast of George West, not far from Lagarto, where Dodson first attended college, and it provided him with a compelling sense of place that guided his early development as a nationally renowned folklorist. Following his service in World War I and a brief initial sojourn on the faculty of the University of Texas, he returned to Live Oak County to manage the vast Rancho de Los Olmos owned by his uncle, noted cattleman James Madison Dobie. There, J. Frank Dobie gained new perspectives of life on a South Texas ranch, and they in turn influenced his first significant ventures into the collection and documentation of regional folklore. He returned to the university in 1921 but used his Los Olmos experiences as the foundation for his first book, *A Vaquero in Brush Country*, published in 1929. Through it and subsequent writings that captured the rich literary flavor of regional culture, and through his mentorship of friends and students like Dodson, who shared his passion for folklore, he created a legacy that continues to this day. An Official Texas Historical Marker in Live Oak County marks his birthplace and interprets his significant literary contributions.

MARKER LOCATION

Live Oak County Courthouse, 301 Houston St., George West.

Sources: Francis E. Abernethy, "James Frank Dobie," *New Handbook of Texas*, vol. 2, pp. 662–63; Birthplace of J. Frank Dobie, Live Oak County, THC marker files.

5 TOO MANY BARRELS OF OIL

Less than a generation after the Spindletop gusher blew in at Beaumont in Southeast Texas and gave rise to the modern oil industry, rampant oil exploration in the Permian Basin of West Texas created a new wave of prosperity, permanently changing the region's way of life. Sandwiched between Spindletop in 1901 and the discovery of the vast East Texas oil field in the 1930s, the West Texas oil boom of the 1920s set the stage for a new era in Texas history, one rooted in underground wealth, industrial innovation, and rapid development.

Following the phenomenal success of the Spindletop boom and the resulting establishment of major corporations such as the Texas Company (Texaco), J. M. Guffey Petroleum Company (Gulf Oil), Magnolia Petroleum Company (Mobil), and Humble Oil Company (later Exxon), as well as pipeline and refinery operations, oil exploration quickly expanded into other areas of the state. By the 1920s, large fields in North Texas, the Texas Panhandle, Southwest Texas, and Central Texas produced both oil and natural gas in record amounts. The state's economy, primarily based on agriculture, began to change as the newly discovered oil fields became more and more profitable. Boomtowns sprouted across Texas as workers left farms and ranches to pursue riches in the new industry. As historian Roger Olien noted, "Model-T and Model-A Fords, with boxes and suitcases strapped to their trunks, rear seats filled with children and household goods, became familiar sights in most parts of Texas during the first three decades of the twentieth century. Ragtowns, tent cities, and shotgun houses were as common in the oil patch as dog-run houses in the countryside and mail-order bungalows in towns. Gushers and forests of drilling rigs replaced herds of longhorn cattle as symbols of Texas life."[1] By the time the Permian Basin oil bonanza began with the discovery of the Big Lake Oilfield in Reagan County in 1923, scores of oil exploration companies operated in a number of states. Major discoveries brought national and international companies, as well as independent operators, to West Texas, and with them came large drilling ventures and thousands of workers and their families. Drilling in two of the most prolific fields in the region—the McCamey Oilfield in Upton County and the Hendrick Oilfield in Winkler County—began in 1925 and 1926, respectively, and immediately affected the population in surrounding areas. The town of McCamey, its very existence rooted in the oil patch, began in September 1925, days after the first well in the McCamey field came in. A group of investors organized a townsite company on the route of the Kansas City, Mexico, and Orient Railway to serve as a supply point for the developing oil field, and settlement began almost overnight. A post office opened in March 1926, and the town incorporated in December. Prior to the discovery of the McCamey Oilfield, approximately 250 people lived in Upton County. Within six months of its founding, the boomtown swelled with more than 10,000 people living in tents and hastily built frame shacks. Activity brought about by the Hendrick Oilfield similarly affected the Ward County town of Monahans. Founded in 1881 as Monahan's Wells when Thomas J. Monahan dug a water well to supply a stop on the Texas and Pacific Railroad, the town remained a small settlement with fewer than 200 citizens until 1926. With the nearby oil discovery and the resulting need for a railroad supply and shipping point to support the drilling operations, Monahans boomed with hundreds of new citizens as well as expanded businesses to serve the growing community.[2]

By the end of 1927, the massive daily production from hundreds of wells in the heart of the Permian Basin caused a new problem that had to be solved quickly and efficiently in order to avoid devastating circumstances. Companies pumped too much oil out of the ground too quickly, and without adequate storage facilities or pipelines to ship the vast amounts of crude to refineries, they had to scramble to address the issue of overproduction.[3] Although a number of companies built large 55,000-barrel tanks in which to store oil until it could be shipped out, with production averaging 50,000 barrels per day at the height of the boom, storage capacity lagged far behind demand. One company operating in the region, Roxana Petroleum (a subsidiary of Royal Dutch/Shell, an early and influential leader in the worldwide oil industry) faced the problem of what to do with its overabundance of West Texas oil by turning to Shell engineers in California for help. While the Shell Pipeline Company busily built new lines from West Texas fields to the refineries in Oklahoma and Houston, the West Coast operations remained active, as well. Massive crude oil storage tanks recently built in California proved to be the inspiration for solving the Texas dilemma.

Shell's chief engineer, J. A. Wheeler, arrived in Texas in late 1927 to begin plans for constructing two tanks based on the California model, one to be built in Monahans and the other some sixty-five miles east in McCamey. Wheeler brought in additional Shell engineers to assist with the design and measurements—the team reportedly included a Chinese engineer named Dana Young, who calculated the tanks' volume and other details with an abacus—and contracted with a California construction company to oversee the project.[4] According to Wheeler's plan, the two huge tanks would serve as short-term holding reservoirs, and upon completion of Shell's new pipelines the company would pump the oil to the refineries. To accomplish its goal of building the tanks within ninety days, the company hired hundreds of local workers who lived in tent cities near the construction sites, earned fifty cents an hour, and worked twelve-hour shifts, seven days a week. According to one account, the work proved so difficult several laborers died during the project.[5]

Construction on the Monahans tank began first, in January 1928. Records indicate work on the McCamey tank commenced soon after, with the work at both sites overlapping in time and accomplished under the supervision of the same team of Shell engineers. Using hand-operated and horse- or mule-powered equipment, the crews excavated tons of dirt from an eight-acre area at each site and then used the displaced soil to form twenty-foot-high earthen walls in massive oval-shaped configurations. Horse-drawn rollers

Million Barrel Tank, Monahans, circa 1940s. Standing inside the concrete tank years after its failure as an oil storage facility, these local citizens are dwarfed by the enormous size of the structure. The tank stood abandoned for decades as various individuals and organizations tried to convert it into a useful public venue.
Courtesy Ward County Archives, Monahans.

packed the bottoms and sides of the interiors, and after workers installed miles of wire mesh to reinforce the floors of the tanks, they lined them with a thin layer of concrete. Large creosote-soaked wooden piers, eight inches square and placed fourteen feet apart, stood like a forest of trees inside each tank, supporting a massive domed roof that overhung the sides to prevent evaporation of the precious crude oil. With a nod to the unpredictable and often dangerous Texas weather, workers fitted the roofs with a complex maze of lightning rods as a fire prevention measure. A set of 175-foot towers placed near the tanks held more lightning rods, and, as an additional fire protection plan, generators pumped a layer of noncombustible carbon dioxide gas into the tanks to fill the space between the wooden roof and the top of the oil.[6]

Completed within the company's ninety-day schedule, each tank cost approximately $250,000 to build and could store more than one million barrels of crude oil. As it turned out, however, each was filled to capacity only once. For several days and nights in late June, as the Shell engineers watched and supervised the operation, crude oil flowed into the tanks and the levels rose. Before the oil reached the top, though, a major problem occurred. The tanks, so carefully planned and built, seemingly with every design detail considered by the engineering team, leaked. The engineers had failed to take into account the porous limestone foundation of the earth underneath the tanks, and when the crushing weight of the oil filled the reservoirs, the ground shifted and settled, causing the tanks to crack and the poured concrete sections to separate along the lines of asphalt caulking. Attempting to stanch the leaks, crews tried to patch the cracks with a gelatinous mixture of linseed oil, gasoline, and muriatic acid. When that failed, they pumped water beneath the floors, theorizing the lighter-weight oil would float above the base of water, but both water and oil continued seeping into the earth. With an estimated five hundred barrels of oil escaping from each tank daily, and as additional new pipelines became operational and ran from West Texas oil fields to distant refineries, lessening the need for the immense storage facilities, company officials finally decided to cut their losses with the big tanks and abandoned the project in 1929. Workers emptied and cleaned the tanks, and lumber from the immense wooden roofs eventually found new life as building material for nearby houses.[7] An accident during the dismantling of the roof resulted in the death of another worker in the summer of 1935.[8]

In operation for less than two years, the million-barrel tanks nevertheless served their immediate purpose of solving a major storage dilemma, and Shell engineers and executives considered them a modest economic success. Company officials estimated the cost of building and using the tanks amounted to 23 cents per barrel, at a time when West Texas crude oil was selling for 75 cents a barrel. Acceding to that formula, they reasoned they came out ahead by a more than two-thirds margin, at least until the price of oil dropped dramatically at the outset of the Great Depression.[9]

As Permian Basin oil exploration and drilling continued and settled into a permanent industry and way of life in West Texas in the following years, the two abandoned million-barrel tanks stood as silent monuments to the region's early boom years. Similar to the ones that preceded them in California, the Texas tanks later appeared clearly visible in aerial photographs and satellite images taken nearly a century after their construction.[10] Located on private property, the abandoned McCamey tank sits adjacent to dozens of modern oil storage tanks, their smaller round images looking like offshoots of the enormous earthen oval of the 1928 engineering experiment. Images of the Monahans tank, showing a large cut in one end of its oval shape, reveal different surroundings that allude to its adaptive use as a tourist attraction and museum. Behind those aerial views lies a decades-long tale of varied efforts by Monahans citizens to turn their million-barrel white elephant into a source of community pride.

Plans to convert the Monahans tank for recreational uses date to as early as 1936, when local physician Dr. W. O. Rehmeyer tried to purchase the site from the Shell Oil Company. Dr. Rehmeyer wanted to develop a park, but the company declined to sell the property.[11] Nevertheless, local teenagers often used the tank for dances, and in 1937 local entrepreneurs and city officials tried a different tack—they thought the big oval would lend itself perfectly to adaptation into a baseball stadium. With dreams of hosting a minor league team in a unique home field setting, they launched a campaign in the local newspaper to solicit support from citizens and to persuade Shell to donate or sell the tank to the city. Their plan called for filling the floor of the tank with new soil, on top of which they would plant a grass field, and installing bleacher seats into the sloped sides of the structure. Ultimately, however, Shell officials elected not to participate in the venture, and the baseball promoters instead obtained a site west of town from the Humble Oil Company for their new ball field. Although ownership of the tank remained with the Shell Oil Company, various citizens groups continued to use it into the 1940s and early 1950s. The local press billed the tank, the site of numerous square dances, as the world's largest dance hall.[12]

The most colorful period of the tank's history began in 1954, when a local citizen and town promoter named Wayne Long finally convinced Shell to sell the property. A former resident of Corpus Christi on the Texas Gulf Coast, Long moved to Monahans with his wife Amalie in 1950 after his doctor recommended a hotter, drier climate for his health. The Longs invested in a number of real estate ventures and at various times operated a drive-in theater and a trailer park. Wayne Long quickly immersed himself in the life of his new hometown and became active in a number of community organizations and civic clubs. His propensity for practical jokes reportedly earned him both admiration and derision from his new neighbors, but most admitted he was an effective, if sometimes abrasive, town promoter.

In 1953, while serving as chairman of the Monahans Chamber of Commerce tourism committee, Long tried to broker a deal whereby the Shell Oil Company would lease the site of the million-barrel tank to the city for a nominal fee, and the city would in turn develop the property into a public park. When the deal fell through, Long made an offer to buy the tank himself, and Shell accepted. He planned to fill the tank with water, stock it with fish, and market it as a fishing, swimming, boating, and even waterskiing lake. He built a boat ramp at one end of the oval where the Shell Company had cut an opening to haul out timbers from the dismantled roof in 1929. Then he started drilling for the water that would be necessary to fill the tank. Ironically, nine of the eleven wells he drilled struck oil instead. "There was not enough oil for Wayne to grow rich from," his widow, Amalie, later told a reporter for the *Monahans News*, "just enough to mess up his plans." Still, with two wells successfully drilled to provide adequate water, Long proceeded with his plans, cleaning out years of accumulated debris to prepare the tank for its new life as a lake. As he began to fill the tank with water, though, he encountered the same evaporation and seepage problems that plagued the oil storage operations thirty years earlier. Undaunted, he continued with his venture, and four years later he had his lake filled and ready for customers. Long and his wife dubbed the new attraction Melody Park—named for their dog—and it opened on Sunday, October 5, 1958, with an extravagant show by professional water skiers from Austin. The Longs charged four dollars per ticket for admission, and the event drew a sizable crowd. But even as the spectators enjoyed the show, Long saw his dream evaporating along with the water in the lake. Most accounts report the park opened and closed on the same day, with the waterskiing show serving as both its grand opening and its

Million Barrel Tank as Melody Park, 1958. Local entrepreneurs Wayne and Amalie Long spent years converting the tank into a water recreation park, an enterprise that failed almost as soon as it opened. This photograph of the grand opening festivities on October 5, 1958, shows professional water skiers brought to West Texas from Austin for the occasion. Courtesy Ward County Archives, Monahans.

swan song. Long hired engineers to solve the leakage problem, but nothing worked. His plan for a fishing operation also failed when the fish died because there was no vegetation in the lake to supply the oxygen they needed to survive.

Disillusioned and in financial straits, the Longs, like the Shell Oil Company before them, finally gave up and abandoned the tank. Once again the huge structure sat empty, a big hole in the ground on the outskirts of town. Generations of high school kids skipped classes and hung out at the tank, leaving layers of graffiti in their wake. Following Wayne Long's death in 1980, Amalie Long retained ownership of the property for a few more years and then donated it to the Ward County Historical Commission, setting the stage for its next incarnation—a community museum.[13]

Monahans's Million Barrel Museum owes its existence, at least in part, to Deolece Parmelee, a teacher at Monahans High School in the early 1960s. Keenly interested in local history, Parmelee helped research and write *Water, Oil, Sand and Sky: A History of Ward County, Texas,* published in 1962 by the Monahans Junior Chamber of Commerce. As sponsor of the Monahans Junior Historians chapter, she encouraged her students to explore local history and suggested the million-barrel tank as a topic for in-depth study. Some years later, after Parmelee moved to Austin and joined the staff of the Texas State Historical Survey Committee (later the Texas Historical Commission) to work with the Official Texas Historical Marker program, and after some of her former students graduated and became active in Ward County historic preservation efforts, the million-barrel tank once again surfaced as a topic of community interest. At a statewide history fair in Austin in 1975, Monahans Junior Historians took third-place honors with their scale model of the oil storage tank, depicting it during its construction with an accompanying diorama that included tiny human and animal figures and an adjacent tent city. Proudly recalling the event years later, Elizabeth Heath, longtime chair of the Ward County Historical Commission, said, "It wasn't so much that we won third. It was the fact that with the exhibit we asked the question—What's next for the Million Barrel Tank?"[14]

In the early 1980s, plans began taking shape for the Texas Sesquicentennial, a statewide celebration of the 150th anniversary of Texas independence. State officials encouraged communities to join the festivities by planning projects that would feature local history and also tie in with statewide historical themes. For Monahans citizens, the answer was clear—their history was the history of Texas oil, and what better way to tell that history than with a new museum? First, they acquired the Holman House, a former hotel run by the J. R. Holman family during the oil boom era. Eugene Holman (1895–1962), one of the family's six children who grew up in the house, studied geology and went to work for the Humble Oil and Refining Company, becoming the corporation's chief geologist in 1926 at the height of the West Texas oil boom. A respected leader in the worldwide petroleum industry, he became president of Standard Oil of New Jersey, then the world's largest oil company, in 1944.[15] With the acquisition of the Holman House, relocated a number of times since its 1909 construction, the county historical commission had the genesis of a local history museum. In 1984, Amalie Long donated the tank and the surrounding acreage to the

Aerial view, Million Barrel Museum, circa 1987. Viewed alongside the Holman House and the museum's Meadows Amphitheater, the Million Barrel Tank looms as the largest manmade feature in Ward County. Courtesy Ward County Archives, Monahans.

preservation group. With their long-sought vision of making the tank into a heritage tourism attraction finally within sight, the group moved the Holman House to the tank property and began raising funds for the new museum.

After thousands of hours of volunteer labor, as well as financial donations from individual citizens, businesses, corporations, and foundations, the dream turned into reality and the Million Barrel Museum opened on May 30, 1987.[16] Among the museum's features, in addition to the renovated Holman House, are a four-hundred-seat amphitheater built into the side of the tank wall, exhibits of antique farm and oil drilling equipment, a railroad caboose, the original Monahans city jail building, and a windmill. The historic tank, with its new amphitheater, now hosts numerous community events including barbecues, cowboy poetry readings, dances, and school reunions. Many former students who return to the site search for signs of their youthful mischief in the graffiti on the walls. One couple even told a museum volunteer about the time they cut class at Monahans High School and went to the tank for what turned out to be an auspicious day. On a nostalgic visit

Graffiti on wall of Million Barrel Tank, 2008. Years of youthful mischief gave way to an officially sanctioned annual event beginning in 2002, when museum staff invited Monahans High School seniors to leave their marks on the abandoned tank. Visible at left is a concrete base that originally supported the timbered roof system. Photograph by Cynthia J. Beeman.

years later with their four children, they photographed their oldest son standing next to graffiti that revealed their names and the scrawled notation "love" and admitted it was the site of his conception on that fateful day when they played hooky from school.[17] In 2002, museum officials turned the practice of writing on the tank walls into a new community tradition, sponsoring an annual Graffiti Day for Monahans High School seniors.

In 1988, years after Deolece Parmelee retired from the Texas Historical Commission, her old friends in Monahans applied for an Official Texas Historical Marker for the Million Barrel Tank. Dedicated in March 1989, the marker adds to the interpretation of the site and serves as a state-sanctioned witness to the historical significance of the long-ago experiment that, but for the efforts of a tenacious town promoter and generations of dedicated local historians, might have become a mere footnote in the lore of the early twentieth-century West Texas oil boom. Attending the marker dedication, Amalie Long told a newspaper reporter, "I think Wayne would be proud."[18]

MARKER LOCATION: 400 E. 4th Street, Monahans

Second only to Spindletop in tales of legendary Texas oil wells, Santa Rita No. 1, discovery well of the Big Lake Oilfield, opened the Permian Basin to large-scale oil exploration and brought a financial windfall to Texas universities. In the Texas Constitution of 1876, the state legislature set aside one million acres in West Texas as an endowment to fund higher education. Substituted for previous legislation that designated better agricultural lands along the state's developing railroad network for the educational fund, the West Texas land provision seemed at the time to hold little promise for financial reward. But Rupert P. Ricker, a University of Texas (UT) Law School graduate and World War I veteran, believed the 1917 discovery of the Ranger Oilfield west of Fort Worth pre-saged the location of large mineral deposits in West Texas. Taking advantage of a little-known state law that allowed individuals to lease public lands, Ricker applied in January 1919 to explore for oil on 431,360 acres in Reagan, Irion, Crockett, and Upton counties.

With the lease papers filed, Ricker scrambled to raise the fil-ing fee of ten cents per acre—$43,136 due within thirty days—by subdividing the lease and selling interests in his venture. Failing to attract enough investors to cover his costs within the allotted time, he sold his dream to Frank Pickrell, a friend from his days in the army who lived in El Paso. Pickrell and his business partner Haymon Krupp, a Jewish Lithuanian immigrant whose success as a merchant in El Paso made him one of the city's most prominent businessmen and philanthropists, paid the filing fee and hired geologist Hugh Tucker, who chose a site near the Kansas City, Mexico, and Orient Railway line west of Big Lake in Reagan County to drill the first well. The partners incorporated the Texon Oil and Land Company and named Krupp as president and Pickrell as vice president, intending to sell stock to finance their drilling opera-tion. When stock sales failed to generate the required financial capital, Pickrell and Krupp devised a plan to sell small interests in a section of the lease. They raised enough money to purchase

Reconstructed derrick at the Santa Rita Oil Well, 2007. Discovery well of the Big Lake Oilfield, the Santa Rita well, named for the patron saint of impossible causes, is legendary in the history of Texas oil. Its proceeds, along with those of thousands of other wells in West Texas, flowed into a fund to benefit higher education through the University of Texas and Texas A&M University systems. Photograph by Randy Mallory.

used equipment, hired Carl Cromwell as driller and Dee Locklin as tool dresser, and began drilling a test well in January 1921.

Pickrell traveled to New York to find more investors. Two women who considered taking a risk on the venture reportedly consulted their priest, who told them if they decided to invest they should invoke the assistance of Saint Rita of Cascia, patron saint of impossible causes. As the story goes, the ladies decided to invest and gave Pickrell an envelope filled with rose petals, instructing him to scatter them on the well in the name of Saint Rita. Returning to West Texas, Pickrell climbed to the top of the platform and performed the requested rite as drilling continued on the well. Finally, on May 28, 1923, more than four years after Rupert Ricker initiated the lease, Santa Rita No. 1 roared to life, filling the West Texas sky with a gusher of oil. With Santa Rita No. 1 as its impetus, and to the surprise of many who thought the land useless, the Big Lake Oilfield attracted scores of wildcatters, and West Texas oil wealth began to fuel the state's Permanent University Fund (PUF)—the fund created by the provision in the 1876 Texas Constitution.

In 1939, Texas historian and UT professor Walter P. Webb headed an effort to relocate the famous well's derrick and drilling rig to the university's Austin campus, where he envisioned a permanent memorial exhibit. Dismantled and moved there, the timbers and equipment languished in an outdoor storage area for almost two decades. According to a 1958 article in the school newspaper, the *Daily Texan,* the drilling rig with its oil-soaked timbers survived the years of exposure to the elements, but the wooden derrick lay in ruins and could not be reconstructed. Nonetheless, workers reassembled the drilling rig and placed it in a prominent corner of the campus (San Jacinto Street and 19th Street, now Martin Luther King Jr. Boulevard) along with interpretive plaques and a recorded message to convey its history and significance to the university. Webb, serving as president of the American Historical Association that year, called the meeting to order with a gavel carved of wood from the derrick.

Deolece Parmelee, director of research at the Texas State Historical Survey Committee, wrote a brief history of the Santa Rita No. 1 well on the occasion of a historical marker dedication at the well site in November 1965. Titled "Saint of the Impossible Smiled, and UT was Rich," the article appeared in newspapers across the state. Members of the UT Board of Regents, on a three-day tour of West Texas university lands, attended the dedication ceremony along with national, state, and county elected officials. Dee Locklin sat on the platform with other dignitaries and after the ceremony regaled reporters with tales of working on the original well. Although Santa Rita No. 1 stopped producing in 1990, millions of dollars from West Texas oil wells continue to flow to the PUF, benefiting schools in the University of Texas and Texas A&M University systems. "Since the day the saint of the impossible smiled on Reagan County," Parmelee wrote in 1965, "multi-millions in royalty dollars have aided the cause of Texas education. Arid pastures that nobody wanted to buy from the university before 1923 now teem with drill rigs and new wells are brought in with great regularity. But none has quite the drama of Santa Rita No. 1."

MARKER LOCATION
US 67, 13 mi. W of Big Lake

Sources: Martin W. Schwettmann, Santa Rita (Austin: Texas State Historical Association, 1943); Walter Rundell Jr., Early Texas Oil (College Station: Texas A&M University Press, 1977); Conoly Cullum, "The Saint of the Impossible Blesses Texas," Texas Parade, Apr. 1959, pp. 42–45; Carl Coke Rister, Oil! Titan of the Southwest (Norman: University of Oklahoma Press, 1949); Deolece Parmelee, "Saint of the Impossible Smiled, and UT Was Rich," Denton Record-Chronicle (article distributed by Associated Press), Nov. 4, 1965; "UT's 'Big' Rig Gets New Home: Santa Rita Well Moved to Campus," Daily Texan, Sept. 19, 1958; Julia Cauble Smith, "Santa Rita Oil Well," New Handbook of Texas, vol. 5, p. 890; Vivian Elizabeth Smyrl, "Permanent University Fund," New Handbook of Texas, vol. 5, pp. 154–55; Natalie Ornish, "Haymon Krupp," New Handbook of Texas, vol. 3, pp. 1163–64.

6

"WE SHALL COME REJOICING"

With religious pedigrees that reach back to celebrated Protestant camp meetings of the Old South at places like Shoulderbone Creek, Georgia; Sandy Creek, North Carolina; and Cane Ridge, Kentucky, and arguably even to the Great Awakening of eighteenth-century New England and beyond, the rural tabernacles of Texas have a history far greater than would first appear. They evoke memories of earlier times, when residents of dispersed rural settlements regularly gathered beneath the sheltering roofs of the great wooden tents—or the thatched roofs of their predecessors, the brush arbors—for religious and social events. The brush arbors are gone, but wooden tabernacles can still be found in all regions of the state, although their numbers have dwindled significantly over the years. The relatively few that remain are now largely endangered due to harsh Texas weather, redefined functions, inadequate maintenance, vandalism, and neglect. Vernacular in design and most commonly consisting of a massive roof structure—either gabled or hipped—resting on posts and with open sides, most began as temporary structures and have far outlived their original ecclesiastical purpose. Some still have earthen floors and contain either faded antique pews or handcrafted benches more rigid in design, while others reflect degrees of adaptation over the years with concrete floors and folding chairs. A few remain as revered community landmarks, preserved for their cultural identity, historical associations, and architectural integrity.

Each tabernacle had its unique history, but in general the structures represented an association with early religious services, in their myriad forms, as well as aspects of social interaction and community determinism. Some served as integral links in the architectural evolution of church "plantings," providing a transitional phase from open fields, tents, or brush arbors to enclosed sanctuaries. Even with completion of new buildings, though, many tabernacles remained in church use as welcome refuges from the heat in the days before air conditioning. Other tabernacles existed where there were no church buildings, serving primarily as central shelters for protracted religious gatherings known as camp meetings, where worshipers came great distances and stayed for days and even weeks.

Many accounts of pioneer settlement and rural life include references to the protracted camp meetings often associated with tabernacles. Elise Waerenskjold, a Norwegian teacher who migrated to Texas in 1847, provided one of the earliest descriptions: "I must tell you a little about camp meetings, which are the most extraordinarily odd form of Christian worship that any person can imagine. Somewhere in the woods they build a shed—that is to say, a roof which rests on post, but has neither walls nor floor; there are a few logs to sit on, as well as a raised platform that serves as the pulpit. There are five preachers present—at times even more than that—who continue preaching day and night for a whole week. The people in the vicinity congregate around the camp and remain there, some in wagons and tents, and others in small log houses which they have constructed for their own comforts there." Providing details of the religious practices and worship services, she continued:

> But, later on in the evening the women folks wandered
> out into the forest for the so-called secret prayers; the men
> folks went in another direction for the same purpose. They
> alternately sang psalms and poured forth long prayers—
> which various ones present speak responsively. They became
> so inspired on these occasions that one after another they
> began to sing and cry out as loudly as they were able, clap-
> ping their hands, "Glory! Glory!" They began pounding on
> the ones nearest, laughing and crying—in short, conducting
> themselves like perfectly insane people. At the evening service
> the same comic behavior took place, and the preachers exerted

themselves to the highest ecstasies. At these camp meetings people are baptized, married, and tendered the Lord's Supper.

Waerenskjold concluded by observing, "On the whole, it must be said that the feelings that the whole comedy aroused were nothing less than devotional."[1]

Emotions ran deep at the camp meetings, and it was the job of the preachers to seek their release so the spiritual healing, redemption, and salvation could begin. Attendees, for the most part, were on personal journeys, seeking insights, comfort, and direction. Preachers and church elders structured the services accordingly, providing a well-planned mix of lively singing, preaching, praying, responsive reading, "witnessing," and exhorting that built in crescendo fashion to an eddy of personal decision-making. The messages, generally straightforward and basic, stressed eternal judgment, the conviction of the human spirit, and the condemnation of personal sins, but they also led ultimately to a narrow path for salvation. These were evangelical meetings, designed to rescue lost souls and spread the Christian gospel, hopefully lighting the flames of another great community revival in the process. Each tabernacle held that potential in the eyes of those who gathered there to worship.

Camp meeting services provided attendees with what psychology professor Louis Fairchild called "a socially accepted 'emotional jumping-off place.'"[2] While some gatherings were relatively staid and uneventful, many more, especially in the early days, resulted in the human drama of uncontrolled joy as individuals "got religion." The signs of transition from lost to saved ranged from clapping, singing, shouting, dancing, and "speaking in tongues" to even stronger and more demonstrative manifestations of total spiritual surrender as Fairchild described: "Men jerked as though they would be scattered into atoms; the long hair of women snapped and cracked like a whip. Some threw themselves around as if battered by a stormy sea; others fell like trees toppled from the force of strong winds. The fallen lay as soldiers slain in battle, and they might remain there for hours, motionless and apparently breathless. Others trembled and convulsed, their extremities cold to the touch."[3] The tabernacles often contributed to the drama, their cavernous ceilings reverberating with the sounds of salvation, their timbers creaking in the wind and heat, and their roofs sounding as a chorus of drums from the rain. In the evenings—in the days before electricity—coal oil lanterns, torches, or burning pine knots placed around the perimeters cast strange shadows that added to the mystical feel of the event.

With time, the protracted camp meetings gave way to shorter seasonal revivals as the advent of cars, the development of more focused communities, and the construction of permanent church facilities made the overnight camps unnecessary. Worshipers instead left for their homes after the evening services and, if the spirit moved them, returned the following day. The protracted meetings that lasted weeks thus gave way to events of two to four days in duration with fewer and briefer services. Nevertheless, the revivals, just as the camp meetings before them, produced their own memories and provided their own unique historical sense of time and place, as folklorist and educator William A. Owens richly described through his memory of one at a crossroads arbor between Crockett and Madisonville in East Texas sometime in the mid-twentieth century: "I stood outside at the back and breathed again the mixed smell of drying willow leaves, of oak sawdust six inches deep on the ground, of coal oil flares shedding their reddish glow against the outer edges of darkness, on men and women scrooched together on oak plank benches, on children asleep on patchwork quilt pallets. Services had started and the preacher, a white-haired, white-bearded man in white shirt and black trousers, was talking. At the moment his voice was quiet, gentle for a revivalist. From what he said I knew he was Baptist, probably Primitive or Landmark. At the proper time he would shout in anger, not at the sinner—for him there would be compassion—but at the devil and his power to drag the sinner down."[4] And, Owens added, as the preacher continued to build his argument on through the sermon, interspersing it with scriptures, supplication, and spontaneous song while calling sinners to the mourner's bench, deacons echoed their approval with repeated "amens." "Women wept softly," he wrote. "Workers pleaded in soft voices with those who had not yet 'given themselves to the Lord.' A man laid his hand on my arm and leaned close: 'You been born again?' I nodded. He moved on. Then the preacher reminded them of the saints who had gone on before."[5]

Similar scenes played out regularly in brush arbors and tabernacles across the state well into the twentieth century, providing religious focus and identity for communities. To maximize the number of participants, revival planners generally scheduled them around prevailing agricultural cycles: for farmers that was after the "laying by" of crops (following planting and hoeing) in late summer or following harvest in the fall; for ranchers it could be after the spring branding season or before the fall roundups. Planners also took into account such factors as "the elements": summer services required a ready supply of cardboard fans, and the cycle of the full moon provided optimum night vision. Despite the serious and purposeful nature of the tabernacle services, though, they also provided entertainment in rural areas, and residents often attended regardless of personal denominational preference—Baptists, Methodists, Presbyterians, Disciples of Christ, Nazarenes, and others commonly joined together. So meaningful were the gatherings that they regularly attracted visitors from nearby towns as well. While they managed to draw people together, however, most services remained racially segregated in the custom of the time.

Music served as a key attraction for many who participated in the tabernacle gatherings, and it came in many forms, from musical instruments and featured performers to the unaccompanied, shaped-note singing in the manner known as sacred harp. Revival songs generally related directly to the emotional ebbs and flows of the services, ranging from lively and exuberant to serene, pleading, and prayerful. They conveyed uncomplicated messages with tunes and lyrics easily recognized, remembered, and experienced. Popular revival songs such as "I'll Fly Away," "Softly and Tenderly," "Blessed Assurance," "I Surrender All," "The Old Rugged Cross," and "Just a Closer Walk with Thee" reinforced important themes from the sermons, while others like "Bringing in the Sheaves" evoked images familiar to rural families:

Sowing in the morning, sowing seeds of kindness,
Sowing in the noontide and the dewy eve;
Waiting for the harvest and the time of reaping,
We shall come rejoicing, bringing in the sheaves.[6]

With time, the music and the message moved indoors, to nearby towns or out through the airwaves, and the grand old tabernacles that survived the transition began serving other purposes. Many continued to function as community focal points, providing shelter for funerals, weddings, political gatherings, school programs, family reunions, homecomings, and summer chautauquas, as well as the occasional church service or Sunday school class. Others, adaptively reused for agricultural purposes, became pole barns or equipment storage sheds. Most, however, survived only for a brief time following the end of their original function. Those that remain part of the cultural landscape thus take on added historical significance as distinct building types strongly representative of religious history and community development.

Thanks to the work of preservationists, local historians, families, congregations, and others, a number of Texas tabernacles are now interpreted for heritage tourists and others through Official Texas Historical Markers. The largest collection of those is in Erath County, in the north central part of the state, which has four:

- BLUFF DALE TABERNACLE: The small community of Bluff Dale, originally known as Bluff Springs, is situated along the North Paluxy River in the eastern part of the county. South Carolina native Andrew Jackson Glenn migrated to the area from Georgia in the 1880s, and later, when a rail line was built through the area, he donated the present townsite east of the earlier location. The community showed great economic promise in its early years and by the first decades of the twentieth century boasted a bank and newspaper. The tabernacle dates to circa 1906 and that period of prosperity. Sited on a small hill above the town, it features a massive hipped roof resting on large squared beams. Although residents constructed it adjacent to the Baptist church, it served all local denominations and provided space for camp meetings and revivals through the 1940s. It became the site of an annual homecoming in 1950 and is still used for other community functions as well. Electrified in the 1920s and enlarged, repaired, and restored over the years, the structure reflects the heyday of Bluff Dale, which peaked in population in the years before World War II. The Texas Historical Commission (THC) designated the Bluff Dale Tabernacle a Recorded Texas Historic Landmark (RTHL) in 1982.[7]

Hillside view of Bluff Dale Tabernacle, 2008, Bluff Dale, Erath County. Photograph by Cynthia J. Beeman.

Seating in the Bluff Dale Tabernacle, as is typical in many similar structures, ranges from homemade benches, such as this one, to more modern pews donated by or purchased from local churches.
Photograph by Cynthia J. Beeman.

- LINGLEVILLE TABERNACLE: On the opposite side of the county is a tabernacle associated with the smaller rural settlement of Lingleville, which also dates to the mid-nineteenth century. It is named for early settler John (or Jacob) Lingle. Local Baptists provided the site and initial funding and joined with Methodists and Presbyterians in 1913 to build the community structure and its handmade benches as a more lasting alternative to earlier, temporary brush arbors. As originally constructed, the Lingleville Tabernacle measured approximately sixty feet by seventy feet with a wood-shingled hipped roof supported by rounded rustic timbers. A central cupola provided vent space for the roof, and a wooden stage occupied space on the south side. First lit by lanterns and then by carbide and gas lighting systems, it received electricity circa 1938. The Lingleville Homecoming began in 1952, and early funds raised through the event paid for a new metal roof over the shingles and the removal of the cupola in the process. Later changes included reduction of the stage and the replacement of original wiring. The Lingleville Homecoming Committee provided funding for a marker, and in 1983 the THC designated it an RTHL.[8]

- MORGAN MILL TABERNACLE: Ten miles north of the Erath County seat of Stephenville is the settlement of Morgan Mill, with historic ties to the 1870s, when M. C. Laughlin and J. R. Billingsley established a grist mill there. It is named for George Morgan, a later partner in the milling operation. The community tabernacle, built to supersede earlier brush arbors, dates to 1910. Local congregations—Baptist, Methodist, Presbyterian, Church of Christ, and Nazarene—joined together to construct the building for their summer revivals and other meetings. Kerosene lanterns provided the original lighting but became an early hindrance to worship services when they attracted blister bugs and other annoying insects. The addition of electric lights, which proved less attractive to pests, and the tactical use of pesticides minimized the problem. As with other tabernacles, its religious use declined with the advent of air conditioning in local churches, but it continued in service as a community gathering place, the site of numerous events over the years, including homecomings and other reunions. The Morgan Mill Tabernacle, awarded an Official Texas Historical Marker (subject marker) in 1994, features a hipped roof with distinctive wood plank brackets on perimeter support posts.[9]
- PECAN CEMETERY TABERNACLE: With graves dating to 1880, Pecan Cemetery ten miles southeast of Dublin predates the founding of the nearby Purves community in the 1890s. It began on the farmstead of J. W. McKenzie, who in 1884 deeded the initial acreage for the establishment of the burial ground and a church. Friendship Baptist Church remained in operation until 1915, when it disbanded. In 1922, local residents

used lumber from the sanctuary to construct the tabernacle at the cemetery. Partially enclosed on one end, with diagonal board bracing on corners at the other end, the rectilinear structure exhibits bungalow influences in the design of the shingled roof that incorporates both hipped and gabled lines, as well as exposed rafter ends. The structure is used primarily for funerals. The THC approved the RTHL designation for the Pecan Cemetery Tabernacle in 1996, and in May of the following year local families, former residents, and friends gathered to dedicate the marker. Appropriately, the service included the singing of two spirituals evocative of earlier tabernacle evangelism: "Onward Christian Soldiers" and "Amazing Grace."[10]

The tabernacle at Morgan Mill, Erath County, exhibits unique flared bracing at the support posts that visually provides an anchor for the massive roof. Photograph by Cynthia J. Beeman.

The small tabernacle at Pecan Cemetery, near Purves community,
features a roof with elements of both hipped and gabled design.
Photograph by Cynthia J. Beeman.

While the tabernacles of Erath County represent four variations
on a theme, they also provide insights into local values. Years ago,
residents and friends of the small rural communities of Bluff Dale,
Lingleville, Morgan Mill, and Purves made the long-range commitment to keep the structures much as they were in their periods
of greatest historical significance and also to extend their viability despite significant cultural and social changes over the years.
Through the medium of historic preservation, the keepers of the
tabernacles now afford others the opportunity to experience at
least part of the rich history associated with the great wooden
tents. Those who know them only as artifacts from the past can
nevertheless marvel at their engineering and massing, and com-
prehend their complexities, for they are not simple vernacular

structures as they might first appear. And, against the unique architectural backdrop, visitors can try to imagine what it must have been like when communities came together for the purpose of revival. For others who experienced firsthand the tabernacle meetings of decades past, they remain touchstones of emotions, with memories of beloved family and friends, resolute preachers, spirited music, and maybe even life-changing decisions.

Why should we linger and heed not His mercies . . . ?[11]

MARKER LOCATIONS
Bluff Dale Tabernacle: Glenn and Holmes streets, Bluff Dale
Lingleville Tabernacle: FM 219 S of FM 8, Lingleville
Morgan Mill Tabernacle: Intersection of US 281 and FM 1188, Morgan Mill
Pecan Cemetery Tabernacle: 8 mi. SE of Dublin on FM 219, then 1.5 mi. S on CR 291 (Pecan Cemetery Road)

WAUGH CAMPGROUND

A few miles northeast of Caldwell in Burleson County is an Official Texas Historical Marker commemorating the site of Waugh Campground, a longtime Methodist camp meeting and revival site named in honor of Bishop Beverly Waugh (1789–1858), the first Methodist bishop for Texas. There, in 1865, Mississippi native and Civil War veteran Benajah Harvey Carroll (1843–1914), the son of a Baptist preacher, experienced his personal conversion as a Christian. Ordained a Baptist minister the following year, he preached in rural churches and at revivals in Central Texas while also farming and teaching school. In 1871, he became pastor of the First Baptist Church of Waco, a position he held until 1899. Under his dynamic direction it became one of the foremost Baptist congregations in the state, and the Rev. B. H. Carroll rose to prominence as a powerful and influential preacher, religious writer, and denominational leader. A tireless proponent of Christian education and Prohibition, he served as a trustee of Baylor University and a founder of what became Southwestern Baptist Theological Seminary, where he served as both a teacher and school president. He is buried in Oakwood Cemetery in Waco.

MARKER LOCATION
1.5 mi. E of Caldwell on SH 21, then 3.5 mi. N on FM 2000

Sources: Waugh Campground, Burleson County, THC marker files; J. A. Reynolds, "Benajah Harvey Carroll," *New Handbook of Texas,* vol. 1, p. 989; Claudia Hazlewood, "Beverly Waugh," *New Handbook of Texas,* vol. 6, p. 861.

ZEPHYR GOSPEL TABERNACLE

Ironically, the historic tabernacle in the small Brown County town of Zephyr, whose name harkens back to Zephyrus, the Greek god of the west wind, owes its existence to high winds. On May 30, 1909, a tornado ripped through the community, destroying a number of structures, including a tabernacle dating to circa 1898. The following month, with financial assistance from local churches, residents built the present structure on the site using the same overall dimensions. It has since been used for revival services, gospel singing conventions, political rallies, school programs, and other community events. The structure needed extensive rehabilitation in the 1970s, so the Zephyr Home Demonstration Club took on the project as part of the U.S. Bicentennial celebration. Important funding came from a grant awarded by the Massachusetts company Bird and Son (later Bird Corporation), a leading supplier of building materials founded in 1795. Modifications to the 1909 structure included a paved floor, new roof shingles, and electrification. In the bicentennial year of 1976, the Texas Historical Commission designated the Zephyr Gospel Tabernacle a Recorded Texas Historic Landmark.

MARKER LOCATION
1 block E of US 183 on SH 218, Zephyr

Sources: Zephyr Gospel Tabernacle, Zephyr, Brown County, THC marker files; Merle Bond Tilly, "Zephyr, Texas," *New Handbook of Texas,* vol. 6, p. 1152.

Zephyr Gospel Tabernacle, Zephyr, Brown County.
Photograph by Randy Mallory.

(opposite) This interior view of the Zephyr Gospel Tabernacle provides detailing of a pew, as well as the intricate framing system that supports the massive hipped roof. Photograph by Randy Mallory.

7 THE MUSIC MAN OF SCHULENBURG

Carl Morene was the type of individual who quietly went about his business, a good neighbor who worked hard, treated people fairly, and contributed where he could to the quality of life in his adopted hometown. He was a Mason, a Lion, and a member of the American Legion. A quiet and gentle man, he never ran for political office, and he sought neither fame nor special recognition. Everyone in Schulenburg who knew him, it seemed, thought of him as a kind, generous, and decent man. Had those remained the defining elements of his life, he would no doubt have been remembered warmly as an upstanding citizen and a valued friend to many. But an extraordinary set of circumstances he could not have anticipated brought him new opportunities and challenges, and the unselfish manner in which he responded changed his course in life and made him something of a local legend in the process.

Carl Thomas Morene was born on November 13, 1887, to Swedish-immigrant parents in the small southwestern Fayette County community of Muldoon, platted as a railroad town only the year before. His father, A. F. Morene, worked for the railroad, and the family moved often as a result. In 1896, when the family lived at Lyon's Station in Burleson County, Carl's mother passed away; he was only eight at the time. His father died in Gonzales County four years later, and so Carl left school at the end of the eighth grade to seek work. In 1909, he joined the U.S. Navy and served four years. Tradition holds it was in the navy that he learned the electrical trade. During World War I, he joined the U.S. Army and served as a private in the 304 Repair Unit of the Motor Transport Corps. Following the war, he started his career in the electric utility business, operating a light plant at Nixon in Gonzales County. He joined the

Central Power and Light Company in 1924 and worked in Hallettsville before moving to Schulenburg in 1928 to run the company's operation there.[1]

Schulenburg, located south of LaGrange in Fayette County, began as a railroad town in the 1870s and early on attracted immigrant settlers of German, Czech, and Austrian descent. It experienced steady growth as a center of agricultural commerce over the years, and by the late 1920s had approximately 1,500 residents. At the time, it was common for local electrical utility companies to be associated with ice plants, which required large motors to freeze vats of water, so Morene first set up office in the ice plant. A bachelor, he lived in a room of the relatively new Von Minden Hotel, operated by Irwin and Leonida Speckels. He devoted long hours to his work, even on weekends, and during his spare time returned to his room to read or to visit in the lobby with fellow lodgers, many of whom were drummers (traveling salesmen). When the city moved to establish a municipal utility program, it acquired the local Central Power and Light facilities and hired Morene as city manager over electric power, water, and wastewater. From his office at 719 Upton Street he managed the maintenance operations, personally handling electrical instrumentation repair in the back of his office and compiling at his own expense a large technical library for use by municipal crews. Carl Morene enjoyed his work and his friendships with co-workers, and he looked forward to a long association with the city.[2] He had a dependable job and lived a productive life, but by the 1930s, as the nation found itself in the middle of the Great Depression, what had once been dependable and productive became more uncertain as society struggled to adapt to the changes.

The Schulenburg school district, like the town and surrounding rural area it served, experienced steady growth in the early decades of the twentieth century. Faced with the loss of tax revenues brought on by the economic downturn, though, school officials faced tough budget decisions. Looking for ways to minimize expenses, they came to the realization they would have to cut existing programs, including longstanding ones that not only provided educational opportunities for students but proved popular with local residents as well. One of those was the Schulenburg High School Orchestra, which under the leadership of director Hugh C. Berry had gained regional notoriety for its performances, even appearing on a Houston radio station. At the time, marching bands were a relatively recent phenomenon in Texas public schools, and not every district had one. Even rarer, though, were orchestral programs like the one at Schulenburg. Despite its successes and uniqueness, though, the program gave way to broader economic decisions by the school board, which discontinued the paid directorship in 1933.[3]

Carl T. Morene was among those Schulenburg residents who believed strongly that the loss of the school music program would be detrimental to the students and the community, so he offered an alternative plan for the board's consideration. Perhaps motivated by circumstances surrounding his own brief period of childhood and his lack of a complete public school education, but certainly by his love of children, Morene offered to serve as the orchestra's unpaid director in order to keep the program going. Given his full-time responsibilities to the city, though, his offer required a new system outside regular school hours. Board members realized the innovative plan afforded a possible solution for the students and their families and that if it proved successful would take some of the pressure off the board. In their view, they had little to lose, so they voted their approval. The wisdom or folly of their vote, they believed, would soon be known.

Just how or when Carl Morene learned to read and play music remains unknown, but he had those basic skills. It turned out he also possessed the fundamental characteristics of a great teacher, exhibiting patience, resourcefulness, enthusiasm, perseverance, and a genuine interest in his students. While he had much to offer as a leader, the program he inherited—at least at first glance—had drawbacks. It was small, with thirty or so students, and obviously lacked the budgetary support for travel, sheet music, and other program essentials. Additionally, at the height of the Great Depression, few students could afford the cost of musical instruments, and in a largely agrarian community such as Schulenburg, extracurricular programs often meant significant sacrifices for farm families, who relied on their children for chores and fieldwork.[4]

But none of the challenges the program faced in 1933 deterred Carl Morene, so with the confidence, enthusiasm, and integrity that typified his character, he eagerly assumed the leadership as a volunteer. He began immediately by working to retain former members and personally recruiting other students to join the orchestra. As he did throughout his directorship, he took a proactive approach, trying either to fill a particular gap in the ensemble or determining which instrument fit the talents of an individual student best. Gloria Rektonik Baker remembered, "Someone told Mr. Morene I loved music, and one day he asked me if I might like to play the French horn."[5] Bill (Milton) Koehler, whom the director started on trumpet and then moved to bass fiddle and later to trumpet again, provided another perspective of the recruitment process: "My dad had been the cornetist for the Moravia Symphony Band for many years, playing for all the feasts and dances which were so popular during the 1930s. Dad wanted me to learn the cornet also, but somehow I just wasn't interested." When Morene personally sought him out, though, and asked him to join the orchestra, "Well, it really meant something, having him make the request, and I agreed without a second thought." But, Koehler concluded, "Somehow I still wonder if he and my dad hadn't schemed up about the matter."[6]

As Carl Morene redefined the structure of the program, his remarkable generosity soon became evident. He offered individualized lessons at his office in the evenings after work (he referred to beginner classes as "the monkey cage"), never accepting pay, and much in the same manner in which he built the city's technical library he began investing his own money. If the orchestra needed new sheet music, he purchased it himself. If an instrument proved too costly for a student, he often bought one or loaned one of his own. "He would spend an hour or two teaching me to read notes and play the cornet, which was his to begin with," Oscar Gresser recalled in 2004, adding, "I later purchased the cornet, which I still have today."[7] And on occasion when Morene felt the instrumentation called for a particular "voice," he acquired the instrument first and then recruited the right player later, as he did when he purchased a harp because of the special quality it brought to the music. The day of the purchase he recruited Angie Pratka to join the orchestra as a harpist, which she did successfully. After she graduated in 1936, her sister Beatrice took up the instrument, playing it until her graduation four years later.[8] Morene also provided transportation assistance as needed, utilizing his own car and student drivers who picked up their classmates as he prepared for rehearsals. Orchestra practice took place in the school auditorium on Monday and Wednesday nights, and the beginners practiced on Saturday nights. Later, with the implementation of gasoline rationing during World War II, he used his own ration stamps to help with student transportation. If a student wanted to be in the orchestra, he did what he could to make it happen.

Impressed with the progress of the band under its new leadership, the school board secured a special Texas teaching certificate for its director in September 1934. Clearly touched by the gesture and the vote of confidence it represented, Morene observed, "I had never expected to have a teacher's certificate because of the lack of school education I have had. I never graduated from high school."[9] Collectively, the orchestra also gained recognition from the board, the student body, and the community while it grew in stature as the pride of the Schulenburg Shorthorns. Each Monday morning during the academic year, the group performed at schoolwide assemblies in the third floor auditorium (all grades were in one building at the time), featuring a diverse repertoire that included classical works, patriotic songs, and rousing marches. It also held public concerts, played at local events, performed on the radio, and conducted concert tours to such nearby towns as Yoakum, Shiner, Gonzales, and Waelder. Under Morene's guidance, the group fared well in regional music competitions, winning high honors at long-standing interscholastic events in Seguin and Kingsville.[10] And at a school assembly in February 1938, the orchestra presented perhaps one of its most memorable performances when it debuted an original work entitled "Shorthorns Forever," with words and music by Carl Morene, which the student body immediately adopted as the official school song.[11]

Carl T. Morene in his band director uniform.
Courtesy Ray Gouldsberry, Schulenburg.

JHORTHORNJ FOREVER

Word/ and Mu/ic by
C. T. MORENE

SCHULENBURG HIGH SCHOOL

PUBLI/HED BY
/CHULENBURG HIGH /CHOOL
/CHULENBURG, TEXA/

A reproduction of cover art for the sheet music of "Shorthorns Forever," the Schulenburg High School song. The Carl T. Morene Memorial Fund republished the music in 2004 in association with efforts to commemorate the life of the beloved band director. Courtesy Schulenburg Independent School District.

Despite increasing demands on his time as the orchestra program grew, Morene continued his full-time work with the city, and there he also had opportunities to influence the lives of young people. One was Archie Scott. Only three when his father passed away, Scott was raised by his widowed mother, who ran the local telephone exchange across Upton Street from the city utility office. When he was about ten, Scott first "met" Morene in the middle of that street after a car hit the boy as he darted across without regard for oncoming traffic. Morene immediately came to his rescue, and from that encounter a friendship grew. Scott later sought his assistance with building a crystal radio set and received the help he needed, even though the city manager knew little about such projects. But through that collaboration Morene came to appreciate his young friend's inquisitive mind and technical interests and so began teaching him the electrical supply business. After school, Scott would visit the city office, where he worked side by side with his mentor, by then a father figure as well, repairing meters and other equipment in the back shop. And although Morene taught his young friend enough musical basics for him to serve as bugler for the Boy Scout troop, he never tried to recruit him for the orchestra. Instead, he offered him a paid job with the city. In the late 1930s, while still in high school, Scott worked as a "grunt," literally learning the business from the ground up by digging holes for utility poles. The money he earned, as Morene fully realized when he offered the job, went toward his eventual college education. Through the years the two became lasting friends, and on the day Scott returned to Schulenburg from service in World War II, where he saw intense action at places like New Guinea, Okinawa, and Pelileu, he went by to visit "Mr. Carl." As a veteran himself, Morene no doubt understood the adjustments to come. Scott returned to his old job briefly but eventually headed off to college.[12]

As the war drew to a close in the mid-1940s, communities gradually refocused energies on redevelopment and new growth, and local pride took on added significance, especially for returning service personnel. Within that context, Carl Morene planned for a new musical program at Schulenburg High—a marching drum and bugle corps to perform on the field with the pep squad during halftimes at Shorthorn football games. Such groups represented a normal progression in high school music programs across the state, and as with most the Schulenburg corps initially utilized simple movements and configurations, often playing pieces in a stationary concert formation. The repertoire and presentations increased in sophistication over the next few years, and the drum and bugle corps soon evolved into the high school marching band, all the while under Morene's continued leadership.[13]

The year 1947, which marked the beginning of the marching band, proved to be a memorable one at Schulenburg High as the football team, under Coach L. L. Blakeney, completed an undefeated season and headed into bi-district playoffs against Port Acres (Jefferson County). The teams met in competition at Yellow Jacket Stadium in Port Arthur on what proved to be a miserably cold December night marked by rain, sleet, and ultimately plenty of mud. The band and much of the community attended to provide support, and the team gave its best, but the game ended in a 6–0 loss for the Shorthorns, bringing their impressive season to a close. During the Christmas holidays that followed, Carl Morene fell ill with a cold, most likely brought on by the harsh elements he faced during the playoff game, and his condition deteriorated into pneumonia, resulting in his hospitalization at Hallettsville. There, on January 17, 1948, at the age of 60, the man whom his adopted hometown of Schulenburg came to embrace as "Mr. Music Man" quietly passed away. News of his death stunned the residents of Schulenburg and devastated his students. Mourners gathered for his funeral service two days later in the school gymnasium, the only building in town large enough to accommodate the crowds. Band members served as the honor guard, and the American Legion conducted the graveside service, where three of his trumpet players performed "Taps" in a final and respectful salute to their director.[14]

Carl T. Morene left a lasting legacy in the lives of his many students and friends, and they never forgot his kindness, patience, friendship, direction, or dedication over the years. Early in a new century, as many reached their personal senior years—as opposed to their academic senior years of the 1940s—they often reminisced about the "good old days" and talked of ways to honor their beloved director. From a multiclass reunion in 2002 emerged a plan that in scale and creativity clearly reflected Morene's ideals. Individual elements included the commission of an original commemorative work of art, refurbishment of his gravesite, and interpretation of his contributions through placement of a memorial plaque at the high school and an Official Texas Historical Marker at the cemetery. For the artwork, the committee selected Texas sculptor Lawrence W. Ludtke (d. 2007), whose resume included monuments at the U.S. Air Force Academy, Gettysburg National Military Park, Lyndon B. Johnson Presidential Library, Texas A&M University, and the Pentagon. Working closely with the committee, Ludtke utilized a bas relief format in his design of a memorial plaque for city hall and a medallion to adorn a new gravestone. As the work progressed, committee members under the direction of Mildred Klesel Bohlmann finalized the marker application, carefully documenting details of Morene's life and providing the requisite analysis to demonstrate the historical significance of his contributions to the city, school district, and community.[15]

Work on all aspects of the commemoration plan, including the necessary fundraising, came to a successful conclusion in 2005, and in November of that year, only a few days after his birthday, hundreds of citizens, friends, former students, city workers, and dignitaries gathered in front of city hall to honor Carl T. Morene. The dedication ceremony included proclamations, recognitions and speeches, the playing of "Shorthorns Forever," the unveiling of the memorials, and remarks by artist Ludtke, who spoke of lasting friendships he made in the course of the project and concluded with "Ich bin ein Schulenburger," much to the appreciation of those gathered that day. Afterward, the Shorthorn band performed a musical tribute, and in a fitting final salute to the Music Man of Schulenburg, trumpeter Austin Lebeda respectfully and reverently closed the ceremony with "Taps."[16]

MARKER LOCATION: Schulenburg City Cemetery, corner of Schultz Ave. and Eilers St., Schulenburg

"SHORTHORNS FOREVER"

Words and music by Carl T. Morene; debuted and approved as school song, 1938; copyrighted 1946 by Schulenburg High School; based on the tradition that graduates of Schulenburg High are neither ex-students nor former students, only "Shorthorns Forever."

All Hail! The glories of the school we love,
Colors of orange and black;
And Shorthorns so true in spirit,
In class, and on field and track.
For we will hold in hearts forever more,
Sweeter as the years go by;
Mem'ries of pals and comrades,
Of dear old Schulenburg Hi!

PART TWO
PASSING THROUGH TEXAS

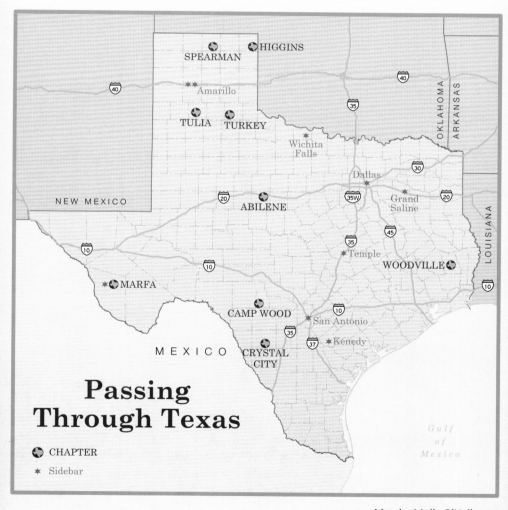

Passing Through Texas

🜋 CHAPTER

✳ Sidebar

Map by Molly O'Hallovan

8 LINDBERGH LANDED HERE

In 1975, the Texas Historical Commission (THC) received an application from the Real County Historical Commission requesting an Official Texas Historical Marker for an event that occurred in the small town of Camp Wood in March 1924. Fifty years afterward, many townspeople still remembered the event, and others had grown up hearing about it—a pair of young barnstorming pilots spent about a week in the small Hill Country town. One of the pilots was Charles Augustus Lindbergh, who just three years later would become the most famous man in the world.

Upon initial evaluation of the marker application, THC historians leaned toward rejection of the request, citing their reluctance to mark sites according to a "George Washington slept here" syndrome. Deolece Parmelee, THC marker program historian, wrote on the staff evaluation form, "The Sam Houston bedroom, the Lincoln bedroom, the many inns that are marked because 'George Washington slept here' have just about saturated the nation with accounts of casual visits by the great of this world. However, the people in Real County do live lives of quietness, and they think the visit of Charles Lindbergh to their county before he had his wings as an army pilot was of great importance."[1] However quiet the life in Real County, its citizens did indeed believe their brush with aviation history in the person of Charles A. Lindbergh was significant. So, too, did the citizens of a number of other Texas communities, as evidenced by the fact the pioneer aviator is mentioned in or is the subject of at least eleven Official Texas Historical Markers, including the one the THC eventually approved for placement in Camp Wood after the applicants provided additional information. When Charles Lindbergh made his famous New York–to–Paris flight in

1927, the concept of hero worship arguably rose to an intensity never before seen and rarely matched since. Its local manifestation in Texas resulted in the placement of historical markers conveying a "Lindbergh landed here" syndrome in seven counties. Despite the hero worship, the fact is Texas figured prominently in Lindbergh's early flight training, and experiences in Texas towns both before and after his famous record-breaking flight offer a glimpse into his life—public and private, glorious and tragic—in the years before World War II.

Born February 4, 1902, in Detroit, Michigan, Charles A. Lindbergh grew up on a farm near Little Falls, Minnesota. As a boy, he exhibited an affinity for mechanics, and as a teenager he became captivated by the idea of flying. He enrolled at the University of Wisconsin intending to study engineering but left after two years to pursue his dream of becoming a pilot. He took flying lessons in Nebraska and soon joined other pioneers in the often dangerous, sometimes lucrative career of barnstorming. Lindbergh bought his first airplane, a Curtiss JN4-D "Jenny," in Americus, Georgia, in April 1923, despite the fact he had not yet flown solo.[2] To gain soloing experience, he flew short trips around the Americus airfield for about a week after taking delivery of his new plane.

Texas had become a draw to the young flier, and when he took off from Americus bound for his home in Minnesota, he managed to put the Lone Star State on his itinerary. "While learning to fly in Nebraska," he wrote, "I discovered that nearly every pilot in existence had flown in Texas at one time or another during his flying career. Accordingly I decided that, at the first opportunity I would fly to Texas myself and although I traveled a rather roundabout way from Georgia to Minnesota, my course passed through Texarkana en route."[3] Lindbergh encountered challenges along the way, at one point flying about a hundred miles off course due to the lack of reliable air route maps and dealing with frequent repairs to his plane after hard landings and other mishaps caused minor damage. Despite the unplanned delays, he landed in Texarkana, achieving his goal of flying in Texas, and continued on to Minnesota where he resumed barnstorming.

Fascinated by the mechanics of flying almost as much as by the

act itself, Lindbergh longed to fly a variety of machines, including the latest models then being used by the U.S. Army Flying
Service. For that reason, in the fall of 1923, he chose to enlist as a
Flying Cadet. He wrote to the War Department in Washington,
D.C., and received a response telling him to report to Brooks Field
in San Antonio by March 15 of the following year. With months
to spare, he decided to barnstorm his way through the Midwest
and then on to Texas. Attending an air show in St. Louis, Missouri,
he saw the latest military aircraft on exhibit and conducted flying
lessons for a few student pilots, one of whom bought his Jenny.
Another of his students, St. Louis automobile dealer Leon Klink,
owned a Canadian version of the Curtiss Jenny airplane, dubbed
a "Canuck." The two pilots decided to take the Canuck and "make
a pleasure flight through the south, barnstorming only enough to
make current expenses, if possible."[4] After a few minor mishaps
caused by too-soft landing fields in Kentucky, Mississippi, and Alabama, they had a more serious accident in Pensacola, Florida, that
required them to spend a week at the Naval Air Station replacing
the plane's landing gear and propeller. They flew on to Louisiana
and then to Houston, where they installed additional fuel tanks to
enable them to fly the Canuck for longer stretches without stop-
ping to refuel. With only a few weeks left on their schedule, they
decided to continue their flight west; Lindbergh planned to go as
far as time would allow and then return to San Antonio by train.
With passenger air flight still in its infancy, private pilots did not
have access to accurate air route maps in 1924; instead, they often
used railroad maps to navigate their way across the United States.
Mistaking the Nueces River for the Rio Grande, which according to
their map was the only river with a railroad track running along its
northeast bank, the pilots followed along the track until it ended
near Camp Wood, at which time they realized their navigational
error. Lindbergh landed the plane in the town square. He figured if
the wind was just right, and if he managed to maneuver between
two telephone poles and over an intersecting road, he could safely
take off again from the square the next morning. The townspeople
offered food and shelter to the barnstormers, and Lindbergh later
reported that although wind conditions were ideal for them to

depart the following day, Klink had learned of a dance to be held that evening and persuaded his friend to stay over another night.[5]

The morning after the dance, with the wind blowing from the right direction and with Lindbergh at the controls, the pilots prepared to depart. Lindbergh related, "One of the town streets was wide enough to take-off from, provided I could get a forty-four foot wing between two telephone poles forty-six feet apart and brush through a few branches on each side of the road later on. We pushed the ship over to the middle of the street and I attempted to take-off. The poles were about fifty feet ahead and just before passing between them there was a rough patch on the street. One of the wheels got in a rut and I missed by three inches of the right wing tip. The pole swung the plane around and the nose crashed through the wall of a hardware store, knocking pots, pans and pitchforks all over the interior."[6] Storeowner Warren Puett, along with dozens of other people, came running. "The hardware dealer told us that he and his son thought an earthquake was taking place," Lindbergh wrote. "But instead of being angry, he appeared quite pleased. When we tried to pay for the damage we'd done, he refused to accept a cent. It had been an interesting experience, he said, and the advertising value was worth much more than the cost of the few boards needed for repairs." The following day, a small item in the newspaper in nearby Uvalde read, "A small plane landed in the street of Camp Wood and wrecked the wall of a store. The pilot was Charles A. Lindbergh."[7]

Damage to the plane was relatively light—a broken propeller and a clipped wing tip—but Lindbergh and Klink remained in Camp Wood for three more days waiting for a new propeller to arrive from Houston. They stayed at the Fitzgerald Hotel and following repair of the Canuck, Lindbergh took the Fitzgerald family for rides in the airplane to thank them for their hospitality before he and Klink continued their journey west. They made it only as far as Maxon, an isolated settlement along the Southern Pacific Railroad between Sanderson and Marathon in Brewster County, before trouble struck again. They damaged a wing when they hit a Spanish dagger plant while trying to get airborne after a landing in the desert. Klink rode the train 250 miles to El Paso to fetch repair supplies while a local rancher took Lindbergh in, but by the time Klink returned to fix the plane, eight more days passed. The two men patched up the Canuck as well as they could and flew back to San Antonio in time for Lindbergh to begin his Army Air Service training.[8]

Lindbergh wrote numerous accounts of his army training in San Antonio. He landed the beat-up Canuck at Brooks Field, thinking he and Klink could repair it within a few days so Klink could travel on to the West Coast. The post commander, however, took issue with the disreputable appearance of the plane and ordered them to remove it from the field at once. They flew it to Stinson Field, a small commercial airfield nearby, to complete the final repairs. Klink departed, and Lindbergh began what he would later call his most important educational experience.

Officially inducted as a Flying Cadet on March 19, 1924, he quickly learned that the "wash-out" rate among cadets was very high. Reports from earlier classes indicated that less than 40 percent would make it all the way through training at Brooks, and of those, only about half would survive the next step—advanced training and eventual earning of wings at nearby Kelly Field. Lindbergh, a formerly unmotivated scholar who had dropped out of the University of Wisconsin, found himself inspired to study. "Before," he wrote, "I'd always gone to school because I had to go, because it was considered the proper thing to do. Here, I realized, I was going to school because I wanted to learn, to complete the course, to gain my Air Service bars and wings. I studied after classes, through the week ends, often far into the night. At times I slipped into my bunk with swimming head, but I had the satisfaction of watching my grade average climb slowly through the 80's and into the 90's, until I graduated second man at Brooks and first at Kelly." Although an accomplished pilot with skills honed through precise military instruction, Lindbergh nevertheless experienced a mid-air collision shortly before his graduation at Kelly Field. After two weeks at Ellington Field near Houston for gunnery instruction, several Kelly cadets were flying practice pursuit maneuvers when Lindbergh and another pilot each positioned their airplanes to "attack" an "enemy" plane. The two pursuing planes collided and became

Charles A. Lindbergh, autographed U.S. Army Air Training School graduation portrait, 1925. Despite academic struggles and flying mishaps, including a mid-air collision with another student pilot, Lindbergh graduated first in his class at the U.S. Army Advanced Flying School at Kelly Field in San Antonio. Courtesy Lindbergh Picture Collection, Manuscripts and Archives, Yale University Library.

entangled; both pilots parachuted to safety, and as they floated to the ground they watched their planes crash and burst into flames. Within an hour, they were back in the air in new airplanes.[9]

On March 14, 1925, Lindbergh graduated from Advanced Flying School at Kelly Field, one of only 19 of the original 104 cadets in his class who enlisted at Brooks Field a year earlier. Commissioned a second lieutenant in the Air Service Reserve Corps, but not called for active duty, he left San Antonio and returned to St. Louis. There, he went to work for the Robertson Aircraft Company as a barnstormer, flight instructor, and test pilot. The following year, when the company secured a contract to fly the U.S. mail, Lindbergh became an air mail pilot and pioneered the St. Louis–Chicago route.

About that time, he began planning to win the Orteig Prize, an offer by a New York businessman to pay $25,000 to the first pilot to fly nonstop from New York to Paris. A number of American and European pilots had perished in pursuit of the prize, but Lindbergh believed with the right equipment he could succeed and claim not only the prize money but also the distinction of being the first person to accomplish the feat. Believing excessive weight contributed to the failures of previous attempts, he determined to have a special barebones plane built and to make the journey alone. He prevailed on a group of St. Louis businessmen to sponsor his quest, and with completion of the Monocoupe plane by the Ryan Aeronautical Company of San Diego, he named it *Spirit of St. Louis*. After months of careful planning and personally overseeing construction of the airplane, twenty-five-year-old Charles A. Lindbergh embarked on his historic flight from Roosevelt Field on Long Island, New York, on the morning of May 20, 1927. Thirty-three and a half hours later, he landed safely at Le Bourget Field near Paris, at 10:21 P.M. local time. He set a new world record, and the resulting fame changed his life forever.

The magnitude of the crowds that gathered at Roosevelt Field to watch him depart amazed Lindbergh, but the throngs that awaited his arrival in Paris completely overwhelmed him. He instantly became an international sensation, the press covering his every move. For the daring but shy young flier, the crush of

Charles Lindbergh, at age 23, earned a commission as second lieutenant in the
Air Service Officers Reserve Corps in March 1925. Just over two years later, he
became the most famous man in the world when he flew solo nonstop from
New York to Paris. Courtesy Lindbergh Picture Collection, Manuscripts and
Archives, Yale University Library.

attention was almost too much to bear. Nevertheless, he agreed
to travel throughout the United States in the *Spirit of St. Louis* on
a publicity tour sponsored by the Guggenheim Fund for the Promotion of Aeronautics. That three-month tour, in which he visited
forty-eight states and ninety-two cities, brought him once again
to Texas. Beginning July 20, 1927, in Long Island, the tour wound
through the Northeast to the Midwest, out to the Northwest and
down the West Coast, then through the Southwest before September 24, when he reached El Paso, Texas. Two days later, after a
stop in Santa Fe, New Mexico, the famous plane and its even more
famous pilot landed in Abilene, Texas.[10]

As was the case in cities throughout the *Spirit of St. Louis* tour,
Lindbergh hero worship was in full bloom in Abilene, and hundreds of people representing seventy-one West Texas towns spent

weeks planning for the event. A parade of cars wound through town from the airfield to a downtown plaza, local bands entertained the crowds, and dignitaries gave speeches and presented gifts to the distinguished guest of honor. The local newspaper, in a special edition issued that evening, reported the crowd was the largest ever assembled in Abilene. A potentially embarrassing moment for Lindbergh occurred when, after alighting from the plane and walking to the car waiting to carry him and Texas First Lady Mildred Moody (a native of Abilene) into town, he saw a "throne," fashioned from a velvet- and flag-draped chair, attached to the vehicle. "Please," he said to Mrs. Moody, "I would much rather not ride up there. I would appreciate it if you would let me ride on the back seat with you." With the chair quickly removed and the flag retrieved and draped over the back of the car, they began their ride into town during which Lindbergh reportedly told his hostess, "I am willing to do almost anything—I don't mind sitting where they can see me—they have come a long way and are entitled to see me if they want—but I can't go those thrones." After giving a brief speech in which he praised the ideal flying conditions and the potential for developing civil and military aviation in Texas, he returned to the airfield and departed for Fort Worth, the next stop on his itinerary. His visit to Abilene had lasted one hour and thirty-six minutes.[11]

Later that year, on a goodwill tour of Latin America for the U.S. government, Charles Lindbergh met Anne Spencer Morrow, daughter of the U.S. ambassador to Mexico. Anne, an accomplished writer, graduated from Smith College in May 1928, and a year later the couple married. Lindbergh taught his wife to fly, and she earned a pilot's license and became his co-pilot on many journeys around the world. Together, they charted air routes from Canada and Alaska to Japan and China, an expedition she wrote about in *North to the Orient,* the first of her many best-selling books. Anne gave birth to the couple's first child, Charles Augustus Lindbergh Jr. on June 22, 1930. Less than two years later, on March 1, 1932, the boy disappeared from his crib in the family home in Hopewell, New Jersey. The kidnapping case became known as "the crime of the century" and plunged the publicity-wary couple into the glare of the international press. After an intense and harrowing ten weeks, police discovered the child's body in a shallow grave a few miles from the house. A coroner determined the baby died from a blow to the head the night he was taken from his bed. As the investigation into the kidnapping and murder stretched into the next two years, the Lindberghs struggled to resume their lives.

Retreating to the Morrow family estate in Englewood, New Jersey, for a time, during which their second child, a son named Jon, was born, the couple sought to avoid the media spotlight. By the spring of 1933, they began flying again, promoting transcontinental passenger air travel. During a flight from California to Washington, D.C., on May 6, they encountered a sudden severe sandstorm in the Texas Panhandle and made an emergency landing in a remote area near Amarillo. Unaware their delay had caused a massive search, they spent the night in their plane and continued on to Kansas City the following morning. Lindbergh made light of the situation, but Anne, in her diary, recounted her terror at flying in the blinding storm, only to have her fears calmed by her husband's skillful control of the airplane.[12] They soon began planning their next major expedition, a trip to survey and map transatlantic air routes between America and Europe. Departing in July, they traveled through the end of the year before returning home.

In September 1934, the Lindberghs flew to California to visit Anne's sister and brother-in-law. Staying at a ranch owned by well-known humorist and aviation enthusiast Will Rogers, the two couples relaxed together for only a few days before receiving word from New Jersey on September 19 of a break in the kidnapping case. The police had arrested a German immigrant carpenter, Bruno Richard Hauptmann, and were preparing to present the case to a grand jury. The Lindberghs' emotional return trip to New Jersey once again included an encounter with citizens of a small Texas town.

Late in the morning of September 24, on a farm just outside the Hansford County town of Spearman, Vi Whitson heard the unmistakable noise of an airplane and went to her back door to investigate. As she watched, the small plane landed in a nearby pasture and taxied to the fence surrounding her yard. As the pilot alighted,

*Anne Morrow Lindbergh (in cockpit) with Charles A. Lindbergh, May 1931.
Following their marriage in 1929, Anne Morrow Lindbergh took flying lessons
from her husband and served as his co-pilot on many flights around the world.
Her chronicles of their travels, many based on her personal diaries, became
best-selling books and made her an internationally renowned author.* Courtesy
Lindbergh Picture Collection, Manuscripts and Archives, Yale University
Library.

he asked politely if she would mind if he parked his plane in her yard for a while. Running low on fuel and wanting to check a minor misfiring in the engine, Lindbergh opted to land in a rural area in order avoid the inevitable attention the couple's arrival in a larger city would cause. News of Hauptmann's arrest had re-ignited the press frenzy, and he wanted to travel back to New Jersey as inconspicuously as possible. Mrs. Whitson offered refreshments to her unexpected guests and flagged down a passing motorist, who agreed to convey a request for fuel delivery to a service station in nearby Spearman. Lindbergh checked on the motor, and Anne invited Mrs. Whitson to sit with her in the plane. As the two visited, Mrs. Lindbergh said, "I am acquainted with the strong winds that you have in the Panhandle. We were forced down in a windstorm west of Amarillo last year."

News spread quickly in Spearman. A number of schoolchildren saw the plane flying low over the town, and with confirmation of the Lindberghs' landing, teachers dismissed their classes to allow students to view the plane and watch it take off two hours after its landing. The local newspaper reported the event with a front-page story headlined "Lindberghs Visit Spearman" that included photographs of the famous fliers and their airplane, along with members of the Whitson family. The enterprising owner of the Continental Oil Company, from whom the noted aviator purchased fuel, took out a large ad that read "'I'll Use Conoco' said Col. Charles A. Lindbergh at Spearman Monday."[13]

The couple continued their journey east, and Charles Lindbergh, with the eyes of the world upon him, calmly testified before the grand jury two days later. In 1935, in a sensational trial covered by hundreds of news organizations, a jury convicted Hauptmann of the kidnapping and murder of the Lindbergh baby and sentenced him to death. The Lindberghs, after receiving threats on the life of their second son, and no longer able to deal with intrusive press coverage during and after the trial, moved to England later that year and remained in Europe until the outbreak of World War II. Fame turned to infamy for Charles Lindbergh when he visited Germany as war clouds gathered and publicly praised Nazi Germany's military strength, particularly with regard to its air force. Returning to the United States in 1939, he became the primary spokesman for the America First isolationist organization that sought to keep America out of the war. Reviled by many Americans who earlier hailed him as a hero, Lindbergh also earned the lasting enmity of Pres. Franklin D. Roosevelt. Despite the aviator's strong isolationist views, he offered his services to the U.S. military following the Japanese attack on Pearl Harbor and the U.S. entry into the war but was rebuffed by Roosevelt. He nevertheless worked for the war effort as a civilian, eventually traveling to the South Pacific to train U.S. Navy pilots on ways to conserve fuel in order to enable longer flights. Also, as a civilian, he flew fifty combat missions.

Lindbergh's tarnished reputation gradually improved after the war. In 1955, he wrote an account of his life and his record-breaking 1927 flight in the Pulitzer Prize–winning book *The Spirit of St. Louis*. In addition to serving as a consultant to the U.S. Air Force, he became heavily involved in scientific research, conservation, and wildlife preservation efforts worldwide. Diagnosed with cancer, he planned his own funeral before his death at his home in Hawaii on August 26, 1974, and was buried in a simple grave on the island of Maui. Anne Morrow Lindbergh became one of America's most beloved writers, publishing five volumes of her diaries and letters, as well as books of poetry and essays, including fascinating accounts of her travels with her husband. Her 1955 book of inspirational meditations, *Gift from the Sea*, was an international best seller. She survived her husband by more than a quarter century, dying at age 94 in 2001.[14]

By any measure, Charles A. Lindbergh and Anne Morrow Lindbergh lived extraordinary lives. The fact that so many Texans have sought to commemorate their special connections to the Lone Star State with historical markers is a testament to their lasting legacy. And while all of America can rightly claim the Lindberghs—hero worship or not—they hold a special place in Texas history.

Official Texas Historical Markers about Lindbergh

Lindberghs Land at Spearman, 0.4 mi. S of Spearman on
SH 207, Hansford County

Charles A. Lindbergh in Texas, SH 55, Camp Wood, Real County

Lindbergh in West Texas, US 83 and SH 36, Abilene, Taylor
County

Official Texas Historical Markers that Mention Lindbergh

Brooks Air Force Base, Hangar 9, 8008 Inner Circle Dr.,
Brooks AFB, San Antonio, Bexar County

Edward H. White II Memorial Hangar, 8008 Inner Circle Dr.,
Brooks AFB, San Antonio, Bexar County

Kelly Air Force Base, Duncan Dr., 100 yards SW of
Billy Mitchell Blvd., San Antonio, Bexar County

"Kelly No. 2" Flight Line, 205 S. Luke, San Antonio, Bexar County

Stinson Airport, 8535 Mission Rd., San Antonio, Bexar County

Love Field, inside Love Field Airport terminal, Cedar Springs Rd.
at Mockingbird Ln., Dallas, Dallas County

First Transcontinental Air Service to Texas Panhandle/Amarillo
Municipal Airport, inside terminal, Amarillo Municipal
Airport, 10801 Airport Blvd., Amarillo, Potter County

Kell Field Air Terminal, Motor Pool Dr., Sheppard Air Force Base,
Wichita Falls, Wichita County

9

PYRAMIDS ON THE ROAD TO MONTE NE

In its original form, William Harvey's promotional plan for his remote property in northwestern Arkansas differed little from other tourism endeavors in the early days of automobile travel. The difference came, as with all his enterprises, through the scope of his plans. A relentless promoter of himself and his iconoclastic interests, Harvey worked only on a grand scale, undeterred by what others thought of his ventures. To him, the plan seemed simple: build and promote a resort of the first class in the backwoods and develop a network of improved roads, all of which would lead to the site. Later, he modified that plan somewhat to include a run for the U.S. presidency and preparation for the end of the civilized world.

A colorful and eccentric character, viewed by some as a visionary and economic pragmatist and by others simply as a charlatan or egocentric promoter, William Hope Harvey (1851–1936) consistently presented an image of unquestioned determination and focus. The career route he took to Arkansas, though, proved much less direct, resembling in many respects the meandering back roads near his Ozark home. One historian aptly described Harvey as a rolling stone, recognized widely for both his "grandiose idealism" and "heroic failure."[1] His substantial successes paled in comparison to his unrealized schemes.

A native of the Buffalo hamlet in what is now West Virginia, Harvey studied law and became an attorney at age nineteen. He moved soon after to Ohio and practiced in the towns of Gallipolis and Cleveland and later in Chicago. In 1884, giving way to the wanderlust that marked his adult life, he and his wife, Anna R. (Halliday), whom he met and married in Ohio, moved their family to southwestern Colorado. There, he operated a successful mining operation near Ouray known as the Silver Bell. When the price of silver declined dramatically, ironically in part because of increased production in western mines, he moved to Pueblo, Colorado, where he returned to the practice of law and engaged in real estate. At Pueblo, Harvey became a promoter, helping develop the city's Palace of Minerals to showcase the mining resources of the state. From there, he moved on to Denver and then to Ogden, Utah, where he staged an event modeled on the Mardi Gras of New Orleans, but it proved to be no rival for its Louisiana counterpart. Rocked by his promotional failures, as well as the economic Panic of 1893, Harvey eventually moved his family back to Chicago, and there, in addition to his legal practice, he embarked on a new venture, one that drew heavily on his experiences in law, mining, and promotion.[2]

Long interested in economics and opinionated to a fault, Harvey developed deep-seated personal beliefs about the underlying reasons for the nation's financial decline, including an almost obsessive distrust of the gold standard, which he viewed as a singular threat to long-term productivity. As a result, he enthusiastically embraced tenets of the growing bimetallism movement that advocated a monetary system based on both gold and silver. From his Chicago base and using his own publishing houses, Harvey wrote a series of popular financial books and pamphlets that stressed such principles as the free coinage of silver. Among his most successful publications was *Coin's Financial School* (1894), an allegorical treatise in which a fictional but thinly veiled Professor Coin (i.e. Harvey himself), depicted in both illustration and text as a youthful Chicago financier, lectured a class of fledgling entrepreneurs "to lead them out of the labyrinth of falsehoods, heresies and isms that distract the country."[3] Publication of the book and others in a special financial series earned its publisher the lasting nickname of "Coin." They also brought him considerable wealth, as individual publications regularly sold in the hundreds of thousands, and related activities such as paid speaking engagements and the lucrative sale of special silver badges increased accordingly.

Harvey's public battle against monometallism gained a wide audience among so-called silverites, who valued the straightforward economic pronouncements in his publications. Among those who took special notice was the nation's most outspoken political opponent of the gold standard, William Jennings Bryan, who in 1896 served as the Democratic candidate for president against Republican William McKinley. (Bryan ran against McKinley in 1896 and again in 1900, both times unsuccessfully.) At Bryan's request, Harvey joined the campaign as a financial advisor, and he became chairman of the Democratic Party's Ways and Means Committee as well. Bryan relied heavily on Coin Harvey and his financial book series, especially *Coin's Financial School,* about which the presidential candidate noted, "It is safe to say that no book in recent times has produced so great an effect in the treatment of an economic question."[4]

In the years following the presidential election of 1896, though, the political climate changed, in large part because the economic situation showed steady signs of improvement, making Harvey's dire predictions and unprecedented solutions seem outdated to the general public. National interest in the free silver movement, especially among Democrats, also declined. Harvey and Bryan parted ways prior to the next election cycle, and Harvey moved from Chicago to the backwoods of northwestern Arkansas near the town of Rogers, an area he first visited during the campaign. There, relying on his experience in real estate and promotion, he embarked on a new and ambitious project that proved to be, literally, monumental.

Coin Harvey christened his new endeavor Monte Ne, a name he said came from Indian words for "mountain water." His plan called for an expansive and first-class, yet somewhat rustic, retreat along the lines of Adirondack Great Camps. While the project consumed much of his creative and physical energies in the early twentieth century, he continued to rail against political and economic injustices he perceived, using his own publishing company to promote the teaching of character building in schools and to call for an end to such financial practices as taxes, rents, and usury. His influence and his audiences, however, declined dramatically. He was not yet through with politics, but for the time being he concentrated his most creative efforts for his resort.

Postcard of William "Coin" Harvey's amphitheatre (erroneously denoted in card caption as the pyramid) at Monte Ne, near Rogers, Arkansas. Much of Harvey's resort, which he viewed as the initial focal point of the Ozark Trails, is now beneath the waters of Beaver Lake. Curt Teich photo postcard courtesy Dan K. Utley.

Harvey began his development of Monte Ne at a time of transition for recreational travel; while railroad excursions to resorts remained *en vogue* among elites, others turned to the automobile as a preferred means of vacation travel. At the time, though, most existing roads, especially away from cities, remained relics of horse and buggy days—meandering two- and four-rut paths that afforded severely limited access during bad weather. Designed primarily for rural families and seasonal market access, they proved inadequate for the demands of a burgeoning traveling public, and Harvey realized that in order for his resort to flourish, he needed to tap into a more dependable transportation system. When his efforts to secure better roads from local officials failed, he built a railroad spur and utilized transportation via the White River as well, but those experiments also proved limiting. What he envisioned was a network of paved—or at least all-weather—roads that would route travelers from main lines to Monte Ne. Never one to think small, he saw no reason to restrict his vision to northwestern Arkansas; instead, he enlisted the aid of others in neighboring states to help with his promotion. In so doing, Harvey tapped into an existing program known as the Good Roads Movement.[5]

While the Good Roads Movement is most commonly associated with the beginning of the Automobile Age, it originated as an effort by bicycle groups, most notably the League of American Wheelmen, which began the *Good Roads Magazine* in the 1890s to promote better transportation for its members. At the same time, agricultural groups such as the Grange, lobbying for improved market access for farmers, influenced the federal government to establish a Bureau of Public Roads within the Department of Agriculture. As these and other transportation efforts moved forward, the automobile became the preferred means of personal travel and steered discussion and planning in a new direction. Soon, there was talk of interstate travel and even transnational travel, and with it, improved communication and commerce. While the federal and state governments worked to define their respective roles in such endeavors, private organizations sprang up to promote possible routes and lobby for financial assistance. In the days before the federal program of numbered highways, among the best known of the early named road associations promoted such routes as the Lincoln Highway (from New York City to San Francisco), the Dixie Overland Highway (from Savannah, Georgia, to San Diego, California), the Meridian Highway (from Winnipeg, Manitoba, to Mexico City), and the Old Spanish Trail (from St. Augustine, Florida, to California). Add to that list the name of the Ozark Trails (OT), the brainchild of Coin Harvey.[6]

The Ozark Trails Association (OTA) formally organized at a Monte Ne convention attended by sixty-three delegates on July 10, 1913. Harvey's original concept, worked out in the years preceding, included only four states: Arkansas, Missouri, Kansas, and Oklahoma. "My personal interest in the Ozark Trails," he wrote, "is that they all lead to Monte Ne, where we have a delightful resort where many are interested who live in the four states. Of course all the towns we pass through are equally interested in this road proposition, and that gives us cooperation." He further noted, "My inclination runs toward doing something of a progressive nature that will promote the collective good."[7] Regardless of his motive, Har-

vey clearly understood the potential for returns on tourism invest-
ments, and he stood ready to provide direction for the promotional
marketing necessary to make the endeavor successful. To that end,
he traveled the region extensively, meeting with civic groups to
promote good roads and tourism, recruiting new members for
the organization, and building up competition among cities and
regions vying to be included in promotional materials. The association did not build roads and bridges, as some other groups did;
instead, it called for improvement of existing routes for eventual
linkage to other routes. It also supported establishment of state
highway programs, an emphasis that, ironically, eventually led to
the demise or incorporation of the named highways.[8]

Coin Harvey put forth great effort for the association's annual
meetings, reminiscent of political conventions, complete with
spirited music, rousing speeches, promotional parades, platform
discussions, and territorial "boosterism." His work and the support
of his followers paid off quickly, and by 1916, when the OTA held
its convention at Springfield, Missouri, thousands attended. The
year proved to be a significant one in highway development, as
Congress authorized the Federal Aid Road Act, signed into law by
Pres. Woodrow Wilson. The law provided for states and the federal
government to share equally in the funding of road construction
projects, potentially a major economic development for ongoing
projects such as the Ozark Trail.

To spread the impact and enthusiasm of the 1916 convention
even further, while also targeting marketing strategies on key
regions, the association held shorter interim gatherings known
as adjourned meetings. With each gathering the excitement
grew among member cities, but those who hesitated or cautioned
restraint often found their communities left out—the "official"
routes thus changed regularly depending on the amount of local
support. While the OTA began as a regional effort, it soon grew to
incorporate other states, including Texas, when members chose to
extend the system to hook up with the National Old Trails Road
(Ocean-to-Ocean Highway) at Las Vegas, New Mexico, thus becoming part of a transcontinental route.[9]

Cities on proposed routes across the Texas Panhandle quickly joined in the OT effort, and Texas figured prominently in leadership, planning, and programmatic considerations that ensued. In 1916, Oklahoma City hosted the largest OTA gathering—an adjourned meeting—with attendance estimated at more than ten thousand. Speculation thus spread that the 1917 annual convention would be even larger, resulting in an unprecedented economic boost to the city lucky enough to be selected host. Although each state could nominate one city, it soon came down to a choice between Tulsa and Amarillo, with Tulsa at a disadvantage because no precedent existed for successive meetings in the same state. Cyrus Avery of Oklahoma magnanimously carried the day for Amarillo when he nominated the Texas town, noting Tulsa's willingness to wait its turn as host and adding, "the purposes of the association would be better served if the meeting went to a western city where they have more promoting to do than we have."[10]

Following the meeting, the OTA group in Amarillo, headed by J. L. Pope, began preparing in earnest for the convention, scheduled for June 1917 and anticipated to attract fifteen thousand visitors, the equivalent of the city's entire population only seven years earlier. Pope personally hit the roads, traveling all stretches of the OT and utilizing old-fashioned community boosterism and salesmanship to promote Amarillo. Back in the Panhandle, local planning for lodging included the use of schools, cooperative efforts with homeowners, and development of a tent city with full amenities, including electricity, plumbing, a restaurant, shops, and an auditorium tent. For entertainment, officials proposed rodeo events, baseball games, concerts, automobile races, and a carnival. At stake was not only Amarillo's future as a viable convention city and tourist destination, but also the possible designation of the central route across Texas—the Amarillo route—as the official one for future promotion.[11]

The 1917 convention lived up to its billing and planning, attracting well over ten thousand visitors—an impressive number, albeit slightly less than the attendance for the Oklahoma City meeting. Coin Harvey presided, as he always did in the formative years of the association, and as expected, attention centered on the official route, which coalesced along the central line that included Tulsa,

Oklahoma City, Amarillo, and Las Vegas. Ironically, the route no longer centered on Monte Ne, although the resort remained tangentially connected via a side route; the program Harvey started and nurtured had grown well beyond his original vision, adapting to more modern influences. What became evident at the Texas meeting was that an official route excluded significant cities, some of which had active promotional tourism programs, leaving them few alternatives save the development of other routes and regional associations. In effect, streamlining of the OTA program began to isolate it from many of the successful local endeavors it had cultivated, supplanting the competitive factor central to its early growth. The new focus, coupled with increased involvement of governments in road development, presaged a coming decline in such private programs, but those factors failed to concern the Ozark Trailers, as the promoters were known, in 1917. The meetings in Oklahoma City and Amarillo represented high water marks for the program, and few saw any reason the excitement would not continue.[12]

Sometime in the months following the Panhandle meeting, the OTA developed a new system of signage for the official route. Earlier directional markings included fence posts painted with the OT logo in white and green, the official trail colors, or small signs attached to telephone poles. Planners sometimes utilized special markings or codes on the signs to provide additional information, such as approaching turns or intersections. Detailed guidebooks or log books based on mileage between roadside landmarks—businesses, intersecting roads, cemeteries, buildings, and geographical features—and including photographs, maps, and information on local sites, also helped travelers navigate the oftentimes confusing route.

By 1918, though, the association sought roadside directional signage on a grander scale through the use of large concrete obelisks it called pyramids. In the days before a centralized numbering system for roads, private trail markers were not unusual, but what was unique about the OT markers was their height. Designed for placement at, or even within, key intersections, the monumental pyramids included painted information on destinations and

*Ozark Trails Guide
Book cover art, 1932.
Courtesy Dwayne
Jones.*

Ozark Trails "pyramid," Tulia, Swisher County.
Photograph by Randy Mallory.

driving distances for the motoring public. Some even had electric lights for nighttime travelers. As Nan Lawler noted in her thesis on the OTA, however, the pyramids proved to be obsolete before their completion, given their emphasis on one route, their confusing and inconsistent information, and other factors, but they nevertheless served as focal points of local pride, reminders to visitors of a community's commitment to tourism and progress.[13]

The pyramids' design, not coincidentally, reflected Coin Harvey's new emphasis at Monte Ne. Convinced the world was in its final days, he planned for a 130-foot pyramid (obelisk) that would mark his burial site but, more importantly, preserve a record of the world's decline for any future civilization that might somehow evolve post-annihilation. A plate attached to the monument would instruct any future survivors, "When this can be read, go below and find the cause of death of a former civilization." Inside would be collections of materials depicting the growth of the civilized world from its beginning to its untimely end in the early twentieth century. There would also be a book he would write, outlining what he believed were the causes of the global failure. With the same energy and focus he exhibited with his other endeavors, Harvey developed detailed plans and promoted his end-time philosophy widely as he also raised funds for the project.[14] As it consumed more of his time, he spent less effort on the OTA, which, although it regularly paid homage to the founder, nevertheless started to pass him by in theory and direction.

At its 1920 meeting in Pittsburg, Kansas, with Harvey's blessing, the OTA chose its first new leader, James Elmer Swepston (1879–1949) of Tulia, Texas. A native of Rains County in East Texas, Swepston taught school at Decatur and served briefly as president of the short-lived Western College in Artesia, New Mexico, before moving his family to Tulia in 1912. There, he opened an abstract office and actively participated in civic and political affairs, serving on the school board and as a founder of the West Texas Chamber of Commerce before his election as Swisher County Judge in 1920, the year he assumed leadership of the OTA. Although Swepston's management style differed from Harvey's, including open admission of program inadequacies, he followed many aspects of the founder's model, personally visiting cities along the OT to promote programs and objectives.[15]

Unfortunately for Swepston, he took control of the OTA at a time of declining participation for not just that group but other named road associations as well. As larger cities withdrew from the programs, opting for their own tourism promotions, and as the federal government developed a system of numbered roads and centralized road planning through state commissions, the associations—at least in their original forms—became irrelevant. With the OTA, Swepston also had to contend with infighting among association members, barely managing to survive a planned takeover by recalcitrant delegations from New Mexico and Oklahoma during the 1921 convention in Shawnee, Oklahoma. Attendance at subsequent meetings fell to less than a hundred, and by the time of the 1924 meeting in Duncan, Oklahoma, even the most dedicated association members realized the end was imminent.[16] The following year, work began in earnest on a new road, to be designated numerically as U.S. 66, that would, in its course from Chicago to Los Angeles, incorporate key elements of the Ozark Trails, including much of the route across the Texas Panhandle. The driving force behind the route planning—the man who came to be known as the "Father of Route 66"—was Cyrus Avery, who years earlier nominated Amarillo as the site for the OT convention. Thanks in part to his efforts, both Amarillo and Tulsa remained prominent points of interest on the new highway.[17]

With the advent of the new highway system and the improvement of local roads, the Ozark Trails pyramids gradually disappeared from the cultural landscape. Highway workers dismantled most of them, paving over the remains or using the concrete rubble as fill. A few survived as local landmarks, testimonies to community pride, while others outlived the communities they once promoted. While no accurate records exist for the total number of pyramids, there were perhaps hundreds at their peak of service. OTA leaders planned sixteen for Texas, but how many actually existed remains in doubt. What is known is that four Texas pyramids survive in the early part of the twenty-first century: those at Tulia, Swisher County; Wellington, Collingsworth County; Tampico,

OT

OZ RK
T AIL
N←S

INSON
23 E.

MANGUM
50 E.

CHICKASHA
140 E.

WELLINGTON
TEXAS

Ozark Trails monument, town square, Wellington, Collingsworth County.
Courtesy Texas Historical Commission. Photograph by Brett Cruse.

Hall County; and Dimmitt, Castro County. All are now designated State Archeological Landmarks, a legal distinction that allows the Texas Historical Commission to review any developmental plans. An Official Texas Historical Marker at the ghost town of Tampico interprets the story of the Ozark Trail in that part of the state, and one at Tulia tells the story of the OTA and the role J. E. Swepston played in its leadership.[18] The markers, like the historic routes and accompanying pyramids they interpret, are reminders of the early connection between tourism and good roads. Although short-lived, the OTA influenced interstate planning efforts, promoted better highways, brought large numbers of people together to network tourism efforts, and played a key role in development of the nation's iconic Mother Road, Route 66.

Although the marker at Tampico refers to OT founder Coin Harvey, his story remains more closely associated with his Arkansas home of Monte Ne, where he is buried alongside his son. In his later years, Harvey rekindled his passion for politics, and at the age of 80, following a "national convention" of the Liberty Party at his resort, he ran for U.S. president, losing in dramatic fashion to Franklin D. Roosevelt in the 1932 election. Harvey died four years later, leaving behind an elaborate masonry amphitheatre and a partially constructed pyramid (both now listed in the National Register of Historic Places). The resort property eventually gave way to real estate developments and the waters of Beaver Lake, impounded in the 1960s. While architectural vestiges can still be seen, particularly in drought years, the most accessible reminders of Coin Harvey's lasting contributions remain the OT pyramids along the roads he envisioned leading to Monte Ne.

MARKER LOCATIONS: The Ozark Trail at Tampico, 9.3 mi. NE of Turkey, off SH 86 near FM 657; and Ozark Trails Association, Maxwell and Broadway, Tulia

Ozark Trails monument, Tampico, Hall County. This photo shows the pyramid prior to recent refurbishment by local citizens. Courtesy Texas Historical Commission. Photograph by Brett Cruse.

Ozark Trails monument, courthouse square, Dimmitt, Castro County. Courtesy Texas Historical Commission. Photograph by Brett Cruse.

THE NAT

Isolated vestiges of Route 66, the celebrated successor route to the Ozark Trail across the Texas Panhandle, can still be found in small towns, as well as places once considered towns. The largest concentration of related properties, though, remains in Amarillo, where the route merged temporarily with the city's Sixth Street (6th Avenue). In 1994, local residents succeeded in having the U.S. Route 66–Sixth Street Historic District listed in the National Register of Historic Places at the state level of significance for its relevance to contexts of transportation and community planning and development. The district included eighty contributing buildings, and many still retain features easily identified with the era of "America's Main Street." One building of particular note is known as the Nat. It began its life in 1922 as a natatorium, or indoor swimming pool, thus the name, but in 1926 the owners refurbished the building as a dance hall, complete with a ballroom of maple flooring over what had been the pool. The change coincided with the birth of Route 66 as a major highway of tourism and adventure, and the club and the road literally grew up together. Local residents and travelers alike made the Nat the most celebrated nightclub in town, and during its heyday from the 1920s to the 1960s it successfully spanned the popular music evolution from big band swing to rock and roll. Performers who played the Nat included such greats as Louis Armstrong, Count Basie, Harry James, Benny Goodman, Elvis Presley, and Buddy Holly. It closed as a club in the 1960s, but the building remains a landmark sought out by fans of Route 66. Two Official Texas Historical Markers—one for the Nat and one for Route 66 in Amarillo—provide interpretation for the iconic road, and for its lasting economic and cultural influence in Texas.

MARKER LOCATIONS

Amarillo Natatorium (The Nat), 2705 W. 6th Ave., Amarillo; and Route 66 in Amarillo, 6th Ave. between Georgia and McMasters streets, Amarillo

Sources: Paul H. Carlson, *Amarillo: The Story of a Western Town* (Lubbock: Texas Tech University Press, 2006); U.S. Route 66–Sixth Street Historic District, Potter County, National Register of Historic Places files (hereafter cited as THC NR files); Amarillo Natatorium and Route 66 in Amarillo, Potter County, THC marker files.

10 A GATHERING IN THE WOODS

The East Texas Piney Woods, a vast area of evergreens and hard-woods dominated by several varieties of pine, represent the southwestern limits of the great southern forest. As William L. Bray observed in a 1904 survey of Texas forest resources, "Like a vast wave that has rolled in upon a level beach, the Atlantic forest breaks upon the dry plains—halting, creeping forward, thinning out, and finally disappearing, except where, along a river course, it pushes far inland."[1] Before reaching the plains, though, the East Texas Piney Woods cover all or part of forty-eight counties, an area estimated as roughly the size of Indiana. One of the most heav-ily forested counties, and thus a perennial state leader in timber production for decades, is Tyler County in Southeast Texas. Located north of Beaumont, south of Lufkin, and west of the Neches River, it is an area rich in natural resources and forest history as well. Its abundant streams, heavy rainfall, and rich sandy-loam soils are ideal for the propagation of pines, and they grow in abundance throughout the county, both commercially and naturally.

The forests have long defined the people, institutions, and heri-tage of Tyler County. The county seat of Woodville—named for Gov. George T. Wood and not the ubiquitous stands of timber, as some might believe—annually hosts the Dogwood Festival, a cel-ebration of natural woodland beauty and the advent of spring but also a reflection of cultural existence in the Piney Woods. The ear-liest Native American residents relied on the woods for food, fuel, and shelter, as did pioneer settlers who followed. But many early settlers, initially drawn to the area for agricultural purposes, also viewed the trees as obstacles to development of farmlands and pasturage. There were limited early efforts to exploit the forest resources, but it was not until rail lines began piercing the region, providing increased commercial viability in the latter nineteenth century, that a bonanza era of timber production developed.

At the time, Tyler County was at the center of a predominant longleaf pine belt that reached westward from Louisiana across parts of a dozen Texas counties. Longleaf pine forests were unique, unlike any in existence at the time—or since. According to forest historians Robert S. Maxwell and Robert D. Baker, the ecosystem was almost overwhelming to travelers and pioneers, with trees four to five feet in diameter reaching 100 to 150 feet in height. And, as they noted, "The forest floor under the great longleaf trees was clean, and the forest was described as parklike. Here the combination of sandy soil and woods fires had eliminated most competing growth, and the traveler walked or rode through the forest without difficulty."[2]

One of the limitations in the historical interpretation of landscapes, both cultural and natural, is that at times they are difficult to differentiate. Such is the case with the story of timber production in East Texas, particularly where longleaf pines once existed. While a few of the trees can still be found in isolated pockets or in stands where new plantings are carefully protected and cultivated, they remain anomalies in the present environment of subsequent-growth loblollies and other varieties valued for quicker growth and thus economic viability. Commerce, rather than nature, influences the cultural landscape in an area of such abundant harvestable resources. And so travelers to Tyler County today view impressive woodland stands with thick vegetative undergrowth, unaware the scenery that serves as the backdrop for every vista, from rural areas to small towns, is largely a reflection of the region's cultural history. There was a time, only a few generations past, though, when the resource was almost completely depleted.

The boom era of timbering in East Texas, which existed roughly from the 1880s to the 1920s, represented a "cut out and get out" philosophy. Sawmills proliferated and virgin stands of trees disappeared at a time when such forest conservation measures as selective cutting and reforestation, designed to provide sustainable yields over time, were only emerging theories of practice.

This photograph of a worker on Thompson Lumber Company land in East Texas dramatically portrays a typical native longleaf pine stand of timber from the bonanza era. The massive trees, high canopies, and relatively clean forest floor are in marked contrast to the faster growth habits of pine forests in the area today. Courtesy Texas Forestry Museum, Lufkin.

Consumer demands of unprecedented growth in the Gilded Age thus favored immediate supply over long-term investment in natural resources, and Texas timber helped fuel the growth, both regionally and nationally. The result of such a system seemed inevitable, and indeed, few stands of native trees remained as the natural resource harvest came to a close. By 1917, state forester John H. Foster wrote of the virgin longleaf forests in the past tense, observing they "were in class by themselves among the timber regions of the world," and then adding, "The greater part of these forests has now been cut."[3] But there were also signs of change in the early decades of the twentieth century as it became evident the situation was potentially reversible, at least in part, and Tyler County suddenly found itself on the front lines of the evolution.

To appreciate how emerging national trends began to converge on the timber fronts near tiny Woodville in the spring of 1909, it is important to understand broader historical contexts of conservation and scientific forestry. Both were in their infancy at the time, and what public national discourse there was often centered on natural resource programs of Theodore Roosevelt, U.S. president from 1901 to 1909. An avid outdoorsman and longstanding political advocate of natural resource preservation, Roosevelt focused national attention on the need for solutions to problems associated with unchecked economic development. With regard to natural resources specifically, he relied heavily on close friend and advisor Gifford Pinchot. Born to wealth in New England and educated at Exeter Academy and Yale University, Pinchot conducted postgraduate work at L'École Nationale Forestière in Nancy, France, but soon returned to the United States determined to seek what he believed to be more practical forestry experience. Through family connections with the noted landscape architect Frederick Law Olmstead, he secured a job at Biltmore, the sprawling estate of George Vanderbilt near Asheville, North Carolina, where he oversaw development of the first systematic professional forestry program in the United States. He later became a federal forester and in 1898 rose to chief of the Division of Forestry in the U.S. Department of Agriculture. He and Roosevelt became friends during the latter's governorship in New York, and they shared a common vision for a strong federal role in conservation. As Pinchot biographer Char Miller noted, "As with many of their generation, they were appalled by the human destruction of nature everywhere visible in early-twentieth-century America. The solution, they believed, lay in federal regulation of the public lands and, where appropriate, scientific management of those lands' natural resources; only this approach, guided by appropriate experts, would ensure the lands' survival."[4] In response to Pinchot's influence, Roosevelt restructured and strengthened the national forestry program in 1905, establishing it as the U.S. Forest Service (USFS) and naming Pinchot as first chief forester. Through his new central role in the administration and with strong support of the president, Pinchot set about defining a federal conservation concept. Central to the new initiative was his realization that a unified approach encompassing diverse programs around a central conservation focus provided the strongest administration. "When the use of all the natural resources for the general good is seen to be a common policy with a common purpose," he wrote, "the chance for the wise use of each of them becomes infinitely greater than it had ever been before." And, he added with emphasis, "The very existence of our Nation, and of all the rest, depends on conserving the resources which are the foundations of its life."[5]

With his systematic and centralized approach, Pinchot raised the level of the national forestry program from virtual obscurity to the front lines of conservation efforts in short order. He not only worked to strengthen federal control of public lands, a move not without some measure of controversy, but he also developed new means of outreach to timber companies through emphasis on forest products research and the establishment of experiment stations. Additionally, he promoted forestry education, which he viewed as fundamental to change, to spread the effectiveness of progressive scientific forestry practices and provide a steady supply of trained personnel for government programs.

Pinchot's interest in formal forestry education stemmed from his own personal experiences when he made the decision to pursue a career in the field. Unable to find adequate training at home, he studied in Europe, but he had a vision of something similar and yet distinctive in the United States. When programs at Cornell University and the Biltmore Forest School proved limiting, he and close friend Henry Solon Graves planned for a program at their alma mater, Yale University. Pinchot's father, James W. Pinchot, provided necessary funding, and the Yale Forest School (now Yale University School of Forestry and Environmental Studies) began in 1900 as a postgraduate program with a curriculum heavy in applied forestry and field experience. Graves served as the first dean, and the Pinchot family provided for summer training facilities on estate land at Milford, Pennsylvania. Field schools were integral to the educational concepts of the Yale model.[6]

And that brings the story back to Tyler County. Within a few years of its founding, the Yale Forest School administration began providing opportunities for field training outside Connecticut and Pennsylvania in an effort to give its students a broader perspective of forestry issues in the nation. This was in keeping with Pinchot's plan to develop a distinctly American school focused on American needs. To that end, the school required each student, in the last semester of study for the master of forestry degree, to spend time in the "lumber woods" to receive training in logging operations, topographic surveying, timber valuations, and plan development for all manner of timber operations. In 1906, the senior class worked at Waterville, New Hampshire, on lands owned by International Paper Company. The following springs, students worked in southern Missouri with the Missouri Lumber and Mining Company, and in central Alabama with the Kaul Lumber Company. In the spring of 1909, Yale forestry students traveled once again to the South, working in East Texas in association with the Thompson Brothers Lumber Company. The site for the Tyler County camp was a few miles southwest of Woodville at a place called Mooney's Lake (later Twin Lakes). It included a mess hall, bunkhouse (most students slept in tents, though, due to the warm weather), and swimming facilities at the lake, a former mill pond. A tram line operated nearby. Students worked at the camp and also three miles north of town at the company's vast Doucette mill. Now only a

The commercial center of Doucette, the Thompson Brothers Lumber Company mill town in Tyler County, circa 1899. Yale Forest School students worked in Doucette as part of their summer training. Courtesy Texas Forestry Museum, Lufkin.

small community with a few hundred residents, Doucette was at the time a lumber boomtown, thanks to the Thompsons, with a population larger than the county seat of Woodville.[7]

The Thompson family established one of the earliest successful timber operations in East Texas during the antebellum, pre-railroad days. Georgia native John Martin Thompson, considered the patriarch of the enterprise, came to the Republic of Texas with his parents and siblings in 1844. He and his father, Benjamin Franklin Thompson, and brother, William Wirt Thompson, started a sash mill in northern Rusk County in 1852, and it grew steadily as the area's population increased. The company expanded operations with new partners and experienced dramatic growth in the 1880s with establishment of a large mill in Trinity County, part of the timber-rich longleaf pine belt. As investors such as Ben Foster of Kansas City, Missouri, provided additional capital, the company expanded into other uncut areas of East Texas. Thompson Brothers Lumber Company moved its headquarters to Houston in 1906, with J. Lewis Thompson as president, the same year it acquired the Doucette mill, an operation that dated to 1891 under various owners. By 1909, the Thompsons were major players in the East Texas lumber industry, along with John Henry Kirby and W. T. Carter.[8]

In the spring of 1909, seniors of the Yale Forest School made their way to New Orleans by boat (the *Comus*) and then overland to the camp near Woodville that would be their home for almost three months. Among the twenty-nine students were several who developed noteworthy careers in forestry, including many who joined the fledgling U.S. Forest Service during its formative years, rising to important levels of responsibility. Five of the students, though, deserve special recognition: Frederick A. Gaylord, R. Chapin Jones, Edgar D. Hirst, Joseph C. Kircher, and Aldo Leopold. The first three rose quickly in the field of forestry to become state foresters within a few years of their master's work at Yale. Connecticut native Gaylord, a descendant of Elihu Yale on his mother's side, graduated with honors from his ancestor's namesake school and later became state forester of New York; Jones, of Iowa, worked for the U.S. Forest Service and the Pennsylvania Railroad before becoming an assistant state forester in Maryland and state forester in Virginia; and Hirst, born in Ohio, became state forester of New Hampshire the year he graduated from Yale. Illinoisan Joseph Casimir Kircher joined the U.S. Forest Service immediately upon graduation, serving first as a forest assistant in the Coconino National Forest in Arizona. Rising fast within the agency, he became the first regional forester for Region 8, an administrative area of the U.S. South that reached from Virginia to Texas. Kircher played a prominent role in the successful association between the USFS and the Civilian Conservation Corps, a New Deal program established in the 1930s during the first administration of Pres. Franklin

D. Roosevelt to address depleted resources and provide work for young men. During World War II, he also gained attention in Texas for his approval of a plan to use German prisoners of war to cut timber downed by an ice storm.[9]

The best known of the Yalies at Woodville, though, was Aldo Leopold. Born in 1886 in Burlington, Iowa, he developed an early interest in the natural history of his region and spent countless hours observing and documenting its woods, prairies, and wildlife. Seeking to learn more, he majored in forestry at Yale University. There, and later with the USFS, he became a follower of the utilitarian conservation model espoused by Gifford Pinchot, although, as biographer Curt Meine observed, "Leopold did not so much absorb the Pinchot doctrine as adopt it by default." Over time, however, he developed his own profound and focused environmental philosophy, based on what he termed a "land ethic" that argued for a break from the stranglehold of economic determinism in land use to one based on expanded considerations. "A thing is right when it tends to preserve the integrity, stability, and beauty of the biotic community," he wrote. "It is wrong when it tends otherwise."[10]

Leopold was a prolific writer, even as a young man, and his letters and notes provide an important perspective of student camp life in East Texas. Writing home, he noted, "It is really a beautiful region. . . . If you could see the full moon tonight, sailing high over the towering pine-trees, you would like it, too. I have decided, again and again, that it is worth all the trouble of the mosquitos and fleas and snakes and pigs, and more too." Interpreting his writings, Meine observed, "The naturalist in Leopold reemerged during these weeks in Texas. Both at work and in his free time, Aldo began to explore the woods with old-time enjoyment and newfound enthusiasm."[11] Within himself, even during those days, he felt an inner struggle not fully resolved by his chosen career of forestry. Over time, he came to be regarded more appropriately as the father of wildlife conservation whose inspirational and thought-provoking writings on natural history were reminiscent of Henry David Thoreau. Sadly, Leopold did not live to see the overwhelming success of his landmark work, *A Sand County Almanac;* he tragically died of a heart attack in 1948, shortly before its publication, while helping a neighbor fight a grass fire near his home in Wisconsin.

Had the story of the 1909 Yale Forest School camp near Woodville ended with the last of the fieldwork in June, it would no doubt still have someday warranted an Official Texas Historical Marker. Its role in the national sweep of scientific forestry, its relation to the emerging role of forest conservation even as East Texas sawmills worked steadily to turn the last of virgin pine stands into boards, its close association with early forestry education efforts of Gifford Pinchot, and its remarkable impact on state and federal forest administration for decades through the careers of the students who worked there all speak to historical significance. But there is another aspect of the story that is equally compelling and perhaps even more significant in terms of its eventual impact on Texas forest history.

While the students camped and worked in Tyler County, they had a rare opportunity to witness a small and informal but unprecedented gathering of foresters and lumbermen brought together to determine if there was common ground for the seemingly divergent interests of conservation and timber production. Those advocating for conservation were the elites of scientific forestry, including U.S. Chief Forester Gifford Pinchot, Yale Forest School Dean Henry Solon Graves, and professors Ralph Bryant and W. H. Uhler.

Representing the timber interests were several prominent lumbermen, most notably three—J. Lewis Thompson of Houston, John Barber White of Kansas City, Missouri, and John C. Kaul of Birmingham, Alabama—who served on the Conservation Committee of the Yellow Pine Manufacturers' Association, one of the nation's largest trade associations for the lumber industry. To Pinchot and Graves, committee chair White, who went by the honorary title of "Captain," was a key player. He was a man of considerable influence in the association but also an industry leader who publicly voiced his support of conservation measures, particularly the concept of selective cutting, the careful harvesting of older trees to provide more space for younger stock. Equally important to the

A photograph from the gathering of government foresters and lumber
industry leaders near Woodville, 1909. Dignitaries on the front row include
Missouri lumberman John Barber White (second from left), U.S. Chief Forester
Gifford Pinchot (third from left), one of the Thompson brothers, believed to be
Alexander Thompson of Doucette (center), Alabama lumberman John C. Kaul
(third from right), and J. Lewis Thompson, Houston (far right). Courtesy Texas
Historical Commission marker files.

gathering, given its Texas location, was J. Lewis Thompson, who
also displayed an interest in forest conservation. Other Texas lumbermen, most notably John Henry Kirby, a native of Tyler County,
privately expressed interest in some conservation measures but
opted to avoid public comments. Thompson, it seemed, was the
right Texan at the time to help carry the message to other companies and states. Kaul, who previously hosted Yale forestry students in Alabama, likewise provided important symbolic regional
representation.[12]

The meeting at Mooney's Lake in May, conducted with the college students in attendance, proved to be productive, evidently
void of contention. For whatever reasons—Pinchot's stature
within the federal government, the willingness of the lumbermen to consider a means of ensuring sustained productivity, or
the enthusiastic representation of the future foresters from Yale—
the meeting moved along steadily. Pinchot served as moderator.
Although he then represented a new administration (William

Howard Taft assumed the presidency in March 1909), Pinchot had no reason to anticipate a major shift in policy. Later, when disputes between the two over environmental policies and management caused an irreparable rift, the president fired Pinchot, replacing him with Graves. But in May 1909 there remained the promise of a unified federal purpose based on the successes and popularity of Roosevelt's conservation agenda. An aura of optimism prevailed, due in part to the leadership of Roosevelt and Pinchot in recent national and international conservation conferences. One, held in Washington with the nation's governors the previous year, resulted in a Declaration of Conservation that recognized "private ownership of forest lands entails responsibilities in the interests of all the People" and acknowledged support of "the enactment of laws looking to the protection and replacement of privately owned forests." Such a statement would not have gone unnoticed by politically astute lumbermen like those participating in the Tyler County discussions.[13]

Under Pinchot's leadership, the foresters and lumbermen soon reached what the chief forester believed was the first conservation accord agreed to by lumbermen and foresters. The *Dallas Morning News* reported, "This is the first conference of the kind ever held, and, as Mr. Pinchot described it, is the first time the Forestry Service has ever co-operated with the lumber manufacturers touching the conservation of forestry, and in that respect he counts it the most forward and important step and greatest accomplishment the Forestry Service has yet made, and from this beginning he hopes to see ultimately complete harmony of sentiment and action between the government and the timber land owners and lumber manufacturers to the end that the timber resources may be conserved in cutting timber and also that the forests may be reproduced from time to time."[14] Whether or not it was the first, it was certainly among the earliest such efforts. It called on the association to support state and federal legislation to discourage the practice of clear cutting and promote selective harvesting; develop systems for forest fire prevention and control; and establish an equitable means for taxation of private forest lands. Members of the Conservation Committee agreed to report the recommendations of the gathering favorably to their association for due consideration, marking a major move forward in broader discussions of forest conservation. The gathering in the woods ended as quietly and unceremoniously as it began, and the key players left with the sense that change in a major U.S. industry was not only inevitable and imminent but potentially promising as well.

On June 4, the students struck camp and made their way south to Beaumont, where the following day local officials provided them with a tour to the Spindletop oilfield, a steamer cruise on the Neches River, and a dinner. Soon after, they dispersed for their homes or new jobs. Company and college leaders viewed the East Texas forest school a success. As all of the students took specially administered Civil Service exams at Woodville in May, many of them immediately joined the U.S. Forest Service. There, Pinchot's philosophy continued to guide their work, as well as the mission of the agency, up to the time of World War II—and even beyond. Yale University thus set the standards for federal forestry programs, as Pinchot intended, at a crucial time of development, providing both direction and key personnel. And those national standards also translated to state programs; Pinchot, who served as Republican governor of Pennsylvania from 1923 to 1927, and again from 1931 to 1935, provided political influence at that level as well.

Although the conservation movement continued to grow in the early decades of the twentieth century, change came slowly to the timber fronts in East Texas, and in time the predictable end of the boom era occurred. With timber resources virtually depleted in many areas by the 1920s, and with prices relatively low and some operations moving to the West and Northwest, the region faced an uncertain future. But state officials and forestry leaders eventually embraced conservation measures designed to replenish stock and provide for sustained yields over time. With those changes and others, the forests gradually returned, although the era of the longleaf pine remained part of history. Pine varieties with quicker growth habits and thus shorter investment cycles were the determinants of new industries that in addition to boards produced pulpwood, plywood, and particle boards. In some areas of the Piney Woods, historic sawmilling elements from the past remained partially viable into the latter twentieth century, but they too eventually gave way to changes brought about by economic realities.

The timing of the gathering near Woodville proved to be significant not only to industry but to the formalized development of forestry management and forestry education in Texas. Less than five years later, under the direction of Temple banker W. Goodrich Jones, a dedicated advocate for forest conservation, a group of businessmen met to establish the Texas Forestry Association. The organizational purpose, to lobby for creation of a state forestry agency, resulted in the successful passage of legislation the following year that set up the State Department of Forestry under the auspices of Texas A&M College and also provided for a college forestry program and acquisition of state forest reserves. Vermonter John H. Foster, a 1907 graduate of the master's program in the Yale Forest School, served as the first state forester. The department continued to grow in responsibility and scope of mission, and in 1926 it became the Texas Forest Service (TFS).[15]

While the historical development of the TFS is not the focus of this article, several aspects of its past are worth noting in regard to the Official Texas Historical Marker that now interprets the story of Gifford Pinchot's significant visit to Tyler County. The marker is appropriately sited adjacent to the TFS district office south of Woodville and just two miles east-northeast of Twin Lakes (the former Mooney's Lake, located on private property), where Yale students camped, studied, and listened as foresters and lumbermen came together to find common ground in 1909. Also fitting is that A. D. Folweiler, a Yale graduate who served as Texas State Forester from 1949 to 1967, prepared the marker application. His insights into the significance of the Woodville gathering and his knowledge of available resources were vital to approval by the Texas Historical Commission. In 1986, a sizable group of local historians, interested residents, TFS employees, and timber company personnel gathered at the TFS site to dedicate the marker, entitled "The Yale Summer Forestry Camp and Gifford Pinchot." There, virtually in the shadow of a fire tower that came to symbolize a later era of timber management in East Texas, they reflected on a time when Tyler County was at the forefront of an emerging conservation movement. Among those present at the event was James B. Hull, who became Texas state forester in 1996, retiring in 2008 after a distinguished career with TFS that included service in the Woodville office.

MARKER LOCATION: 3 mi. S of Woodville off US 69 at TFS complex

TEXAS FORESTRY ASSOCIATION

It might seem strange to some that the Texas Forestry Association began in the Central Texas town of Temple, Bell County, in the middle of the Blackland Prairie and more than a hundred miles west of the East Texas Piney Woods. But it might also seem strange that W. Goodrich Jones, known as the "Father of Texas Forestry," was a banker born in New York. When Jones's family moved to Europe for a brief time in the mid-1870s, he had an opportunity to learn about the German model of forest management, and although he later pursued a business degree from Princeton, he remained committed to conservation throughout his life. As a banker in Temple, he advocated the planting of trees and helped establish Arbor Day in Texas in 1889. His work caught the attention of U.S. Forester Gifford Pinchot, who invited Jones to attend the White House Conference on Conservation called by Pres. Theodore Roosevelt. Afterward,

W. Goodrich Jones, circa 1926. The Temple banker and early conservationist is considered the "Father of Texas Forestry." Courtesy Robert D. Baker.

Jones spearheaded the effort to form a state group, and in 1914 hosted a meeting of lumbermen, conservationists, businessmen, and government leaders in Temple to establish the Texas Forestry Association. Jones served as the organization's first president. As a result of its focused legislative efforts, the Texas Department of Forestry (later Texas Forest Service) began the following year through a bill signed by Gov. James E. Ferguson, a former Temple banker. Two Official Texas Historical Markers in Temple—for the Texas Forestry Association and W. Goodrich Jones—help interpret the important role the town played in the conservation of forest resources in Texas.

MARKER LOCATIONS

Texas Forestry Association, Main and 1st St.; W. Goodrich Jones, Jones Park at Ave. H and 23rd St., Temple

Sources: Robert S. Maxwell, "William Goodrich Jones," New Handbook of Texas, vol. 3, pp. 992–93; E. R. Wagoner, "Texas Forestry Association," New Handbook of Texas, vol. 6, p. 335; Site of the Organization of the Texas Forestry Association and W. Goodrich Jones, Bell County, THC marker files.

11 GHOSTS AT MITCHELL FLAT

Marfa (pop. 2,000), the picturesque seat of government for Presidio County, is a town that successfully reinvented itself in recent years as a center of cultural arts and heritage tourism. Drawn by the unmistakable Old West mystique of the regional landscape, visitors seek out contemporary art exhibits of the Chinati Foundation, admire the Second Empire elegance of the restored courthouse, and inquire about local sites and lore associated with the epic 1956 movie, *Giant,* that featured cinematic luminaries Rock Hudson, James Dean, and Elizabeth Taylor. Many also make a nighttime excursion east of town in hopes of witnessing another group of luminaries, the legendary and unexplained Marfa lights that can frequently be seen moving mysteriously across the surrounding plains. Eight miles out of town on the road to Alpine, the Texas Department of Transportation maintains an expansive rest area that doubles as a public viewing area, complete with telescopes—for although the lights are unpredictable in appearance, frequency, and intensity, they are also relatively easy to spot. Also at the viewing area is an Official Texas Historical Marker— perhaps read more by flashlight than any other in the state—that provides background on the phenomenon.

Historical credit for the first recorded sighting of the Marfa lights generally goes to cowboy Robert Reed Ellison, who mistook them for campfires of Apache Indians in the Chinati Mountains while driving cattle through Paisano Pass in 1883, the same year Marfa began as a settlement along the Galveston, Harrisburg, and San Antonio Railway. When Ellison and others later searched the area they found no evidence of Apaches or their campfires, but in talking with other early residents they learned several had experi-

Photo of Mitchell Flat and the Chinati Mountains at dusk showing what is believed to be one of the Marfa lights to the right. Courtesy Texas Department of Transportation. Photograph by J. Griffis Smith.

enced similar encounters. And so too may have the Apaches who earlier called the area home. As folklorist Elton Miles noted in his study of the Marfa lights, they have spawned a large number of what he terms "pseudo Indian legends." Some involve gods utilizing the area later known as Mitchell Flat to store lightning bolts and stars or to provide an ancestral home for the spirits of warriors. One of the more persistent stories, with numerous variations, centers on an Apache chieftain named Alsate, allegedly betrayed by Spaniards and thus eternally committed to starting fires to summon aid from others. And there are a number of pseudo Indian tales, like those later told of pioneers that involve unrequited love, separated lovers, and eternal searches for reconnection.[1]

Despite some cultural diversity in the stories, there are transgenerational similarities with varying details, such as wagon trains replacing Native American camps, and lone cowboys instead of lone scouts. And, as is common in such stories, many reference buried treasure. There are also later personal accounts of encounters with the lights, encounters that in more populated areas might be termed "urban legends." Most involve some plausible but otherwise distant associational connection to the storyteller—a friend of a cousin, for example—who narrowly escaped death or dismemberment while in pursuit of or in panicked flight from the lights. That effort to connect the present to the past is a key element of folklore. According to Miles, "Since the folk mind abhors a missing link in the chain of cause and effect, legend is spawned, sometimes disguised as rumor." But in seeming defiance of legends there are also a number of observers who provided detailed accounts of their own encounters. Jesús Jacquez, a trapper in the Chinati Mountain area, told of times when he and other trappers saw the flashing lights followed by a ghostly terrestrial appearance: "Then we would see a woman up ahead of us . . . signaling for us to follow her into the mountains, where the lights had been flashing. The first time we saw her, we thought she needed help. We tried to call her, but she always started walking back and would wave for us to follow her. Of course no one had the nerve to do that. Every time we made those trapping trips, we always saw the same lights and the same woman." For those who might dismiss folkloric explanations or even historical personal accounts, pseudo-scientific speculation often provides some measure of plausibility. Without scientific evidence, however, the ideas appear as numerous as the legends and myths. They include underground gases, lunar reflections (despite sightings on cloudy nights), mica deposits, static electricity, phosphorous veins, ball lightning, atmospheric light refractions (the Novaya Zemlya effect), magnetic charges, or even "Jack rabbits, whose fur glows because they have run through luminescent brush or have picked up glowworms."[2] Commonly, many who view the lights hasten to point out what they reason are more obvious and therefore logical explanations, including car headlights on distant roads or mercury vapor security lights on remote ranches. Both these and other human causal explanations are quickly dismissed by longtime residents of the area, especially in light of the history associated with the sightings.

Since there is a strong public perception—right or wrong—that no scientifically credible explanation for the phenomenon yet exists, the lights have drawn many well-intentioned researchers, adventurers, and myth debunkers to the Mitchell Flat over the years. According to Miles, "The appeal of the unknown in these lights is strong enough to arouse sensible men to elaborate and expensive investigative action in their determination to conquer the mystery of the Marfa Lights and lay bare their natural disposi-tion. This appeal is as strong as the tug of treasure maps handed down by dying prisoners to Coronado's Children, sending them into the wilderness with canteens and shovels and hearts full of yearning."[3]

Cowboy Ellison and Native Americans whose names remain unrecorded for posterity were among the first to venture out to the site in search of explanation. Those who followed later utilized new technologies and theories to justify their missions. They have included military personnel, geologists, law enforcement officials, and teachers and students, some from nearby Sul Ross State Uni-versity in Alpine. And even though there is a general consensus in stories associated with the investigations that the lights are not easily discernible from directly overhead, airplane pilots have scoured the nighttime landscape over the years, even dropping sacks of flour to mark supposed sources of the light emissions for ground crews. Some researchers have become local legends because of their seemingly indefatigable pursuit of the truth. As Miles described the situation, "They load themselves with survey-ing equipment, they triangulate the lights, they level on them with high-powered binoculars, they walkie-talkie back and forth from planes and pick-ups, they coordinate observations with radio-equipped cars, and they continue to drop sacks of flour despite all the former flour-sack failures."[4]

Over the years, despite unsubstantiated rumors of missing observers, most longtime residents believe the lights, while dis-concerting to visitors, especially when viewed for the first time or while alone, are not to be feared. To many they are simply part of the Marfa landscape. As local rancher Frank Jones observed, "Yeah, the Lights are there, but they aren't bothering us, and we're not bothering them."[5] This laissez-faire approach has led some people to personify the lights, affording them human qualities of mischief, friendliness, anger, or shyness. Kirby Warnock, a Dallas journalist, wrote in 1982 of his efforts to solve the mystery of the lights. He and his brother, adorned with leggings made of PVC pipe to protect against omnipresent rattlesnakes and carrying a camera to document their planned encounter, took a reading with surveying gear and headed out to the flat, leaving a backup crew at the road. "The lights were out, though, and they almost seemed to know what we were trying to do. As if to taunt us, they began to put on a show. First, one would appear and increase in intensity, lighting up the landscape around us, then suddenly split into two lights of equal lumination. The split was not like an amoeba separating, but rather as if one light had been 'hiding' behind the other, then suddenly rose up from behind it."[6]

Today, the Marfa Lights are a major tourist attraction, and they continue to mystify and confound observers much as they did more than a century ago. Nightly, visitors make the pilgrimage to the viewing station east of Marfa and search the skies for evidence of the unexplained. Some succeed in their quest and thus become part of a special community of heritage tourists, each with personal speculations about cause and effect. Until recently, though, few of the visitors had any idea as they gazed across Mitchell Flat toward the backdrop of the Chinati Mountains that another significant set of lights once dominated the area. And even fewer are aware that the two sets of lights occasionally crossed paths, adding another layer to the historical mystery.

On March 27, 1942, only a few months after the Japanese attack on Pearl Harbor, Hawaii, that signaled the entry of the United States into World War II, Maj. Norman L. Callish of the Army Air Forces made an official visit to Marfa. Meeting initially with R. E. Petross and Jack Kelly of the Marfa Chamber of Commerce and then other community leaders, Callish announced plans to establish an airfield and training command center in the vicinity. District Judge

Hunter O. Metcalfe drove the major to several possible locations, including sites on all sides of the county seat. Callish determined two to be satisfactory for recommendation to a selection board that would visit the area within weeks.[7]

In early April, the board selected a site east of town on land owned by Thomas G. Hendrick of Abilene and leased for grazing purposes to W. B. Mitchell and his sons. Although initial plans called for local funding support through bonds, in the end the U.S. government purchased the land outright. Preliminary construction of Marfa Army Air Field (Marfa AAF) began in May 1942, and work on the flight areas—three runways, parking apron, and connecting taxiways—lasted into November. In addition to hangars and maintenance support structures, the base included a hospital, theater, chapel, classrooms, headquarters facilities, and other structures, most of temporary or minimal construction, speed being the motivating design factor. Additionally, work began on auxiliary landing fields: South Field (9 mi. SSE); Ryan Field (26.5 mi. WNW); the Civilian Aeronautics Administration Field (10 mi. NW); Marfa Municipal Airport (9 mi. WNW); and Aragon Field (18 mi. WNW).[8]

In June 1942, Lt. Col. Gerald Hoyle arrived on temporary duty from California to oversee construction of the base and development of an Army Air Forces Advanced Flying School (two engine), part of the Western Flying Training Command out of California. He set up office in the Marfa National Bank while construction crews worked on the new base. A Vermont native and graduate of the University of Southern California, the forty-one-year-old Hoyle was familiar with Texas, having received his advanced flight training at Kelly Field, San Antonio, and even landing at Marfa once due to bad weather while on a flight to El Paso. In 1939, he completed tactical training at Randolph Field, also at San Antonio. With a record of service as a pilot in the Philippines and the Far East and experience in establishing training schools in California and New Mexico, Hoyle had the requisite background for the new assignment, and in August he formally assumed command at Marfa.[9]

Minnesota native Lt. Col. John D. Wynne arrived at Marfa in November as the first director of training. He enlisted in the Army

Air Corps in 1939 and took his basic training at Kelly Field. For his first assignment, he moved across San Antonio to Randolph Field, where he served as flight instructor. Also arriving in November was Lt. Col. F. Hazelton, assigned to Marfa as base executive and personnel officer. A Vermont native who grew up in California and graduated from the University of Southern California, like Hoyle, he apparently had no prior experience in Texas. Most of the early officers lived in the Paisano Hotel, while enlisted men made the Toltec Motel their home.[10]

The first two training planes—an AT-9 and an AT-17—arrived from Roswell, New Mexico, in November. The Cessna AT-17, a twin-engine trainer known as the Bobcat, became the workhorse of the base, and soon others began arriving from installations farther west. The base eventually included more advanced aircraft, including P-38s and B-25s. Flight instructors arrived in late November and early December 1942. The first aviation cadets reached the base on December 4, and flight training began, significantly, three days later on December 7, one year to the day after the attack on Pearl Harbor. The first class, designated 43-B and including 180 cadets, graduated in February 1943.[11]

The rapid development of Marfa AAF had a dramatic impact on the small town, which became a virtual boomtown with the concomitant supply and housing shortages. The Presidio County seat, though, accepted the challenges, with civic leaders calling on residents to support the new installation, just as they had the establishment of Fort D. A. Russell years earlier. As military historian Thomas E. Alexander noted,

[Residents] read of missing aircraft, fatal accidents, and lost lives with genuine sympathy and warmly welcomed all military personnel to become part of the community.... Marfa residents were encouraged by the newspaper to invite servicemen to take part in family Christmas observances. The USOs [United Service Organizations] in both Marfa and Alpine planned Yuletide festivities for those not fortunate enough to be entertained in local homes. Carol singing and taffy pulling were among the diversions offered the soldiers, but of particular interest seemed to have been the huge quantities of food donated to the USO by local citizens. Area businesses provided gift boxes for the festivities, with some parcels containing certificates for free long-distance calls to homes all across the nation.[12]

Through their generosity, both Marfa and nearby Alpine set high standards for wartime support on the home front. During World War II, similar stories played out in countless new and revitalized military towns throughout the nation.

In addition to the regular training, maintenance, medical, supply, guard, band, and headquarters units expected at a large training command, Marfa AAF served as home to two African American units, the 1017th Quartermaster Platoon and the 36th Aviation Squadron, as well as a headquarters company of the Women's Army Corps. The latter provided continuity in command support as servicemen transitioned to overseas assignments. Additionally, under an agreement between the U.S. War Department and the government of China, Marfa AAF provided flight training for Chinese officer cadets beginning in 1944.

Among the servicemen stationed at Marfa AAF were two in particular who enjoyed at least a modicum of celebrity status. One, the up-and-coming Hollywood actor Robert Sterling, was married to the glamorous actress Ann Sothern, who visited him at Marfa and stayed at the Paisano Hotel. Another, born Alfredo Arnold Cocozza in Philadelphia, interrupted a promising operatic recording career upon entering the service but became a popular entertainer during his stay in West Texas, sought out by churches, women's clubs, and other groups for his remarkable tenor voice. Following the war, Cocozza—using the name Mario Lanza—showed early promise as both an actor and singer before his tragic death in 1959 at the age of 38. Celebrated visitors of another sort—captured soldiers of Germany's Afrika Korps—began arriving at Fort D. A. Russell in 1944. The army installation eventually became an adjunct of Marfa AAF, providing other necessary housing for the growing air base.[13]

For several years, pilot training at Marfa AAF remained at high levels, with flights taking place both day and night and classes graduating on a monthly schedule. Given the activity at the Mitchell Flat facility and the regularity of the Marfa lights, it seemed inevitable there would eventually be encounters by the military personnel. One former serviceman who spoke often of the situation was Fritz Kahl, an Iowa native and later Marfa mayor who first heard of the lights when he served as one of the initial flight instructors at the field. "Me and another pilot got a fix on them," he told, "and tried to fly to that spot [in an AT-6 trainer], but when we got up in the air, we couldn't see them. I kept getting lower and lower, until finally the fellow in the back seat started shouting at me to get out of there because we were so low he could see the yucca plants." Admitting in another interview that he chased the lights on several occasions in 1943 and 1944, Kahl added, "My God, there I was, a World War II aviator. Hell, I was twenty-one years old and didn't have any sense, flying airplanes at night out in the hills, right down on the ground. You got to be young. You got to be crazy."[14]

During the war, a period of unprecedented alert for both military personnel and civilians in the United States, the ghost lights caused new concerns, especially for individuals who grew up outside the area and were unfamiliar with them. Once again, as Miles noted, without that missing link of cause and effect, rumors persisted, fueled by heightened fear, anxiety, and suspicion. The remoteness of the Marfa area most likely added to the uneasiness associated with the mysterious lights. Marie Roberts remembered, "In 1943 during World War II, while working at the Marfa Army Airbase, I overheard two young pilots talking about the strange lights to the south. The boys believed that it was a light used to guide German supply planes in. They were sure that the Germans had a large, well-hidden camp and were getting ready to invade the United States by way of Mexico."[15] The young pilots were unaware that similar stories of the lights signaling impending attacks had persisted since Robert Reed Ellison first reported their existence. Then, the possible invaders were Native Americans; during the time of the Mexican Revolution, they were Villistas. In the world wars, they were Germans.

Rumors about the lights persisted during the war, and some individuals even attributed training mishaps to their sinister nature. There were stories that during nighttime flights they aligned to replicate runway lights, instead guiding confused pilots straight to their deaths against the Chinati Mountains. There were also pervasive rumors of top secret and ill-fated investigations of the ghost lights. Common versions included supposed details of disrupted communications, melted vehicles, burned bodies, or investigators rescued alive but hopelessly lost to hysteria. Base postal worker James Mecklin later told of the investigative efforts of "a Major Davidson," who authorized the use of several planes in an elaborate effort to uncover the source of the mysterious lights. "I wasn't in on this," Mecklin noted, "but they told me that for three nights he set up teams out there of four planes, one behind the other, and that they would follow that light."[16] As with similar attempts, the lights failed to cooperate, disappearing as the planes approached, only to reappear some distance away. Thwarted on every sortie, the major finally conceded defeat and eventually left Marfa still curious about what he had experienced.

Amid the investigations and rumors, flight training at Marfa AAF continued at a steady pace. With the war tide turning in late 1944 in favor of the Allies, new rumors began to spread. This time they dealt with the possible closure of the base and the fort, despite official announcements to the contrary. Then, in April 1945 came announcement of a stand-by basis, followed by a letter from the Western Flying Training Command of a "temporary inactivation" to begin in late May. The last graduating cadets received their wings on May 23, and within days, personnel and aircraft relocated to other bases in preparation for the closing. By June 30, though, the War Department apparently reversed itself and announced plans to reopen the facility under the designation 818 Air Base, serving the Troop Carrier Command. Rumors quickly shifted to talk of base expansion and an increased mission, but the subsequent surrender of Japan in August 1945 also meant the eventual end of Marfa AAF. (Officials inactivated Fort D. A. Russell before the war's end.) Despite a few persistent rumors to the contrary, the base closed later that year. Removal of salvageable structures began soon after, with many living on through adaptive reuse as

A recent photograph of what remains of the Marfa Army Air Field main entryway. Photograph by Randy Mallory.

barns, churches, school facilities, and other purposes. In the course of its brief existence, Marfa Army Air Field provided training for more than seven thousand pilots to aid the Allied war effort. It also served as a temporary town for thousands of military personnel, provided jobs for local civilians, and fostered economic promise for Marfa and Presidio County.[17]

Today, just over sixty years after the end of the war, only the limited remains of the entryway, located alongside the highway near the Marfa Lights viewing area, serve as a structural landmark of the base. What was once a major training facility is now an archeological site on private land, inaccessible by the general public. From the air, though, the outline of its runways, roads, and building foundations are clearly discernible among the grasses and scrub brush that have moved back to reclaim the land. At the viewing area, two Official Texas Historical Markers interpret the unique dual history of the site. The first, erected in 1988 through application by the Presidio County Historical Commission, tells the story of the mysterious Marfa lights. The second, dedicated in July 2007 in conjunction with the sixtieth anniversary of the U.S. Air Force through the Texas in World War II initiative of the Texas Historical Commission (THC), commemorates Marfa Army Air Field. Dedication of the latter marker also coincided with a quarterly meeting of the THC and included state officials, Marfa residents, and even former servicemen once stationed there. Special guest for the ceremony was retired U.S. Air Force Maj. A. J. Wigley, of Oklahoma, who provided poignant reminiscences of his service as a Marfa cadet during World War II. That evening, hours after the ceremony, several state commissioners and THC staff members, including the authors of this book, made their way back to the marker site, where they quietly reflected on the significance of the day's events as they watched lights moving mysteriously out over Mitchell Flat.

MARKER LOCATION: 8 mi. E of Marfa on US 67/90.

FORT D. A. RUSSELL

New York native David Allen Russell (1820–64) was a career military officer in the U.S. Army. A graduate of West Point, he served with distinction in the U.S.-Mexico War and, following service in the Pacific Northwest, returned east to lead the 7th Massachusetts Volunteers during the Civil War. Brevetted for heroism in battle and increasingly entrusted with enlarged commands, he saw action in the Peninsula Campaign, the Seven Days Battles, the Battle of Fredericksburg, and The Wilderness Campaign. Wounded at Rappahannock Station, he quickly returned to his command but died during fighting in the Third Battle of Winchester (Battle of Opequon) on September 19, 1864. He is buried in the Evergreen Cemetery in Salem, New York.

Texas was not the first state to have a U.S. Army installation named for General Russell; that distinction goes to Wyoming. Camp Cheyenne, later renamed Fort D. A. Russell, dates to 1867 and construction of the Union Pacific rail line through Wyoming Territory. Troops at the fort initially provided security for the railroad and participated in regional military actions against Native Americans. It remained an active post through World War I, and in 1929 became Fort Francis E. Warren, serving as a training center in World War II before conversion to Warren Air Force Base in 1948. Early fort buildings are still maintained and utilized as part of base operations.

In contrast, the fort in Texas was short-lived. Established as Camp Albert in 1911 and later renamed Camp Marfa, the U.S. Army outpost in Presidio County grew out of concern that fighting associated with the Mexican Revolution could spill over into Texas. As a result, Signal Corps biplanes and cavalry units based at the camp regularly patrolled along the Rio Grande during that time. The mission for Camp Marfa expanded significantly in the following decades, and its remote location proved ideal for combat training maneuvers. In 1930, with the change in the name of the fort in Wyoming, Camp Marfa became the new Fort D. A. Russell. Soon after, though, rumors of its closure began to spread—devastating news for the small town during the Great Depression.

A 1942 photograph of Fort D. A. Russell, Marfa.
Courtesy Texas Historical Commission, National Register of Historic Places files.

Recent photograph of the historic entryway pylons at what was
Officers Row of Fort D. A. Russell. Courtesy Texas Historical Commission,
National Register of Historic Places files.

Mural painted by German prisoners of war, Building 98, Fort D. A. Russell.
Photograph by Randy Mallory.

Temporarily inactive for only two years, though, the post became an artillery training base in 1935 and began serving a broader function in the World War II era. Officially deactivated in 1945 and closed the following year, the fort transferred to private ownership by the end of the decade.

Two Official Texas Historical Markers help interpret the short but complex story of Fort D. A. Russell. The first, a subject marker erected in 1989, provides an overview of the Texas installation's existence from 1911 through World War II. The second, approved by the Texas Historical Commission in 2004, tells the unique story of Building 98, elaborately decorated on the interior with murals painted by German prisoners of war from Field Marshal Erwin Rommel's Afrika Korps. The building marker recognizes the structure's historical and architectural significance and thereby conveys the Recorded Texas Historic Landmark designation that provides a measure of legal protection.

MARKER LOCATIONS

Fort D. A. Russell, corner of First Ave. and Madrid St., Marfa; and Building 98, Fort D. A. Russell, 705 W. Bonnie St., Marfa

Sources: Patricia L. Faust, ed., *Historical Times Illustrated Encyclopedia of the Civil War* (New York: Harper and Row, 1986); Lee Bennett, "Fort D. A. Russell," *New Handbook of Texas,* vol. 2, p. 1096.

12 CHASING THE NEXT FRONTIER

Will Rogers understood the unmistakable rhythms of time and place, and he provided historical identity for an era as few ever have. A unique transitional expression of the American West, he is difficult to categorize, so vast were his contributions. More often than not, he is remembered simply as a humorist, but he was also an actor, a writer, an adventurer, an entertainer, a cultural ambassador, and, perhaps the title he preferred most, a cowboy. The relative simplicity of his demeanor and the "everyman" persona that marked his character endeared him to people across the nation—and around the world—in the decades leading up to the Great Depression. A sense of universal truth permeated his observations on life, and his folksy and neighborly humor served as a mirror to a rapidly changing society. No one, it seemed, from the powerless in the working class to the elites of politics and business, could escape his wit, delivered with such effective good will, sincerity, timing, and purpose—and his signature schoolboy grin—that it could be at the same time both biting and comforting. Regardless, it always seemed welcome or at least appropriate. Even those who sought to label his unique talent were not immune: "When I first started out to write and misspelled a few words, people said I was plain ignorant," he observed, "but when I got all the words wrong, they declared I was a humorist."[1]

Born along the Verdigris River in Indian Territory (near present Oologah, Oklahoma) on November 4, 1879, to parents of mixed Cherokee heritage, William Penn Adair Rogers grew up on the ragged edge of a frontier existence, albeit with certain advantages that afforded him both opportunities and a measure of early independence. His father, Clement Vann Rogers, served in the Confederacy during the Civil War alongside such noted Cherokee soldiers as Stand Watie and William Penn Adair, for whom he named his son. A self-driven, serious man, Clem Rogers became a prominent rancher, landowner, businessman, and political leader during a time of great transition in the Cherokee Nation. Will's mother, Mary America Schrimsher Rogers, despite losing three of eight children as infants, provided a stable home life, one filled with warmth, love, and humor. She had a lasting influence on her son, the youngest of her children, although she died in 1890 just as he entered his teenage years. Will Rogers developed a deep respect for the Native American culture through his parents, but even that was subject to his wit: "My ancestors didn't come over on the May-flower," he is quoted as saying, "but they met the boat."[2]

Motivated more by life experiences than structured schooling as a young man, Rogers proved to be naturally inquisitive but easily distracted and prone to wanderlust. Although a decent student, despite his comical comments to the contrary later in life, he was not innately drawn to the formal regimen of education. Among his favorite early diversions from studies was roping, and he spent countless hours around the ranch lassoing animals, fences, buggies, and even sisters. His mentor on the ranch was Dan Walker, an African American cowboy noted for his roping skills, and Rogers worked with him and copied his technique every chance he got. In 1893, when Will and his father took a load of cattle to Chicago and attended the World's Columbian Exposition, he had the unique opportunity to study the different style of Mexican vaqueros in Buffalo Bill's Wild West Show, particularly the elaborate trick roping of Vincente Oropeza, billed as "the greatest roper in the world."[3] Rogers excelled in this observational, non-traditional type of education, but such interests outside the mainstream of classical studies only served to frustrate both him and his father. Clem Rogers had the means to provide his son with excellent opportunities at a number of respected boarding schools, but none seemed to work for Will. Consequently, he never stayed too long at any one institution. Confiding to his cousin, Spi Trent, he once wrote, "Spi, I Really Try to be a good sport about this school business but I am gaggin at the bit. I cant keep myself inside a school room."[4]

The end of Rogers's formal education came abruptly in March 1898, while he was enrolled at Kemper School (later Kemper Military School) in Boonville, Missouri. A schoolmate, William A. "Bill" Johnson from Canadian, Texas, told him about the possibility of cattle work in the Texas Panhandle, specifically in the area of Higgins, Lipscomb County, where the Johnsons lived until the year before. That idea gave Rogers the plan he needed as a starting point for leaving his schooling behind. Borrowing money from his sisters, even though they knew their father provided him with a comfortable allowance and would strongly disapprove of their assistance, Rogers left Missouri and headed west to learn the craft of the cowboy.[5]

In 1898, the relatively young railroad town of Higgins offered great promise as a cattle-shipping center, and the booming cattle business of the surrounding region meant an abundance of jobs for cowboys, seasoned or otherwise. Young Will Rogers arrived there by train on March 15, 1898, and checked into the Johnson House, a hotel owned by Bill's father. Following his friend's suggestion, he made contact with local rancher W. Perry Ewing, who

Will Rogers as a student at Kemper School, Missouri. Photograph was taken not long before Rogers left to begin his adventure as a cowboy in Texas—and beyond. Courtesy Will Rogers Memorial Museum, Claremore, Oklahoma.

B676E5   **Higgins Hotel, Higgins, Tex.**   Pub. by Word Bros. Leading Druggist.

Historic photo of the Hotel Higgins (formerly the Johnson House) in Higgins, Texas. Will Rogers stayed there upon his arrival in Lipscomb County. Courtesy Wolf Creek Heritage Museum, Lipscomb, Texas.

agreed to hire him on as a hand at his Little Robe Ranch, located twelve miles south-southeast of town in what is now Ellis County, Oklahoma. There, Rogers worked closely with Ewing's teenage son, Frank, who would become a lifelong friend. At the Little Robe, as Arthur Frank Wertheim and Barbara Bair, editors of *The Papers of Will Rogers,* noted, "Rogers wrangled horses, helped in the roundup and calf branding, and joined a six-week cattle trail drive, accompanying four hundred head of cattle 165 miles to Medicine Lodge, Kansas. The trail drive gave Rogers an opportunity to experience the rugged life of a cowpuncher. He guarded the herd at night and got drenched in a prairie thunderstorm and his horse was caught in quicksand at a treacherous river crossing."[6] Will Rogers and Frank Ewing worked well together, and on occasion they took cattle out to rangeland northwest of Higgins, where they stayed in a small cabin on Camp Creek. After Will had been with the family for a while, Perry Ewing sent a note to Clem Rogers asking what he should do with the boy, and the response was that Will could stay on at the ranch if he would work. Despite his enjoyment of the situation, Rogers remained with the Ewing outfit only a few months.

He returned there many times over the next few years, however, to work for several weeks but already he felt the need to seek new experiences. Riding a horse southwest only as far as Amarillo, he joined up with the L. A. Knight outfit out of Plainview. While in that employ, he helped drive a large herd of cattle to Liberal, Kansas. In short order he was on the move again, this time using the rails to reach places like Colorado and New Mexico, and he even spent time with the Mashed O operation near Muleshoe in Bailey County.[7] Later in life, he remembered his first cowboy experiences in the Texas Panhandle with great nostalgia and a genuine respect for the land. In one of his weekly newspaper commentaries from 1934, he wrote, "That plains was the prettiest country I ever saw in my life, as flat as a beauty contest winner's stomach, and prairie lakes scattered all over it. And mirages! You could see anything in the world—just ahead of you—and I eat out of a chuck wagon, and slept on the ground all that spring and summer of '98."[8]

Following a quick return to the home place near Oologah, where he tried for a time to follow through on his father's plan to have Will run part of the family cattle operations, he headed out again, traveling back to Texas and over to Missouri, and even out to California, never staying in one place too long. Relying on his exceptional roping skills, which he honed through his work on ranches, he entered and won a number of steer-roping contests at fairs and other special events throughout the West and Midwest. He even competed against and bested Vincente Oropeza at St. Louis in 1899, although both men eventually lost the steer-roping event to Gus Pickett of Decatur, Texas. During much of his time as a circuit contestant he partnered with rancher, railroad agent, and promoter Zack Mulhall, out of Oklahoma Territory, who recruited talented young cowboys for events he staged.[9] But, even with the independence, travel, and pay associated with his new profession, Rogers again felt the pull of new frontiers. Although his next would be remarkably different from his earlier experiences, taking him from the United States to other continents, it also had—in an ironically strange and serendipitous way—something of a Texas connection, one that would eventually set Rogers on a dramatic new life course.

In 1902, with friend Dick Parris, Rogers traveled to England and then to the vast pampas of Argentina to experience firsthand what he considered the mystery and excitement of the gaucho culture, widely romanticized in the United States as the South American equivalent of the Old West. In short order, though, Parris determined he made the wrong decision and headed home, leaving his friend to pursue the grand adventure alone. Rogers did so with great energy and purpose, working alongside the celebrated gauchos and experiencing their unique customs and perspectives. As always, he used his remarkable skills in human interaction and cultural observation to determine where he might best fit in, but he quickly became disillusioned. The Argentine frontier, he came to realize, like that of the American West he so eagerly sought only a few years before, was subject to the same eroding influences of modernization. What he sought in that regard was not to be found in Argentina.[10]

With the gaucho mystique and another frontier now evaporating for him, Rogers looked around for a suitable replacement, one he hoped would lead somewhere other than north toward home; he was not yet ready to end his quest. He found what he was looking for in an assignment that allowed him to escort a shipment of livestock across the Atlantic to South Africa, where he arrived only months after the end of the lengthy Boer War. After joining up with local outfits for a short time, he traveled to Ladysmith looking for work. There he came across a man who went by the moniker Texas Jack, a name that to Rogers might have evoked the literary flavor of dime novels about the Old West. The association, if indeed it occurred to him at all, was not coincidental as it turned out.[11]

Texas Jack's real name was John B. Omohundro Jr., and he was the owner, promoter, and principal star of Texas Jack's Wild West Show and Dramatic Company, then on tour in South Africa. Little is known of him, but what has been recorded by others is often clouded in legend and otherwise questionable circumstances. His story goes back to the exploits of another Texas Jack who also went by the name John B. Omohundro Jr. The original Texas Jack, like Will Rogers generations later, sought adventures in the American West as a young man. Born John Burwell Omohundro

Jr. (some family records show his middle name as Baker, the same as his mother's maiden name) near Palmyra, Virginia, in 1846, he apparently made his way to Texas as a teenager and became a cowboy. That part of his life story, however, has never been documented, and exactly where and when he worked in Texas remains unknown. By the time of the Civil War, though, he was again in Virginia, and from there he served under the command of Confederate Gen. J. E. B. Stuart as a scout. In the years after the war, he evidently returned to Texas and worked on cattle drives, including one to Tennessee where, according to lore, grateful residents dubbed him Texas Jack.[12]

It was during his early days as a drover that he claimed to have come across the gruesome scene of an Indian raid in Kansas, where he found a young boy—the lone survivor of the family. Omohundro took the child to friends in Fort Worth who agreed to provide foster care and raise him in a good home. Later, the young man simply adopted the name of his rescuer—sobriquet and all— as his own. The original Texas Jack eventually moved to Nebraska and met William F. "Buffalo Bill" Cody, with whom he partnered as a scout, guide, and buffalo hunter. In 1872, the two joined up with Ned Buntline in Chicago and starred in *The Scouts of the Prairie,* a stage production written by Cody and loosely based on western adventures he shared with Omohundro. The lively melodramatic performances included staged skirmishes and fight scenes, complete with villainous characters, discharged weaponry, spellbinding rescues, and the actions of authentic western "heroes," as Buntline, Omohundro, and Cody billed themselves. Separate performances in the show featured special cowboy skills, including rope tricks by Texas Jack—believed to be the earliest example of a roping act on the American stage.[13]

The overwhelming success of the stage venture led to other theatrical offerings and seasons, as well as personal fame, but over time Texas Jack and Buffalo Bill parted ways. Cody, as is well known, continued on as a showman, developing his famous Wild West extravaganzas and performing to enthusiastic crowds throughout the world. Omohundro also remained in theatrics, although somewhat reluctantly and, despite additional notoriety as the hero of popular dime novels, grew to prefer a quieter life. His story ended, at least in part, in Leadville, Colorado, where he died of pneumonia at the age of 33. He is buried in the city's Evergreen Cemetery beneath a tombstone provided by his friend, Buffalo Bill.[14]

The legacy of Texas Jack the showman continued on in the work of his namesake. No doubt borrowing from the success of his rescuer, while also developing his own unique style as an entertainer, Texas Jack the younger knew how to present a program that would appeal to international audiences captivated by the legend and lore of the American West. In Will Rogers, he evidently saw enough talent and authenticity to warrant an investment, and so he offered the young cowboy a feature role in his show as a bronc rider and trick roper. For Rogers, the opportunity provided a clearer focus for the search he started years before in Texas. Writing of the new direction and its significance, Wertheim and Bair noted, "Part circus, part rodeo, part historical melodrama and parade, the Wild West show was a means by which the American West that Rogers had seen as a small child became converted into legend."[15]

Rogers's first on-stage experience as a paid performer failed to reflect star quality, although it provided a memorable lesson in stage fright. Apparently debuted to the audience the night he signed with Texas Jack, he later recalled, "When I got in that ring that night I couldent [sic] slip up on the bank and throw a rope in the creek. I couldent a-doubled that rope up and hit the ground with it. I tangled myself up in that rope so I guess they thought I was doing a Houdini. Finally, when Jack saw I wasent going to be able to choke myself he come in and drove me out." Later in the show, when Rogers appeared rather ignominiously as a bronc rider, he remembered, "It must have been a big hit cause everybody laughed." In addition to his feature performances, he also acted in skits, playing a variety of characters.[16] Although he could not have known it at the time, the defining elements of his future career were coming together quickly in South Africa.

Consistent with his new profession and his role as a feature act, Rogers developed his theatrical persona as "The Cherokee Kid: Fancy Lasso Artist and Rough Rider." He quickly became an audience favorite, twirling two ropes at once and performing such difficult tricks as the "Big Crinoline," a full extension, spinning open loop utilizing as much as sixty feet of rope. His ability to perform the latter, in particular, led to his hiring, although only later did Rogers learn that Texas Jack had neglected to tell him he had a standing reward offer for anyone who could perform the difficult trick. Rogers, as an employee, of course, was not eligible for the prize. Despite that early "oversight," Rogers admired Texas Jack, who became his early theatrical mentor, and he carefully studied his special talents for working the crowds. "Texas Jack was one of the smartest showmen I ever met," he wrote. "From him I learned the great secret of the show business—learned when to get off. It's the fellow that knows when to quit that the audience wants more of." In a letter to his father dated December 15, 1902, Rogers wrote, "I like it fine and Jack himself is the finest old boy I ever saw and he seems to think a great deal of me he is a man about 40 years old and has traveled all over the world showing. . . . It isent [sic] a wild mob like them at home for he dont drink a drop or smoke or gamble and likes for his men to be the same."[17]

Rogers remained in the employ of Texas Jack for eight months, but shortly after joining up, as he gained confidence in his theatrical abilities, he began planning to take his act to a larger venue— one of the major circus companies. He confided in his boss, who supported his idea, and so, in April 1903, the Wild West showman wrote the following general letter of reference:

I have very great pleasure in recommending Mr. W. P. Rogers ("The Cherokee Kid") to circus proprietors. He has performed with me during my present South African Trip and I consider him to be the Champion Trick Roughrider and Lasso Thrower of the World. He is sober, industrious, hardworking at all times and is always to be relied on. I shall be very pleased to give him an engagement at any time should he wish to return.
Texas Jack.[18]

In December 1903, Rogers accepted an assignment with the Wirth Brothers' Circus, which operated in Australia and New Zealand. He left there in March the following year, however, and was back in Indian Territory in April. Texas Jack continued on in South Africa but passed away at Kroonstad in October 1905.[19]

In his six-year pursuit of the frontier—more accurately a journey of self-discovery—Will Rogers traveled to five continents, collected thousands of stories, made countless new friends, earned his independence, and discovered the genesis of his life's calling as an entertainer. Throughout his lifetime, from vaudeville to silent movies, and from talkies to radio and journalism, he built on that remarkable beginning of his professional life, drawing on it continually for inspiration, direction, and humor. The consummate showman, Rogers nevertheless remained accessible to the public through his movies, radio programs, and newspaper columns, and by the 1930s many considered him the conscience of America. The sense of adventure he showed as a young man continued to define his character as much as anything, even to the end. On August 15, 1935, as he and his close friend, the noted Texas-born aviator Wiley Post, traveled in Alaska on a backcountry sightseeing expedition, their plane crashed shortly after takeoff from remote Walakpa Lagoon near Point Barrow, killing them both. So great was Will Rogers's fame that his sudden and tragic death stunned the nation and the world and marked a defining moment for a generation that mourned the loss of a hero for the ages. But, as Will Rogers once humbly noted, "This thing of being a hero, about the main thing is to know when to die. Prolonged life has ruined more men than it ever made."[20]

The memory of Will Rogers lives on in many parts of Texas, where he is remembered as a decent man who appreciated, experienced, and promoted, with great humor, the culture of the American West. Fort Worth's landmark Will Rogers Memorial Center, with its distinctive coliseum completed in 1936, now serves as an entertainment center for that city's expansive cultural district, where it hosts the Southwestern Exposition and Livestock Show among other events. At Texas Tech University in Lubbock, Electra Waggoner Biggs's statue, *Riding into the Sunset,* which depicts Rogers astride his horse, Soapsuds, has been a landmark feature of the campus landscape since 1948. (Other Texas castings of the piece are in Fort Worth and Dallas.)[21] And in the small Panhandle

A photograph of Will Rogers (left) and pilot Wiley Post (right) taken during their ill-fated trip to Alaska, 1935. Courtesy Will Rogers Memorial Museum, Claremore, Oklahoma.

town of Higgins (pop. 406), which began hosting a Will Rogers Day Celebration in 1962, an Official Texas Historical Marker recalls the days when, as a teenager, he first came to the area to start his quest as a cowboy. Throughout his life, Rogers maintained close ties with people in Higgins, especially his friend Frank Ewing. In 1926, when Will Rogers spoke at an Amarillo event, the two former cowboys joined up with Bill Johnson for a reunion. Years later, after Rogers's death, when officials named a stretch of Route 66 at Amarillo in the entertainer's honor, Ewing led off a parade by accompanying a riderless Soapsuds along the way. In 1967, two years after Frank Ewing died, a crowd gathered in Higgins during the Will Rogers Day Celebration to dedicate the Rogers marker, which includes mention of their friendship. Texas Speaker of the House Ben Barnes, a Democrat, provided the keynote address. Will Rogers would no doubt have appreciated that. "I dont belong to any organized Political faith," he noted in a 1930 speech, adding "I am a democrat."[22]

MARKER LOCATION: Park on US 60E, Higgins

WILEY HARDEMAN POST

Late in 1898, the same year Will Rogers began his cowboy adventure in the Texas Panhandle, W. F. and Mae Laine Post gave birth to a son, Wiley Hardeman Post, in the rural Corinth Community south of Grand Saline in Van Zandt County, Texas. Within a few years the family moved west near Abilene, Taylor County, and then again to southwestern Oklahoma. Wiley Post had little interest in school and left after his elementary years, eventually finding employment in nearby oilfields, where he showed a remarkable talent for mechanical work. From the time he first viewed an airplane at a Lawton, Oklahoma, fair in 1913, he pursued a career in aviation. In 1924, he joined up with an air circus as a parachute jumper and soon started taking flying lessons. Two years later, though, while back in the oilfields working to raise funds for his own plane, an accident resulted in the loss of his left eye. Following recuperation, he used part of his workmen's compensation to purchase a used Canuck plane and pay for its repair, and in 1927, he and his first cousin, Edna Mae Laine, who he met during a barnstorming tour at Sweetwater, Texas, used it for their elopement.

Working through his disability, Post became a licensed air transport pilot employed by oil companies, as well as the Lockheed Corporation. In partnership with oilman F. C. Hall, he modified Hall's Lockheed Vega, the *Winnie Mae*, for airspeed competitions and won the 1930 National Air Races. The following year, he and navigator Harold Gatty flew the plane around the world, covering 15,474 miles (using a northern latitude route) in less than nine days, a record time. The feat resulted in a tickertape parade in New York City, a White House visit with Pres. Herbert Hoover, and a special banquet hosted by Will Rogers at his home in Claremore, Oklahoma. Two years later, Post made the global trip again, but solo, completing it in less than eight days. Soon after, he purchased the *Winnie Mae* from Hall and adapted it for stratospheric flight, hoping to exploit what he called the "high winds" (now jet stream) for sustained speeds. Despite the devastating economic conditions of the 1930s, Post received corporate financial backing—principally from Phillips Petroleum and B. F. Goodrich—to develop the first pressurized flight suit and to continue his pioneer work in stratospheric aviation, which resulted in significant innovations for the aviation industry. In 1935, seeking a rest from his work, Post invited his friend, Will Rogers, to accompany him on a trip to Alaska aboard his Lockheed Orion-Explorer.

Only thirty-six years old at the time of his death, Post came to be regarded as a legend in the history of aviation. In the short time from 1930 to 1935, he set air speed records, circled the globe twice, pioneered stratospheric flight, and contributed many significant and lasting innovations in design and mechanics. The *Winnie Mae* and his prototype pressurized flight suit are now part of the collection of the National Air and Space Museum of the Smithsonian Institution in Washington, D.C. An Official Texas Historical Marker, dedicated in 1996 to honor his celebrated life, is located in Grand Saline. Eight miles south, a marker for the Corinth Cemetery mentions his family's early association with the area. Although his parents and other relatives are buried there, Wiley Post is buried in Memorial Park Cemetery in north-central Oklahoma City.

MARKER LOCATION

Garland St. (US 80) and Main St. (SH 17), Grand Saline

Sources: Wiley Hardeman Post historical narrative, prepared by Teresa Lynne Sawyer Lewis, THC marker files; Bobby H. Johnson, "Wiley Hardeman Post," *New Handbook of Texas*, vol. 5, pp. 289–90.

13 ALIEN CITY IN
A STRANGE LAND

Observing the landscape around the South Texas town of Crystal City in Zavala County today, one would be hard pressed to envision the once-bustling city-within-a-city that existed there during World War II. What appeared as a town in the 1940s, laid out in an orderly grid of streets, actually was an internment camp run by the U.S. Immigration and Naturalization Service (INS) under auspices of the Department of Justice. Surrounded by barbed wire fences and guard towers manned by armed sentries, the Crystal City Alien Family Internment Camp covered almost three hundred acres and at its peak housed almost four thousand people. Few physical structures or artifacts remain to suggest the presence of the "town." Its unique history is one of the lesser-known stories of the American home front during the Second World War.

With war raging in Europe in 1940, the United States closely monitored world events but had not yet entered the fray. In June of that year, Congress passed the Alien Registration Act, which required all non-citizens living in the United States to register at their local post offices. Using the registration information, the Federal Bureau of Investigation, under its legendary director, J. Edgar Hoover, maintained files on almost five million people and generated lists of suspected enemy aliens. One outcome of the lists would be the now-infamous internment of Japanese Americans in relocation centers (internment camps) mostly in the western states. At the same time, in a move to secure ports and boundaries of the Western Hemisphere, and in cooperation with government officials in Mexico and a number of Central and South American countries whose support for the Allies' cause it actively solicited, the U.S. government also monitored the presence and activities of immigrants to those countries from Axis nations.

Following the U.S. entry into the war in December 1941 after the Japanese bombing of Pearl Harbor, Hawaii, wholesale roundups of resident aliens in the United States, the territories of Alaska and Hawaii, and Latin America, particularly those of Japanese, German, and Italian ancestry, began in earnest. In January 1942, at a conference of foreign ministers in Brazil, most Latin American countries broke off diplomatic relations with Axis countries and prepared to expel persons classified as enemy aliens. Although most of their ancestors had immigrated to Latin America as farm laborers, many of those identified as "Axis nationals"—particularly among the Japanese in Peru—represented a growing merchant, banking, and business class. Their success and financial strength by the 1930s generated a hostile movement among native business interests who led campaigns to drive them out of business, deny them citizenship (and in some cases rescind citizenship previously granted), and suspend further immigration. In addition to the relocation centers used for detaining Japanese Americans, the United States set in motion a plan to house people expelled from Latin America in a network of internment camps operated by the INS and guarded by U.S. Border Patrol officers.

With many Americans caught in enemy-occupied territory abroad, the U.S. government planned to repatriate detainees to Japan and Germany in a prisoner exchange program. The majority of Latin American deportees, although culturally identified with their ancestral homes, were, after generations in the Western Hemisphere, natives of their adopted countries. Now, stripped of citizenship or legal resident status in the countries from which they were expelled and forced to travel to the United States, they became refugees officially classified as illegal aliens upon entering U.S. territory. Many of them ended up in Texas, where the INS operated three internment camps.[1]

Citizens of Kenedy, a small town in Karnes County about sixty miles southeast of San Antonio, mounted a lobbying effort to convince federal officials to use a former Civilian Conservation

Corps (CCC) facility in their town for a detention center. The INS converted the CCC camp's existing nine barracks for internment use, added two hundred prefabricated one-room cabins (referred to as "victory huts"), as well as a central dining hall and kitchen, latrines, hospital, headquarters building, and staff quarters, and enclosed the compound with a ten-foot-high barbed wire fence and guard towers. Receiving its first large group of detainees in April 1942, the Kenedy camp housed males only, primarily Japanese, Germans, and a few Italians from Latin America, and some Japanese from California. The average population at the facility ranged from about 700 to 1,200. Repatriation from the camp began as early as May 1942, with about 975 prisoners repatriated by the fall of 1944. The internment camp operations at Kenedy ceased in October 1944, replaced by a U.S. Army–run prisoner of war (POW) camp housing German soldiers captured during the Battle of the Bulge. According to one source, U.S. soldiers wounded in the same battle served as guards at the Camp Kenedy POW camp.[2]

The facilities at the Seagoville internment camp in southeast Dallas County contrasted sharply with those at Kenedy and other locations. Built in 1940 as a model minimum-security women's prison, it resembled a school campus with Colonial-style red brick buildings, sidewalks, green lawns, and well-furnished dormitories with kitchen, bathing, and laundry facilities. An educational staff supervised such activities as sewing, weaving, folk dancing, and gardening, and outdoor sports included badminton and baseball. Musical instruments and a well-stocked library afforded cultural activities, and detainees could order clothes from catalog companies such as Montgomery Ward and Sears. Although provided with more amenities than detainees in other camps, people housed in the Seagoville camp worked at various levels as required and never lost sight of the fact they remained there against their will. When first converted by the INS, the Seagoville camp housed about 50 female Japanese language teachers arrested on the West Coast, but soon families of Latin American Japanese and German detainees joined them.[3] One of the smaller internment facilities operated by the INS, Camp Seagoville had a peak population of less than 650.

By 1942, the Justice Department and the INS began planning for a large facility to allow men who had been arrested and detained in camps across the country to be reunited with their families—many who voluntarily joined their husbands and fathers in detention—for the duration of the war. The INS chose the site of a former migratory farm laborers' camp in Crystal City in the arid South Texas plains some fifty miles south of Uvalde for what would become the largest of all the internment facilities in the United States, and the only one specifically designed for families. Built by the Farm Security Administration in 1940, the facility included more than 150 one- and three-room cottages, bathhouses, a clinic, and various utility buildings.4

Immediately upon acquiring the property, the INS began a massive building project. They enclosed the 290-acre site with fences and guard towers and spent more than one million dollars to lay out streets, extend electric and water utilities, and erect more than five hundred structures including additional housing, schools, stores, a hospital, administrative offices, warehouses, and recreation centers. With the improvements largely completed by the end of 1942, the government began moving both German and Japanese families to the site. Thirty-five German families arrived in December 1942, followed by the first group of Japanese families—primarily from Hawaii and Peru—in March 1943. Records indicate the presence of at least one Italian family, as well, but reportedly they were released following Italy's surrender to the Allies in 1943. With the ratio of internees generally that of one-third German and two-thirds Japanese, the camp maintained an average population of about 3,000, with peak estimates placed at 3,500 to 4,000. Acceding to rules of the Geneva Convention regulating treatment of prisoners of different nationalities, officials divided the camp into a German section and a Japanese section. In addition to INS staff and Border Patrol guards, citizens of Crystal City worked at the camp in various professional and administrative positions.5

By all accounts, Crystal City internees essentially lived a small-town existence, although their status as prisoners remained clear throughout their confinement within a barbed wire enclosure monitored by armed guards. They suffered the loss of personal

Aerial view of Crystal City Alien Family Internment Camp, circa 1944–45. Laid out in a grid pattern, the internment camp resembled a small city on the South Texas prairie. The main entrance to the camp is at the bottom right; the large round feature in the upper left is the cement swimming pool built by German detainees. Shown to the right of the swimming pool is the camp citrus orchard. The E-shaped building in the center is the Federal High School; the L-shaped building at the center bottom is the German School. The hospital complex is visible in the lower right corner. Courtesy University of Texas at San Antonio Institute of Texan Cultures #098-0953. Loaned by Betty Fly.

liberties: INS staff censored their mail heavily; they endured the constant illumination of nighttime floodlights visible almost to the Mexican border; and they experienced daily headcounts and occasional personal searches.[6] While most internment centers offered only barracks-style housing, central mess hall dining facilities, and shared bathhouses and latrines, the design of the Crystal

City camp centered on quasi-neighborhoods of "victory huts" and duplex, triplex, and quadruplex houses where families cooked their own meals in private kitchens and shared bathroom facilities only with the other families in their units. Many families used their personal funds, doled out by camp authorities according to various rules and regulations, to plant flower and vegetable gardens, raise hogs and chickens, and maintain beehives for honey. A number of families also built screened porches onto their cottages—"morale-builders" according to U.S. officials.[7]

Daily camp activities revolved around work, school, and recreation. Adults earned ten cents per hour working at jobs in the camp's farming operations, sewing shop, furniture factory, machine shop, schools, laundry, bakery, canteens, warehouses, and administrative offices. Men worked on trucks delivering blocks of ice as well as milk from the camp's dairy to houses throughout the compound, and a number of women trained as nurses' aides in the seventy-bed hospital. According to a rather propagandistic film about the camp produced at the end of the war by the INS and showing various scenes of life within the facility, "Japanese and German girls who were trained by the public health nurses as aides were faithful and dependable helpers." Detainee doctors, including two female Japanese physicians, and nurses also worked in the hospital. The film includes footage of operating room facilities and shows newborn babies in the nursery, with the narrator proudly proclaiming, "Young America! About two hundred and fifty Americans were born in this hospital."[8]

Four schools provided educational opportunities for children and teenagers. In addition to the American elementary school, Japanese and German internees operated separate grammar schools—known simply as the Japanese School and the German School—with teachers recruited from within their own ranks. The U.S.-run Federal High School, staffed by local teachers and administrators recruited to Crystal City by the camp's school superintendent and accredited by the State Board of Education, resembled a typical Texas high school in many ways. In addition to their scholarly pursuits, students participated in choirs, bands, and drama clubs, played team sports, held dances and proms, and published

Japanese children in unpaved street lined with duplexes in Section D of Crystal City Internment Camp, circa 1943–45. Many families detained at Crystal City lived in duplex, triplex, or quadruplex housing units. This photograph reveals small garden plots and clotheslines in the dusty yards of the neighborhood. Courtesy University of Texas at San Antonio Institute of Texan Cultures #098-1007. Loaned by Betty Fly.

a yearbook with the somewhat ironic title of *The Roundup*.[9] The camp even had its own Boy Scout and Girl Scout troops. Competitive and team sports included tennis, track and field, wrestling, volleyball, basketball, soccer, football, and—by all accounts the most popular—softball. With teams of teenagers and adults, male and female, participating, the internees organized a thirty-two-team softball league, complete with "American League" and "National League" schedules and championship playoffs.[10] A cement-lined swimming pool, built by German internees from a large irrigation storage tank, also provided recreational opportunities and a welcome respite from the relentlessly hot South Texas sun. Tragically, two young Japanese girls drowned in the pool in the summer of 1944. Occasionally, under the supervision of guards, residents of the camp received permission to venture outside the fenced perimeter for nature hikes and picnics along the Nueces River.[11]

Cultural offerings included a library stocked with English, Spanish, German, and Japanese books; occasional musicals and plays performed by internees; and regularly scheduled movies. Japanese and German internees congregated in their respective community centers for social interaction, engaging in such activities as arts and crafts and board games, and—in the case of the German center—simply relaxing and visiting with friends while enjoying a beverage in the beer garden. Some of the more than thirty interned priests and ministers attended to the spiritual needs of the families and conducted Christian and Buddhist worship services. Four newspapers, produced with typewriters and mimeograph machines, provided news in English (the *Crystal City Times*), German *(Das Lager)*, Japanese *(Jiji Kai Jiho)*, and Spanish *(Los Andes)*. A "downtown" market district included stores where families could purchase food (fresh fish, meat, vegetables, eggs, bread, and pastries), clothing, household items, canned goods, and sundries. Like the detainees at Seagoville, they also had access to mail-order catalogs from which they obtained goods not available in the camp stores.[12]

As the end of the war approached, U.S. authorities planned for ways to phase out the camp system and deal with the remaining internees. As camps across the country gradually closed, the INS transferred people to other facilities, including the one in Crystal City. Large numbers of detainees, despite the fact they were from second- or third-generation immigrant families and had never been to Germany or Japan, faced repatriation because the Latin American countries that expelled them refused to allow them to return. At the same time, some Japanese families, although not subject to repatriation and allowed to remain in the United States, faced uncertain futures as refugees. Unable to claim citizenship of any country or return to their pre-war professions as bankers, businessmen, merchants, and skilled workers, many became factory or agricultural laborers, in effect reverting to the lower economic status they had worked for generations to leave behind. Of the Crystal City population, 300 Germans traveled in November

1945 to Ellis Island—once the famed port of entry for millions of immigrants coming to America—for processing at the internment camp there and eventual repatriation to Germany. Six hundred Japanese left Crystal City in December 1945 for Hawaii, and 660 Peruvian Japanese transferred to Japan. The last internment camp operating in the United States by 1946, the Crystal City facility continued to house a few hundred people. In 1947, the government paroled the remaining Peruvian Japanese internees, and most of them traveled to New Jersey for jobs at the Seabrook Farms frozen foods factory that employed many displaced Japanese Americans. Early in 1948, the last of the German internees went to Ellis Island or Germany, and the Crystal City Alien Family Internment Camp finally closed on February 27, 1948, almost two and a half years after the formal end of World War II.[13]

Located within the city limits of Crystal City today, the site of the internment camp reveals only a few clues to its history as a significant part of U.S. policy of alien containment during the Second World War. The remnants of a few building foundations are still discernible, and the abandoned hulk of the cement swimming pool, now filled with dirt and weeds, stands as a silent reminder of the cool, refreshing respite it once offered to hundreds of families. Redeveloped with schools, sports fields, low-income housing, and government office structures, the land is now owned by the local school district. A number of former detainees have returned to Crystal City over the years, both individually and in conjunction with formal reunions sponsored by the Zavala County Historical Commission and other organizations. Gathering to remember and reflect on their years in confinement, they renewed old friendships, met each others' families, and interacted in a new way with former camp workers who also returned to share in the memories and forge new relationships based on a spirit of acceptance and equality rather than fear and injustice. Craig Gima, a writer for the *Honolulu Star-Bulletin* whose father, aunt, and grandparents were among the Hawaiian Japanese interned in Crystal City, attended a reunion in 2002. Although his father declined to travel back to Texas to relive his wartime experiences, Gima met many former internees and their families and participated as both a descendant and a reporter. Kay Kaneko, a resident of Kona, Hawaii, who spoke to Gima at the reunion, recalled life as a child in the camp: "It was a unique place," she said. "I've got lots of memories of Crystal City. Some of them were lots of fun, and some are difficult to talk about." Karen Ebel, whose father was a German detainee during the war, expressed gratitude for the public acknowledgement provided by the gathering but also reflected on the injustice of the internment and the fact that the German experience in U.S. internment camps is a lesser-known story than that of the Japanese. Speaking of the German American internees, she said, "We [were] just as loyal as anyone else. We didn't participate in [the] Holocaust. We didn't blow up any bridges and tunnels. We weren't spies. We ought to be called good, loyal Americans." During the reunion, Kaneko, Ebel, Gima, and about 150 other former internees and their families marched as special guests in the town's annual Spinach Festival parade and recited the Pledge of Allegiance to the U.S. flag. Echoing the words of the pledge, the theme of the reunion that year—"And Justice for All"—can now be seen emblazoned in white paint on a large abandoned water tank near the remains of the camp's former swimming pool.[14]

University of Texas professor and architect Alan Taniguchi, who spent a year in an Arizona relocation camp during the war and whose parents and brother were among the Japanese internees at Crystal City, placed a large granite monument at the site of the camp in 1985. Although the monument commemorates only the Japanese experience at Crystal City, part of its inscription provides a poignant and cautionary message: "This marker is situated on an original foundation of a two-family cottage as a reminder that the injustices and humiliations suffered here as a result of hysteria, racism, and discrimination never happen again." On Veterans Day in 2007, as part of its Texas in World War II initiative, the Texas Historical Commission dedicated an Official Texas Historical Marker at the site of the Crystal City Alien Family Internment Camp.[15]

MARKER LOCATION: near intersection of N. Seventh Ave. and E. Holland St., Crystal City

KENEDY ALIEN DETENTION CAMP CEMETERY

Deaths of soldiers on the battlefield, a sad fact of any war, account for only part of the casualties of armed conflict. Civilian losses, as well as the deaths of persons imprisoned in internment camps and prisoner-of-war facilities, are an inevitable corollary of war and add to the overall fatality statistics. Thousands of people spent years away from their homelands interned within the more than seventy POW camps and three alien detention camps in Texas during World War II. Population within the camps fluctuated as many people faced repatriation to Axis countries in exchange for U.S. prisoners, families living in internment camps had additional children, and people died due to various diseases and accidents. In most cases, authorities arranged to bury the bodies of those who died in the camps either in cemeteries at the sites or in nearby community graveyards. They exhumed most of them and returned them to their families in other countries at the close of the war, but some, whether unclaimed by next of kin or for other reasons, remain buried in Texas cemeteries as reminders of the ancillary casualties of war. The Fort Sam Houston National Cemetery in San Antonio contains the graves of a number of Axis POWs whose remains were reinterred following the closing of camps at the end of the war. In Kenedy, the site of an alien detention facility that later served as a POW camp, the burial sites of five people who died while interned as enemy aliens can be seen on the southeast side of the Kenedy City Cemetery. The graves of the five internees—Oskar Bechstedt (1882–1943), Kurt Pellman (1902–42), Herman Richard J. Roedinger (1906–42), Friedrich Hartleben (1869–1943) and Yukihiko Kohashikawa (c.1892–1942)—are marked with simple stones and curbs. Thanks to the efforts of a local group of concerned citizens who recently cleaned, landscaped, and fenced the neglected burial plot, the Kenedy Alien Detention Camp Cemetery received the Historic Texas Cemetery designation and an Official Texas Historical Marker from the Texas Historical Commission in 2005.

MARKER LOCATION

Intersection of DeWitt Street and county roads 328 and 330, Kenedy

Source: Kenedy Alien Detention Camp Cemetery, Karnes County, Historic Texas Cemetery file (hereafter cited as THC HTC files) and THC marker files; Camp Swift, Bastrop County, THC marker files.

PART THREE
TEXANS ON THE NATIONAL STAGE

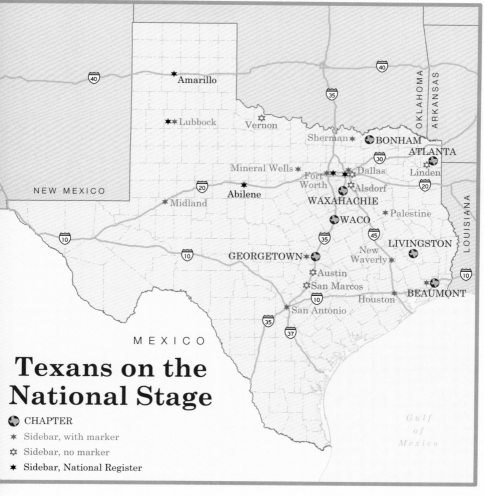

Texans on the National Stage

⬤ CHAPTER
✳ Sidebar, with marker
✿ Sidebar, no marker
✴ Sidebar, National Register

Map by Molly O'Hallovan

14

FIGHTING EVERY
STEP OF THE WAY

Three blocks south-southeast of the Williamson County Court-house in Georgetown and one block off Main Street is a stately but otherwise modest and unassuming house of the Late Victorian era that seems somewhat out of character with encroaching commercial development nearby. A block away is Founder's Park where, tradition holds, early commissioners first met in 1848 to establish the site of the county seat for the newly created county. The home, which anchors an imaginary dividing line between commercial and residential elements of Georgetown, a city known for its exemplary work in historic preservation, reflects integrity and purpose from an era of economic and social progress known as the Gilded Age.

In many ways, the home is a fitting representation of a former resident, Jessie Daniel Ames (1883–1972), an important social reformer of the Progressive Era who began forming the fundamental concepts of her life's work while a resident of Georgetown. An Official Texas Historical Marker in front of the home provides the basics of a national story that began in Texas. Born in Palestine, Anderson County, where her father, James Malcolm Daniel, worked for the International and Great Northern Railroad, Jessie moved with her family to Overton, on the line between the counties of Smith and Rusk, before settling with them in Georgetown in 1893. There, she attended high school and Southwestern University, graduating from the latter in 1902. Two years later, she once again moved with her family when her father accepted a job in Laredo, Webb County. There, she met a young army surgeon, Dr. Roger Post Ames (1870–1914), whom she married in 1905.

Jessie Daniel, circa early 1900s.
Courtesy Texas Historical Commission resource files.

Educated at Tulane Medical School in his hometown of New Orleans, Louisiana, Roger Ames served with distinction in the U.S. Army Medical Corps, participating in the Spanish-American War at the end of the nineteenth century. He served in the Philippines and later in Cuba, where he assisted Dr. Walter Reed in experiments that eventually isolated the cause of yellow fever. Following their marriage, Roger and Jessie made their home in New Orleans, where he worked for the army to combat the spread of malaria. Soon, there were signs the marriage was in trouble. Roger's family, who relied on him for financial support, viewed Jessie as socially inferior and a possible threat to the lifestyle they enjoyed, and their open indifference put undue pressure on the young couple. In addition, Roger and Jessie, despite the birth of two children, experienced a sexual incompatibility that further hindered their relationship.

As Roger's job-related demands increased, the marriage suffered even more, and when he took a new assignment following another outbreak of yellow fever, he sent Jessie and the children back to Texas. In the ensuing years they saw each other infrequently, and eventually Roger moved to Guatemala to avoid responsibilities of marriage and the restrictive demands of his family. There, he worked as a physician for the U.S. Consul and the American Fruit Company. Despite the complications of their marriage, Jessie worked at reconciliation. As she described the strained relationship, "I could not live away from him. I could not live with him. I always returned in hope and joy; I was always sent away in despair."[1]

Jessie visited Roger in Guatemala in August 1914, and it appeared for a time there might be hope for the couple. She returned to Texas optimistic and resolute about their future but also pregnant with their third child. Within months, though, the chance for reconciliation ended when Roger died of a tropical fever. His widow faced an uncertain and difficult future.

Exhibiting the type of optimism often borne of adversity, Jessie Daniel Ames joined with her mother, Laura Maria Leonard Daniel, to manage the Georgetown Telephone Company, purchased by her father shortly before his death in 1911. She first worked as the

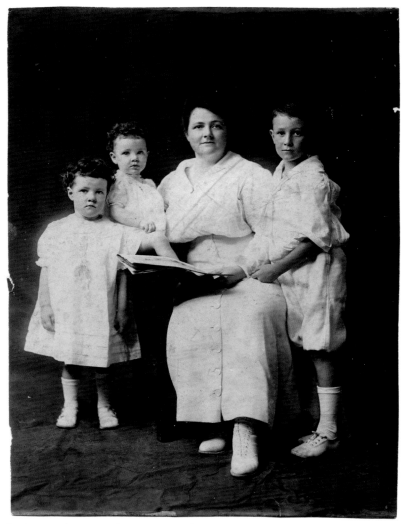

Jessie Daniel Ames with her children, (left to right) *Mary, Lulu and Frederick, circa 1917.* Courtesy Texas State Library and Archives Commission.

bookkeeper but gradually began to take over more management responsibilities. Under her leadership, the company developed as a successful enterprise within a growing and prosperous city.

Outside of work, Jessie developed an interest in civic activities through membership in the Woman's Club of Georgetown, established in 1893. The year of its founding is significant, because it coincided with the World's Columbian Exposition in Chicago, Illinois, an event that, among other achievements, focused attention on women's issues and served as a rallying point for a burgeoning women's movement. The exposition influenced a golden era of women's clubs dedicated to such matters as fine arts, education, libraries, and social reform. Such was the case with the Georgetown group, and when it reorganized in 1917 as a federated woman's club, Ames served as its first president.[2]

Through her work with the Woman's Club of Georgetown, Ames emerged as a leader in social action and reform at the local level, and her education in grassroots activism, coupled with her early successes, came to define the next important phase of her life. As her biographer, Jacquelyn Dowd Hall, wrote, it was during this time a "fierce and unwilling striving propelled her into the public life," where "she retained a consciousness formed in adversity: competitive, insecure, and, in her own words, 'fighting every step of the way.'"[3]

Ames became acutely aware of social justice issues, both locally and nationally. In the Progressive Era of reforms and social justice activism, many women found opportunities, both individually and as part of organizations, to express their concerns, get involved, and offer their unique perspectives on such issues as public health, education, child labor, welfare programs, libraries, and the arts. In so doing, they provided considerable energy and insights, influencing political agendas that, at the time, did not provide them with the right to vote. As a result, it was a natural progression of the social activism of the era to acquire input and voice through suffrage.

Efforts to enfranchise women in Texas date to the mid-nineteenth century, but the idea gained momentum in the late nineteenth and early twentieth centuries through the pioneer work of such leaders as Rebecca Henry Hayes of Galveston and sisters Annette, Elizabeth, and Katherine Finnigan of Houston. The Texas Woman Suffrage Association organized in 1903 and, especially under the later leadership of Minnie Fisher Cunningham, who spearheaded the development of local chapters, began to grow as a recognized political force in the state.[4]

Jessie Daniel Ames was among those who became active in the Texas woman suffrage movement during its formative years. To her, the right to vote was fundamental to her citizenship. "All I wanted was the vote," she noted, because she viewed herself as "the owner of property which votes could tax without the consent of the owners. It was a condition of taxation without representation and I was a female Patrick Henry."[5] Turning her concerns to action, she organized the Williamson County Suffrage Association in 1916. Later, she hosted the organizational meeting of the Georgetown Equal Suffrage League, and those in attendance elected her to serve as the first president.

Given her enthusiasm, energy, and results, Ames soon gained the attention of state suffrage leaders, including Minnie Fisher Cunningham, who became her mentor, Jane Y. McCallum, and Eleanor Brackenridge. Those connections led to her involvement in the Texas Equal Suffrage Association and election as treasurer in 1918, the same year the Texas Legislature, in a special session, voted to grant women the right to vote in state primary elections. Full enfranchisement came the following year.

The timing of the legislature's actions, while an important step for the suffrage movement, nevertheless presented formidable challenges. After Gov. William P. Hobby signed the measure into law, Texas women had slightly more than two weeks to register for the Democratic primary—and Texas was then virtually a one-party state—already scheduled for July 26. In Williamson County, Ames worked tirelessly to meet the challenge, as noted years later: "Mrs. Ames and other sufragettes [sic] spearheaded a massive campaign in Williamson County that resulted in 3,300 women making the trip to the courthouse in Georgetown to register. They came by wagon, hack, and on foot; observers say, 'There's never been anything like it since.'"[6] The year 1919 proved to be equally important for the suffrage movement in Texas as the legislature, once again addressing the issue in special session but this time following defeat of a statewide referendum, voted overwhelmingly to ratify the 19th Amendment to the U.S. Constitution. Texas thus became the ninth state to ratify the amendment that provided for equal enfranchisement for women, and it went into effect the following year. As the idea thus gained significant momentum, the Texas Equal Suffrage Association, at its 1919 convention in San Antonio, formally reorganized as the Texas League of Women Voters (TLWV) with Jessie Daniel Ames elected to serve as first president.[7]

Despite the TLWV's general policy of nonpartisanship, Ames and Cunningham worked to defeat former U.S. Sen. Joseph Weldon Bailey in his bid for Texas governor in 1920. An outspoken conservative Democrat opposed to many Progressive reforms, including woman suffrage, Bailey was a formidable opponent, given his impressive political career, his connections to big business, and his strength as an orator. Ames and Cunningham proved relentless, however, and continued to attack him as best they could. In one notable fight involving the selection of delegates to the Democratic National Convention, the two joined with men on a special resolutions committee that effectively argued for continuation of Wilsonian reforms, prompting Bailey to refer to the group as "six sissies and two sisters." Although Bailey led in the first primary for the governorship, he lost in the runoff to Pat M. Neff, in part because of the newfound political power of women activists.[8]

Ames provided important early leadership for the development of voter education and citizenship training programs of the TLWV, mainstays of the organization's efforts to this day. Her Georgetown colleague, Mary Shipp Sanders, directed sponsorship of citizenship schools in communities statewide, including Georgetown and Taylor in Williamson County. During the presidency of Ames, the TLWV formulated a legislative program that called for reforms in education, employment, and infant care. And, in an initiative that ultimately proved transitional for Ames, the league pressured Governor Hobby to address much-needed penal reform measures by approving an independent and comprehensive survey of the state system through the National Committee on Prisons and Prison Labor. Ames soon received an appointment to the committee's state division, subsequently developing a deep concern for the plight of prisoners, particularly African American women. As a result, she successfully lobbied for establishment of a state training school for delinquent black girls.

The 1920s proved to be another transitional time for Ames, who gradually shifted her energy to matters of civil rights and other social reforms due in part to her disillusionment with political aspects of the women's movement but also to the rise of such organizations as the Ku Klux Klan (KKK) and her increasing awareness of educational inequities. A catalyst for the transition was a Dallas meeting headed by Carrie Parks Johnson, director of Women's Work for the Commission on Interracial Cooperation (CIC) in Atlanta, Georgia. The CIC was a coalition of southern civil rights groups headed by Will Alexander, a former Methodist minister and educator who later served prominently as a leader of New Deal farm programs under Pres. Franklin D. Roosevelt.

Following the Dallas meeting, the CIC organized the Texas Interracial Commission with Ames as chair of the women's committee. She became a paid field worker for the organization in 1924 and later served as executive director of the Texas group. Ames personally directed progressive programs that advocated equality in housing and employment, improved access to the judicial system, and an end to mob violence. To promote the goals of her new organization, she worked directly with civic groups, legislators, newspapers, and local law enforcement officials, including Williamson County District Attorney Dan Moody, whose well-publicized legal victories over the KKK laid the foundation for a later political career that included Texas attorney general and governor.

Impressed with her actions and accomplishments, Alexander soon named Ames the new director of Women's Work for the CIC, and she moved to Atlanta. There, her primary focus was mob violence. Although the number of lynchings of African Americans had declined somewhat in the late 1920s, there was resurgence in the early 1930s, exacerbated in part by the intensity of the economic depression. One incident in Sherman, Texas, involving an African American man accused of raping a white woman, proved particularly influential in strengthening the anti-lynching efforts of the CIC. Historians Wilman Dykeman and James Stokely described the horror of the mob scene in their biography of Alexander: "An infuriated crowd set fire to the building. By late afternoon the courthouse, once considered one of the finest in Texas, was gutted. Some of the mob were still not satisfied their quarry was dead.

They blasted their way into the vault, found the Negro's body, and dumped it through a window to the mob below. A chain was fastened about the neck, and the corpse was dragged through town, hanged from a cottonwood tree, and burned."[9] Alexander's revulsion at the news of the Sherman incident increased his resolve to attack the system of lynching at its root causes. As part of a broader program aimed at education and legal prevention, he set up the Southern Commission on the Study of Lynching, an all-male organization, and later asked Ames to establish a separate women's group with identical objectives. Known as the Association of Southern Women for the Prevention of Lynching (ASWPL), it first met in November 1930 with twenty-six individuals representing such groups as the League of Women Voters, the Young Women's Christian Association, the Parent-Teacher Association, and Methodist, Southern Baptist, and Presbyterian churches. Central to the group's initial work was repudiation of a prevailing view in the South that lynching existed, at least in part, as a means of protecting the virtue of white women.

Ironically an all-white organization due to Ames's belief that such composition made the argument against the protection of white women more effective, the ASWPL was a coalition of women's groups in fifteen states that worked with local officials for compliance and support. Members were on the front lines of the struggle, personally working to defuse the violence, filing detailed investigative reports on the causes of lynchings, and publicly arguing chivalry was no more than a mask for murderers. The organization also published and distributed booklets with titles such as "This Business of Lynching," "Death by Parties Unknown," and "With Quietness They Work."[10]

As anticipated, reaction to the work of the ASWPL was often heated, vindictive, and personal, with much of the vitriolic rhetoric directed squarely at Ames. She received hate mail on a regular basis and was the focus of verbal attacks during public meetings. Opposition even resulted in the formation of a counter-ASWPL group known as the National Association for the Preservation of the White Race. The founder, Mrs. J. E. Andrews of Atlanta, Georgia, proved relentless in her opposition, both in person and in print. In her publication, *Georgia Woman's World,* she directed her wrath at "Mrs. Jessie Daniel Ames of Negro fame, and a few others of the birds of the feather that put on such disgusting appeals to the beast in Negro men." Describing her reaction to a presentation by the ASWPL at a local church, Andrews added: "I told the Ames woman that she was a tool of Negroes; and she is; and that the rest, everyone that applauded that unjust and filthy thing, were the sum [*sic*] of the earth, and they are; and that the preacher who permitted such a beastly thing to be put on in his church was a Judas Iscariot of his Lord and Master and to his race."[11] Opposition to the efforts of Jessie Daniel Ames came not only from outside the organization but from within as well. The league faced internal dissension in part because her preference for education as the best means of lasting reform clashed with more aggressive political measures preferred by other members. Her opposition to federal anti-lynching legislation, for example, put her at odds with her colleagues, as well as such civil rights advocates of the era as Walter White, Mary McLeod Bethune, and Eleanor Roosevelt. Her actions, seemingly contradictory to her earlier work against mob violence, reflect in reality her core conservative values as a child of the Old South. She still adhered to the doctrine of states' rights, especially in opposition to forced compliance. Despite compelling arguments to the contrary by her fellow ASWPL members, Ames remained resolute in her opposition to the legislation. That inflexibility, coupled with a national decline in lynchings, led the group to disband in 1942 in favor of a Southern Regional Council with broader objectives.

Having fought the good fight for many years, Jessie Daniel Ames retired two years later and moved to Tryon, North Carolina. There, she remained active in local issues, participating in Methodist church activities, assisting with African American voter registration drives, and attending a women's study group. She also wrote of her reminiscences and worked successfully for congressional recognition of her late husband's military medical career. She was not particularly close to her children, though. Her son, Frederick Ames, a Houston pediatrician, did not survive his mother. Daughter Mary Ames Raffensterger also became a pediatrician and practiced in Philadelphia. Daughter Lulu Daniel Ames, a victim of polio, lived in Austin, where she ran a newspaper clipping service.

Her health in decline, Jessie Daniel Ames eventually returned to Texas to live with Lulu. She died in an Austin nursing home on February 17, 1972, and was buried in the International Order of Odd Fellows Cemetery in Georgetown, the city where she began her lifetime of crusades for social reform.[12] Despite great personal odds, Ames persevered for the causes she championed and lived to see many of her efforts, particularly in civil rights and education, adopted into successful reform measures in the latter part of the twentieth century. Her legacy is often overshadowed by the accomplishments of others, but her pioneer work remains an integral part of societal rights now considered part of the mainstream culture. Her former home and simple grave provide little evidence of her many accomplishments, but an Official Texas Historical Marker at the site of her former home now interprets the story of the unassuming but undaunted advocate who began her remarkable and nationally significant public service career in Williamson County.

MARKER LOCATION: 1004 Church St., Georgetown

MINNIE FISH

Minnie Fisher Cunningham (1882–1964), mentor of Jessie Daniel Ames, was a leading advocate for woman suffrage at the state and national levels. Born on a farm in Walker County near the town of New Waverly, Minnie Fisher received a degree in pharmacy from the University of Texas Medical Branch at Galveston and worked as a pharmacist in Huntsville, but her encounter with pay inequity, as she noted, "made a suffragette out of me." In 1902, she married Bill Cunningham, a local lawyer and insurance executive. The couple soon moved to Galveston, where she began her work on behalf of voting rights for women, a cause she continued later when she lived in Austin. She actively lobbied western governors for passage of the 19th Amendment and helped establish the National League of Women Voters, serving as the executive secretary in Washington, D.C. Back in Texas in 1928, she ran unsuccessfully for the U.S. Senate on a reform platform and in opposition to the politically powerful Ku Klux Klan but carried only her home county of Walker. In the 1930s, she worked for the Texas Agricultural Extension Service in College Station but returned to Washington in 1939 and served in the Women's Division of the Agricultural Adjustment Administration, part of the New Deal program of Pres. Franklin D. Roosevelt. He is often credited with giving

Minnie Fisher Cunningham, circa 1926. Courtesy Texas State Library and Archives Commission.

her the nickname "Minnie Fish." An outspoken liberal Democrat, she ran for Texas governor in 1944, placing second in the primary to the incumbent, Coke Stevenson. Minnie Fish retired to Fisher Farms near New Waverly in 1946, although she remained active in political causes, including civil rights and women's issues, for many years. She died in 1964 and is buried in New Waverly. An Official Texas Historical Marker at the site of her home in Walker County commemorates her extraordinary life.

MARKER LOCATION

2.6 mi. N of New Waverly on US 75

Sources: Minnie Fisher Cunningham, Walker County, THC marker files; Patricia Ellen Cunningham, "Minnie Fisher Cunningham," *New Handbook of Texas,* vol. 2, pp. 450–51.

COMPANION COURTHOUSES

When Jessie Daniel Ames spearheaded the monumental effort that resulted in the registration of over three thousand women voters in Williamson County during a short period of time in the summer of 1918, the scene played out at the Williamson County Courthouse, completed only seven years before. The noted Austin architectural firm of Charles H. Page and Bro. designed the Classical Revival structure, which features projecting central pavilion entryways on each side flanked by Ionic columns and a central copper dome topped with a statue of justice. Funding assistance through the Texas Historic Courthouse Preservation Program of the Texas Historical Commission, in partnership with Williamson County, allowed for its full restoration in 2007.

Charles H. Page and Bro. designed a number of Texas courthouses still in use, including the one at Palestine in Anderson County, the birthplace of Jessie Daniel Ames. Completed in 1914, the structure is similar in many design respects to the courthouse in Georgetown. Also of the Classical Revival style, but with Beaux Arts detailing, the Anderson County Courthouse likewise features a central dome and projecting entryways with Ionic columns.

Both the Williamson County Courthouse and the Anderson County Courthouse are Recorded Texas Historic Landmarks and are listed in the National Register of Historic Places.

MARKER LOCATIONS

500 N. Church St., Palestine; 710 Main St., Georgetown

Sources: Williamson County Courthouse and Anderson County Courthouse THC marker files and THC NR files.

Williamson County Courthouse, 2008. Photograph by Cynthia J. Beeman.

Anderson County Courthouse, 2008. Photograph by Cynthia J. Beeman.

15 CROSSING THE GREAT DIVIDE

This is a story of music—jazz to be specific—and how one gifted young man from a small Texas town started a revolution in sound that quickly swept the nation. More than a half century after his death, the standards he set continue to influence change and experimentation in popular music around the world. In that sense, his music is forever fresh, modern, and challenging. Through his remarkable talent and interpretation, he pioneered a dynamic new role for an existing instrument, redefining its range and repositioning it within the orchestral landscape, while also helping create a new musical vocabulary. His influence spread from jazz to rock and roll, and even to Broadway. Yet few outside the music world know of his contributions, and even fewer know of the Texas connections that mark the beginning and ending of his brief but significant life. For years, his gravesite remained unmarked, but his fans and those who sought to learn more about his life eventually remedied that oversight, providing for a granite gravestone and an Official Texas Historical Marker in the process. Regardless, he remains an enigmatic figure in musical history, even as new generations rediscover him and marvel at his accomplishments.

Guitarist Charles Henry "Charlie" Christian is a jazz legend, a pivotal figure in American music who, in his personal association with other pivotal figures of his era, helped define and focus a distinct cultural heritage. As musicologist Frederick Grunfeld noted, "There is the guitar before Christian and the guitar after Christian, and they sound virtually like two different instruments."[1] As a guitar pioneer who crossed the great divide between acoustic and electric sound and between rhythm background and solo instrument, Christian was present at a time of fundamental change brought on, in large part, by his unique talent.[2] Because of his legendary status, though, what is known of him is often cloaked in myth, conjecture, misinformation, and misunderstanding. Fundamental elements of his life remain in dispute and, given the nature of the medium in which he performed, may never be known with certainty. Even the personal reminiscences of those who knew him best often provide conflicting information. The best resource for understanding him remains the music he left behind, and music historians continue to analyze those communiqués, providing new insights into Christian's personal history and regional influences.

Born in 1916 in an African American neighborhood of Bonham, Fannin County, known as Tanktown, Christian grew up in a musical family. His father, Clarence Christian Sr., who worked in a number of local businesses, played the guitar, and his mother, Willie Mae (sources differ on her maiden name), played the piano and occasionally accompanied silent films at a local movie theater. Charlie's older brothers, Edward and Clarence Jr., were also musically inclined, as were close relatives on his mother's side. The family's Texas roots no doubt influenced the music Charles (as his family called him; he would pick up the name Charlie later in life) heard as a child, but his musical maturation came on the other side of the Red River. When his father lost his eyesight in 1918, the family moved to Oklahoma City to seek new opportunities. There, the elder Christian earned money for the family as a street musician, playing blues but also light classics and sacred songs. Vernacularly known as *busts,* the impromptu performances along the streets or at individual houses provided meaning and purpose for Clarence Sr., while also influencing his sons who assisted him. Even as a baby, Charles participated to an extent, as his brother Clarence later recalled: "And [my father] would lay that guitar down on the floor, and Charles would sit there and cross his little legs under him, and he would reach and get him a handful of strings. And he'd do that so much he'd be sleeping. . . . And he would sit there and just rake on that guitar until he'd get to sleep." Later, in addition to assisting his father physically, Charles joined in performances as a board beater, loudly dancing on a board to draw a crowd. He also, as might be imagined, developed a strong interest in stringed instruments, showing promise first with the bass fiddle.[3]

In the early decades of the twentieth century, Oklahoma City provided a particularly nurturing environment for young African Americans interested in music. Two important, although seemingly disparate, factors—one formal and structured and the other informal and abstract—nevertheless proved to be complementary and progressive. The first was the work of Zelia Breaux, a dedicated and influential music educator in the city's African American public school system. As director of the music program at Frederick Douglass High School, she implemented a comprehensive, multilevel curriculum that emphasized harmony, theory, and classical fundamentals. Actively involved in every aspect of music education, she worked with students even at the elementary levels to determine which instruments they should play or which programs they should pursue. She offered classes in band, orchestra, voice, folk dance, and piano; planned and directed school concerts and operettas; and produced winning programs that were without equal in the region. In addition, she was part owner of the Aldridge Theatre that showcased local talent and provided a venue for traveling acts, including national celebrities like Bessie Smith, Bill "Bojangles" Robinson, and Cab Calloway.[4]

While Zelia Breaux provided a structure that allowed music to flourish in Oklahoma City at the time, an equally significant informal influence came through the bars and music clubs centered on the 300 block of Northeast Second Street, an area that came to be known as Deep Second or Deep Deuce. Like other celebrated districts that were incubators of early blues and jazz—places like Deep Ellum in Dallas, Beale Street in Memphis, and the corner of 18th and Vine in Kansas City—Deep Deuce was an area of few rules and few inhibitions that offered musicians almost limitless freedom of expression. But even in such a venue there was an implied system. It was the scene of so-called cutting sessions, where musicians tested their mettle against others and earned their place in the artistic hierarchy in late night, after-hour jam sessions that lasted well into the following mornings. The sessions were where young musicians came to learn if they had what it took to succeed or move to the next level and where seasoned pros came to see if they still had it. In a sense, it was an informal school with an unwritten curriculum and its own set of graduates and dropouts.[5]

Deep Deuce also showcased territory bands, groups that survived by traveling regional circuits to expand their fan base while hoping to be discovered. Bands from Dallas, Kansas City, Little Rock, Fort Worth, Omaha, and St. Louis regularly played at such Oklahoma City landmarks as Slaughter's Hall. Among the best of the territory bands were Andy Kirk's Twelve Clouds of Joy (Kansas City), the Alphonso Trent Orchestra (Dallas), and the Oklahoma City Blue Devils. National bands also played at Deep Deuce on a regular basis, taking advantage of the town's central location during transcontinental tours by train or bus.[6]

Both musical factors in play at the time in Oklahoma City influenced Charlie Christian, although he ultimately chose the informal route. As a public school student, he was neither focused nor in regular attendance. While at Douglass High, his brief association with Breaux seemed inauspicious, although ultimately it helped set him on a new course. The teacher strongly suggested he adopt the trumpet as his instrument "of choice"; Christian instead preferred the tenor saxophone. Lacking an interest in the former and the funds to purchase the latter, he chose neither and started spending more time playing baseball, at which he showed considerable promise as a pitcher and outfielder. He also, though, played his father's guitars (Clarence Christian Sr. died in 1926), and he quickly demonstrated promise in that realm as well, even taking lessons. In his pursuit of both baseball and music, Christian began demonstrating an obsessive quality that came to define his later professional career. While avoiding school, playing ball during the day and frequenting the Deuce at night, he developed a love interest in Margretta Christian (no relation), who was thirteen years old when they first met in 1930. Two years later, the relationship took on a new dimension when the teenage couple had a daughter, whom they named Billie Jean. Charlie left school at the age of sixteen in order to support his new family, and soon music surpassed ball as his primary focus. Unfortunately, the relationship proved to be short-lived, and Margretta soon left with their daughter.[7]

Although older brother Edward then enjoyed some success as a bandleader in Oklahoma City, Charlie instead looked to others for direction. Among the strongest early influences on his playing were Ralph "Chuck Big Foot" Hamilton, a trombonist and guitarist who may have been Christian's first instructor, and trumpeter James Simpson of the Blue Devils. Although several years older than Christian, Simpson and Hamilton became his close friends and worked to teach him fundamental techniques of jazz and musical interpretation. Speculation still exists about whether or not Christian ever learned to read music, although there are indications he may have at least known the basics. Other influences— and there were many during Christian's formative years as a guitarist—included his friend Aaron Thibeaux "T-Bone" Walker, a native of East Texas and also an accomplished guitarist, and Lester "Prez" Young, a tenor saxophonist who played with the Blue Devils before gaining national attention. Young, in particular, had a tremendous impact on Christian, who learned to translate his own appreciation for the saxophone to a single-note technique on the guitar. The emerging and distinct Christian style of horn-like sounds referenced the influence of Young. Within the Christian family, the strongest influence came from Edward, who overcame initial reservations about his brother's chosen occupation once he heard him hold his own in late night jams on the Deuce.[8]

Sometime in the early 1930s, Charlie Christian began experimenting with ways to strengthen the voice of his acoustic guitar in the days before the advent of the electric guitar. He began by holding a microphone between his knees to provide amplification, and in so doing helped move the guitar from its traditional support role in the rhythm section, where it enhanced the ground beat, to solo status. Speculation surrounds the invention of the electric guitar, but among the first to record jazz using the instrument in the mid-1930s were George Barnes and Eddie Durham. A native of San Marcos, Texas, Durham later recalled his first meeting with Christian at Oklahoma City in the late 1930s: "He asked me to give him some pointers, like what to do if you want to play the instrument with class and go through life with the instrument. He wanted to know technical things, like how to use a pick a certain way. . . . I said, 'Don't ever use an up-stroke, which makes a tag-a-tag-a-tag sound; use a down-stroke.' It takes an awful fast wrist to play a down-stroke—it gives a staccato to sound, with no legato, and you sound like a horn."[9] Soon after his encounter with Durham, Christian purchased his first Gibson ES-150 guitar, which provided him the range and power to implement his solos effectively.

Charlie Christian perfected his unique style in the latter part of the 1930s through steady work with a number of territory bands, most notably Leonard Chadwick's Rhythmaires and the Alphonso Trent Orchestra, and he also traveled in the band that backed the popular Omaha singer, Anna Mae Winburn. In association with Winburn and Trent, Christian toured extensively throughout the Midwest, from Nebraska to Illinois, Minnesota, and the Dakotas. The economic depression of the 1930s, coupled with the burgeoning jazz scene in Kansas City that drew many of Oklahoma's best musicians, made the tours a necessity for young musicians. A brief but significant venue in that regard was the 1936 Texas Centennial Exposition in Dallas, which attracted jazz musicians from across the country who stayed around to play local clubs. As Christian biographers Wayne Goins and Craig McKinney noted, "many musicians looked at the Centennial as a life raft at a time when clubs and big bands were sinking fast." Although Christian's stint in Texas during the Centennial lasted only two months, he returned to Dallas several times in ensuing years through his association with Trent, who regularly played at the upscale Adolphus Hotel. Unfortunately for Dallas audiences at the time, though, Christian often played bass with the Trent outfit.[10]

As Christian traveled, he came in contact with a number of musicians who were pioneers in what came to be known as southwestern jazz, an amalgam of jazz, country, blues, and the emerging sounds of western swing, which offered its own version of country roots with jazz influences. The integration of sounds, like the integration of the musicians themselves in the segregated Jim Crow era, came largely in after-hour jam sessions in the black clubs and halls. After completing their main gigs, musicians would gather informally to play, trading ideas and experiencing new sounds in the process. These were inventors and experimenters, and their laboratories were places like the Hole and the Rhythm Club along Deep Deuce. There, and in countless other impromptu musical labs across the Southwest and Midwest, diverse cultures came together to create something new, and as a serious student of sound Christian absorbed what he heard and translated it to others through his unique style of music.

Charlie Christian's big break came in 1939, and, as with many of the seminal events in his life, there are several versions of how it occurred. Although sources differ on the details, the basic story involves three central figures: pianist Mary Lou Williams, producer John Hammond, and bandleader and clarinetist Benny Goodman. For background, it is important to understand the pivotal role Goodman played in jazz history. Born in Chicago in 1909, Benjamin David Goodman received basic musical training on the clarinet in a synagogue school and at the Jane Addams Hull House. He grew up in the so-called classical era of early jazz, an era marked by the works of King Oliver, Bix Beiderbecke, Louis Armstrong, Fletcher Henderson, Duke Ellington, and others. Of particular importance to Goodman were the sounds of New Orleans jazz, which African American musicians brought north to Chicago and other cities through traveling acts but also as part of a broad exodus from the South in the early twentieth century. Jazz at the time offered young people a freedom of expression and an escape from the more structured Victorian era that defined the lives of their parents. Goodman biographer James Lincoln Collier noted jazz was "openly emotional, rhythmic and spontaneous." Although it served as a cultural crusade for some, Collier noted, Goodman was not a crusader. For him, jazz was more the destination of a personal musical journey.[11]

Goodman, like Christian, developed his chops in late-night jam sessions where black and white musicians felt free to gather and exchange ideas. Earl "Fatha" Hines recalled, "Most of the clubs and hotels where the white musicians played closed between one and two o'clock, and they'd come down either to King Oliver at the Plantation or where we were [the Sunset]. Benny Goodman used to come with his clarinet in a sack. . . . We all got a kick out of listening to each other, and we all tried to learn. We sat around waiting to see if these [white] guys were actually going to come up with something new or different."[12] Professionally, Goodman pursued his interest in jazz through the medium of dance bands, and over time he became one of the most successful bandleaders in the nation, reaching his peak during the 1930s as the celebrated "King of Swing" thanks to his extensive traveling, recording sessions, and radio performances. At the time, two important events cemented his place in jazz history. The first was his bold and precedent-setting decision to integrate his orchestra. Although black and white musicians frequently played together, either in jam sessions or as part of special performances, and even recorded together, bands remained segregated, and black and white musicians never traveled together, given the societal norms of the era. Goodman helped break the color barrier, though, when he hired Texan Teddy Wilson as pianist and Lionel Hampton as vibraphonist to perform publicly with his band and side groups.

In 1938, Goodman embarked on the second event that led to his legendary status. At the suggestion of publicist Wynn Nathanson, with whom he had worked on the *Camel Caravan* radio shows, Goodman agreed to present his orchestra in concert at New York's prestigious Carnegie Hall on January 16. Although this was not the first jazz concert, as some have claimed, it was nevertheless a landmark event that, in effect, provided mainstream recognition of jazz and the vital role it played in American culture. Within that broader context, the Carnegie concert represented the coming of age or the public debut for jazz, particularly swing. James Lincoln Collier observed, "It should be remembered that even as late as 1938 a good many people continued to see jazz as slightly disreputable, not so much for the sexual associations it once had but because it was a low form of music, somewhat raffish. Carnegie Hall was dedicated to the presentation of higher things, and there was thus a tension between jazz and this sacrosanct hall. . . . But it was precisely this tension which caught the public imagination." The irony of the moment was not lost on the musicians. As the curtain rose, trumpeter Harry James, no doubt expressing what others felt, mumbled, "I feel like a whore in a church."[13]

Emboldened by the success of the Carnegie Hall concert and the new energy of his orchestra, Goodman was at the top of the musical charts in 1939. As a bandleader always interested in experimenting, taking chances, and trying to read the interests of his audiences, though, he continually shifted personnel, hired new sidemen, or replaced players when someone better came along. In order to stay competitive and attract exciting new players, Goodman relied heavily on John Hammond, a highly respected jazz talent scout, journalist, and musical producer. The two established one of the most successful partnerships in jazz history and would later become brothers-in-law when Goodman married Hammond's sister, Alice. Importantly, Hammond knew both the black and white sides of jazz intimately, and in an era of segregation he provided important support for Goodman's effort to incorporate the best talent, regardless of race.[14]

At the time, Goodman's search for new talent took on an edge of urgency after the loss of key players Harry James, Gene Kruppa, and Teddy Wilson, who left to form their own bands. Hammond, then with Columbia Records, accepted the challenge, and while supervising a separate recording session with Mildred Bailey mentioned to pianist Mary Lou Williams that he was looking for a good electric guitarist. Williams, who worked with Andy Kirk and his Twelve Clouds of Joy, knew about Charlie Christian and therefore recommended him as the best she had ever heard. Within months, Hammond booked a trip to Oklahoma City to hear the young performer. Although he remembered the venue as the Ritz Café, later sources indicate it was more likely Ruby's Grill, where Christian performed regularly with Leslie Sheffield's Rhythmaires. Greatly impressed with what he heard, Hammond called Goodman in California and told him he had discovered "the greatest guitar player since Eddie Lang." Goodman responded, "Who the hell wants to hear an electric-guitar player?" "I don't know," Hammond confessed, but added, "You won't believe him until you hear him."[15]

Oklahoma City well-wishers bid farewell to Charlie Christian (second from right) *as he prepares to board the train for his audition with Benny Goodman in California, August 1939. To Christian's left is his brother, Edward.* Courtesy Duncan Schiedt.

Hammond continued to press Goodman to provide an audition for Christian, and the bandleader eventually agreed. The news of Christian's big break spread quickly in Oklahoma City, and fans and friends held a party for him on the eve of his train trip to Los Angeles. Details of the subsequent audition are mired in discrepancies, but what most sources agree on is that the initial encounter between Goodman and Christian did not go well. Whether due to Christian's nervousness, Goodman's reluctance, or Hammond's bad timing, it ended with a less-than-impressive pairing of the two musicians—and with Christian unplugged—on the standard "Tea for Two." Following the brief session, which failed to impress Goodman, Hammond persevered on his own and arranged for Christian to join the outfit that night at the elegant Victor Hugo Restaurant. As Goodman ate between sets, expecting to join his quintet after the break, Hammond and bassist Artie Bernstein ushered Christian through the kitchen and onto the stage, where this time he had an opportunity to set up his amplifier. Apparently outraged when he saw he had been tricked, Goodman knew not to make a scene, so he called for the quintet to play the tune "Rose Room," a West Coast favorite he probably thought would be unfamiliar to Christian. He was wrong. Goins and McKinney describe what happened next: "When Benny finally pointed to Charles to take a ride, Charles made the most of it, which obviously got Benny's attention immediately, for he motioned for Christian to take another, then another, then another." Jazz historian Bill Simon elaborated, noting, "Charlie just kept feeding Benny riffs and rhythms and changes for chorus after chorus. That was Benny's first flight in an electrically amplified cloud."[16]

By most accounts, the impromptu set at the Victor Hugo lasted three-quarters of an hour. Christian, then only twenty-three years old, signed with the Goodman organization immediately for $150 per week, a considerable jump from the $7.50 a week he received in Oklahoma. Within days, the quintet expanded to a sextet, with Christian, Goodman, and Lionel Hampton as featured soloists; the other personnel in the original group were Artie Bernstein on bass, Nick Fatool on drums, and either Fletcher Henderson or Johnny Guarnieri on piano. Just three days after the Victor Hugo audition, the new group performed for the *Camel Caravan* show broadcast from the Hollywood Bowl. Memorable tunes that featured Christian prominently included "Stardust" and "Flying Home," based on Christian's riffs from his Oklahoma days. A later recording of "Flying Home" ironically included "Rose Room" on the flip side.[17]

Over the next year, Christian performed regularly with the Benny Goodman Sextet (which sometimes was a septet) and occasionally with the full orchestra. It was the smaller ensemble, though, that allowed Christian the greatest freedom to express his

The Benny Goodman Sextet at the Lyric Theatre, Indianapolis, Indiana, circa 1939. Members are Johnny Guarnieri, piano; Artie Bernstein, bass; Nick Fatool, drums; Lionel Hampton, vibraphone; bandleader Benny Goodman, clarinet; and Charlie Christian, guitar. Courtesy Duncan Schiedt.

new style of guitar voice. Music historian James Sallis described the sound: "Taking the southwestern blues and saxophone sounds he'd grown up with, Christian bent and shaped them into something truly novel, becoming *the* major soloist regardless of instrument." Goodman biographer Ross Firestone added his own interpretation: "Christian's astonishing technique, harmonic sophistication, unwavering sense of swing and limitless flow of ideas, drenched in the blues but also looking ahead to the modern jazz revolution to come, set the pace for every guitar player who ever heard him, and with the exposure he gained from Benny, all of them did."[18] As with his full orchestra, Goodman shifted the sextet personnel to fine-tune the sounds, producing an even stronger group—including Cootie Williams on trumpet—that recorded landmark arrangements late in 1940. As a result, the sextet, Goodman, and Christian were all at the top of national jazz polls.

That same year, Christian embarked on another important chapter in his career, one that offered him new challenges and even freer expression of his talents. Following the routine he first adopted in Oklahoma, he frequented jam sessions after his regular paying gigs. His favorite New York place, where he became a regular, was Minton's Playhouse on 135th Street in Harlem. There, he teamed up with a new set of jazz pioneers—cutting-edge musicians like pianist Thelonious Monk, trumpeter Dizzy Gillespie, and drummer Kenny "Klook" Clarke. The jazz they played was insider music. This was not jazz for the inexperienced or those caught in the mainstream; this was a new wave of expression that referenced the historic roots of jazz but took it to new extremes. There seemed to be few rules, and the improvisational musicians in Minton's laboratory felt free to separate standard chord structures, disrupt accepted harmonic logic, and mask familiar melodies with new lines. In the process, they created a new musical vocabulary and modern frame of reference that over time came to be known as bebop. And Christian was there at the creation, still out in front of the others.[19]

Christian's long hours and obsession for music, coupled with an otherwise freewheeling lifestyle, took their toll on him physically. Despite a chest X-ray that showed tuberculosis scars, he continued to push the envelope. In 1941, though, he collapsed during a midwestern tour and returned to New York for medical care. Doctors at Bellevue Hospital transferred him to the Sea View Hospital, a sanitarium on Staten Island, for long-term rest and rehabilitation. In the era before miracle drugs, rest and fresh air were primary forms of treatment for tuberculosis. Despite some early hope for recovery, he remained hospitalized for almost eight months, and on March 2, 1942, Charles Henry Christian passed away at the age of 25.[20]

Christian's family and legion of friends and fans mourned his passing at three separate funerals. The first, at Mother of Zion Church in Harlem, drew local musicians, including Benny Goodman. The second, in Oklahoma City, was at Calvary Baptist Church, just a block above Deep Deuce, where Christian grew to maturity as a musician. Appropriately, the service included the song, "My Task," played by the Frederick Douglass High School Band under the direction of Zelia Breaux. And then, finally, Charlie Christian returned to Bonham, Texas. Interment in the Gates Hill Cemetery on South Main Street followed a service at Bethlehem Baptist Church on March 10, 1942.[21] Years later, only a small metal funeral home marker denoted the site, but over time it disappeared.

In the early 1990s, University of Oklahoma student Gary Rhodes wrote and directed a short documentary film entitled *Solo Flight: The Genius of Charlie Christian* that premiered on the Public Broadcasting System. Later shown at the Fannin County Museum of History in Bonham, the film helped raise funds for an Official Texas Historical Marker to go at Christian's unmarked grave, along with a granite headstone. Tom Scott of the museum worked with local residents to identify the correct site for placement. The tombstone bears the apt inscription, "Your music will never be forgotten."[22]

Charlie Christian accomplished much in his short life, and his legacy continues to this day, even though he was in the national spotlight for just two years. As historians, musicians, and jazz fans continue to search for more information on his life, the context of his influence continues to grow. Still, Charlie Christian remains something of a mystery to each generation that encounters his music for the first time. James Lincoln Collier provided a good overview of the guitarist's lasting significance: "The point is that Christian cut the trail down which the new players so easily run. Christian was the one who brought the electric guitar to prominence and showed what could be done with it. Had he not played with the brilliance he did, the lesson might not have taken." And, Collier added, following Christian's "brief flight into the sun," the guitar assumed a dominant central position in popular music, a distinction it maintains to this day.[23]

MARKER LOCATION: Gates Hill Cemetery, near SH 78 and S. Main St., Bonham

CHARLIE'S UNMARKED FRIENDS

While there are many Texans who made lasting contributions to the early history of jazz, relatively few have been immortalized with Official Texas Historical Markers.* Listed here are eight individuals—friends of Charlie Christian—whose contributions to Texas music history would no doubt be worthy of commemoration and who may someday be the subjects of state historical markers. Biographical sketches for these and other legendary Texas jazz performers are included in the *Handbook of Texas Online,* a project of the Texas State Historical Association (www.tshaonline.org).

Eddie Durham (1906–87)—A San Marcos native who played both guitar and trombone, he was a gifted composer and arranger remembered as a pioneer of the electric guitar.

Oscar Moore (c. 1912–81)—An Austin-born jazz guitarist, he performed and recorded with such legendary musicians as Nat King Cole, Lionel Hampton, Art Tatum, and Lester Young.

Oran Thaddeus "Hot Lips" Page (1908–54)—A Dallas native schooled at Corsicana and Tyler, he gained prominence on the national jazz scene as a trumpeter, singer, and bandleader who played with Ma Rainey, Count Basie, Artie Shaw, Bennie Moten, and Pearl Bailey.

Henry "Buster" Smith (1904–91)—A pioneer of what came to be known as the Texas Sax Sound, the Alsdorf (Ellis County) native formed a band with Count Basie, performed with Lester Young and Hot Lips Page, and mentored Charlie Parker, Charlie Christian, and T-Bone Walker.

Weldon Leo "Jack" Teagarden (1905–64)—A seminal jazz trombonist, the Vernon native bested Glenn Miller for lead position in the Ben Pollack band and performed with Benny

*Eligibility for Official Texas Historical Markers is determined through an application process that begins with county historical commissions and is reviewed and approved by the Texas Historical Commission. For more information, visit the agency's website (www.thc.state.tx.us), which includes a list of county historical commission contacts.

Goodman, Louis Armstrong, Bix Beiderbecke, Paul Whiteman, the Dorsey brothers, and other jazz legends.

Alphonso E. Trent (1905–59)—Although a native of Arkansas, he became a legendary leader of a territory band in Dallas whose popular performances at the Adolphus Hotel aired regularly on radio station WFAA.

Aaron Thibeaux "T-Bone" Walker (1910–75)—Born in Linden, raised in the Dallas neighborhood of Oak Cliff, and influenced by fellow Texans Blind Lemon Jefferson and Huddie "Leadbelly" Ledbetter, he became a legendary jazz and blues guitarist billed as the "Daddy of the Blues."

Theodore "Teddy" Shaw Wilson (1912–86)—An Austin native trained in music at Tuskegee Institute in Alabama, the noted jazz pianist performed with Benny Carter, Billie Holiday, and Benny Goodman before forming his own band and later teaching at the Juilliard School of Music.

16 HARVEST OF THE DEVOTED HEART

On the southeast corner of the Baylor University campus in Waco stands the Armstrong Browning Library, a magnificent building housing the world's largest collection of books, papers, and artifacts relating to Robert Browning and Elizabeth Barrett Browning. How this world-renowned library devoted to the nineteenth-century married British poets came to be in Central Texas is a story of the determination and ingenuity of another married couple, Dr. A. Joseph Armstrong and Mary Maxwell Armstrong. Their devotion to academic excellence and literary history created a unique legacy for generations of Baylor students, Browning scholars, and the general public who continue to marvel at the beauty of the building and the magnitude of the collection.

Born in 1873, Andrew Joseph Armstrong grew up in Louisville, Kentucky, the son of formerly aristocratic parents whose families' fortunes suffered reversals after the Civil War. His father died in 1887, but Armstrong's mother instilled in her son and his siblings a love of learning and a strong Christian faith. From an early age, he determined to be a teacher, conducting classes and billing himself "Jo Armstrong, Professor of Greek and Latin" in the pretend classroom he set up for his playmates.[1]

Although eager to further his education following his graduation from high school in 1891, his mother's failing health and reduced financial circumstances required him to work to care for her. He worked in a Louisville bank through his mother's illness and death and finally, at age twenty-six, realized his dream of attending college. He enrolled at Wabash College in Crawfordsville, Indiana, financing his studies with a combination of scholarships and odd jobs. He graduated with a Bachelor of Arts degree in 1902 and accepted a teaching position at Rusk Academy (later East Texas Baptist Institute) in Rusk. Though short-lived because the school was unable to pay his salary, his sojourn in East Texas proved providential when he met a fellow English teacher, Mary Maxwell, the Baylor University–educated sister of the academy president. Returning to Kentucky after a few months, he began a correspondence with her as he worked to earn money to finance graduate studies at Wabash and at summer institutes at the University of Chicago, which she also attended in 1903. After earning a master's degree in 1904, Armstrong taught for three years at Illinois Wesleyan College in Bloomington, where he first offered a course devoted to the poet Robert Browning. He earned a Ph.D. at the University of Pennsylvania in 1908.

Armstrong's first appointment at Baylor University came in 1908, when he accepted a one-year interim teaching position in the English department. Although temporary, the Baylor job allowed him to reunite with Mary Maxwell, who was by then teaching high school English in Waco. Returning once again to Kentucky at the end of the academic year, he joined the faculty at Georgetown College, where he became a popular and revered teacher and where his Browning lectures attracted not only students but also members of the faculty and citizens of Georgetown.

While teaching at Georgetown, Armstrong began a lifelong practice of world travel during his summer breaks from academia. On his first trip abroad in 1909, he journeyed to Italy, where he met painter and sculptor Robert Wiedeman Barrett (Pen) Browning, the sixty-year-old son of Robert and Elizabeth Barrett Browning. Following their marriage—against her family's wishes—in 1846, the Brownings left England and settled in Italy, where their son was born and where Elizabeth Barrett Browning died in 1861. Robert Browning and his son lived in England after her death, but when Pen Browning reached adulthood he returned to Italy, the country his mother loved. Robert Browning died in 1889 while visiting his son in Venice, but rather than being interred next to his beloved wife at the Protestant Cemetery in Florence, his body was entombed in Poets' Corner in Westminster Abbey in London. Pen Browning, sole heir to his parents' literary legacy and worldly

Dr. Andrew Joseph Armstrong, Baylor University campus.
Courtesy Armstrong Browning Library, Baylor University, Waco.

goods, remained in Italy the rest of his life. Armstrong's three-day visit with the artist in 1909 set in motion his eventual drive to amass a significant Browning collection. Utterly devoted to the works of Robert Browning, Armstrong later said, "I have taught Shakespeare and Dante and even Homer, the world's greatest geniuses, and I believe Browning yields the student more than any of these. Outside of the Holy Bible there is no other writing than can as truly furnish a guidance for a practical life on the highest plane."[2]

Armstrong resumed his teaching duties in Georgetown in the fall of 1909 and continued to develop his popular Browning lectures. During this time, his relationship with Mary Maxwell grew closer, and the couple married in Waco in January 1911. They traveled to Europe the following summer, employed as tour guides for a company called Temple Tours, and in December of that year their only child, Richard Maxwell (Max) Armstrong, was born. In the fall of 1912, the family moved to Waco, where Dr. Armstrong began his decades-long career as chairman of the Baylor University English department. While attending to his teaching and administrative responsibilities, the professor also pursued his plan to build a library collection devoted to Robert Browning. He offered a Browning course that quickly became popular among Baylor students.

Pen Browning died in Italy about the same time the Armstrongs moved to Waco, and the following year his estate was dispersed at the famed Sotheby's auction house in London. The auction proved to be a major event, taking place over the course of six days in May 1913. Items offered for sale included Pen Browning's belongings and original artworks, as well as everything he inherited from his famous parents—letters, manuscripts, books, paintings, furniture, jewelry, miscellaneous items, and portraits of the two poets. Unable to attend the auction or to purchase items with his modest professor's salary, Dr. Armstrong nevertheless had the foresight to arrange for a Sotheby's agent to monitor the auction and note in the sale catalogue the names of purchasers and prices paid for each item. With that information, he hoped he would be able to track most items sold at the estate auction and, someday, acquire them for his Browning collection. But first he would have to find a way to finance the acquisitions.[3]

Drawing on their love of foreign travel and their earlier experience with Temple Tours, the Armstrongs decided to establish their own travel agency to book summer educational tours, with profits from the venture to be directed to a Browning collection fund. Armstrong Educational Tours, with offices in Waco and Paris managed by Mary Maxwell Armstrong, became such a success over the years that Baylor University Pres. Samuel Palmer Brooks once introduced Dr. Armstrong as "the man who makes his living directing a travel bureau so that he can afford to be a college professor." The Armstrongs led tours to Europe as well as to South America, Africa, and India, where Dr. Armstrong and his son met with Mohandas Gandhi. "It was a delightful hour," Armstrong remembered, "and you may readily believe it was outstanding in the summer's experience." Approximately four thousand people traveled with Armstrong Educational Tours in a twenty-year period, and the company's gross profits reportedly reached one million dollars one year.[4]

The Armstrongs encountered numerous literary celebrities during their travels, thereby enhancing the experience of their clients and students. Among the most popular tours were the ones billed as Browning Pilgrimages. Dr. Armstrong's biographer, Lois Smith Douglas, described the first Browning Pilgrimage, which occurred in 1929: "A select group of cultured and scholarly men and women, devoted to the poetry and the philosophy of Robert Browning, spent the summer retracing the steps of the great poet, rereading his verse at the spot where he composed some of it, inspired by the same rapturous scenes." Douglas further summed up the Armstrongs' travel ventures:

> The Armstrong Educational Tours, begun modestly in 1912, achieved an auspicious magnitude. With their splendid literary and cultural background coupled with fine business acumen, executive ability and linguistic facilities, both Dr. and Mrs. Armstrong were preeminently fitted to conduct travelers. Possibly, however, Dr. Armstrong's greatest asset

was his enthusiasm for the venture; he earnestly wanted people, particularly his friends and students, to experience the delights he had known through travel. As a result, profit was not the ultimate aim of the Armstrong organization, and it operated on a very reasonable percentage. Because of the constancy of their tours and the rapidly increasing volume of the clientele, they gained an entrée never achieved by the purely commercial travel agencies. Extraordinary courtesies and favors fell to the lot of Armstrong tourists as a result of the fine rapport existent between the Armstrong management and the local guides, hotel managers, foreign embassies, and state dignitaries. Not unusual at all was it for a foreign hotel to fly the American flag when an Armstrong party stopped there.[5]

Despite the popular and lucrative summer tours, Dr. Armstrong's primary academic responsibility remained the teaching of English literature and instilling its lasting influence on the lives of his students. His lectures were legendary, and many students, though awed and at times intimidated by the professor's brusque manner and demanding requirements, nevertheless looked back on their experiences in his classes as the most rewarding of their college careers. To enhance the regular curriculum, to provide unique cultural opportunities for the community at large, and to raise more funds for the Browning collection, Armstrong hit upon the idea of indulging his own fascination with celebrities in a way that would benefit both the school and his personal goals. Over the course of several decades, he arranged for a series of poets, lecturers, artists, and performers to visit Waco and the Baylor campus. The events drew large crowds willing to pay modest admission prices, and Armstrong in effect became a booking agent for numerous celebrities, arranging sweeping southwestern tours for the various artists in order to ensure their appearances in Waco. The roster of speakers and performers varied widely, and included poets William Butler Yeats, Robert Frost, Carl Sandburg, Edna St. Vincent Millay, Amy Lowell, Edwin Markham, and Vachel Lindsay; novelist and playwright Sinclair Lewis; historian J. Frank Dobie; folklorist

John A. Lomax; Antarctic explorers Adm. Richard E. Byrd and Roald Amundsen; opera singers Marian Anderson and Luisa Tetrazzini; the New York Philharmonic Orchestra; and actors Basil Rathbone, Katharine Cornell, and Helen Hayes. Rathbone and Cornell, cast as Robert Browning and Elizabeth Barrett Browning in a production of the Rudolph Besier play *The Barretts of Wimpole Street*, proved the most popular of the traveling performers, playing to a sold-out crowd at the Waco civic auditorium.

Correspondence among the professor and the artists—now a part of the Armstrong Browning Library archives—reveals a wealth of information and a glimpse into the high regard in which the celebrities held Dr. Armstrong. Writing to Robert Frost concerning an invitation to speak in Waco, Carl Sandburg urged his friend to accept, saying, "if you hear anything from A. J. Armstrong at Baylor University, you will make no mistake about cooperating with him on any plans he may have for bringing you south." Recommending the Baylor engagement as a boost to his colleague's career, he went on to say, "At Dr. Armstrong's own school they not only read a man's books before he arrives but they buy them in record-breaking numbers."[6]

Through all the years of teaching, chairing the English department, traveling, and booking speakers and entertainers, Dr. Armstrong never lost sight of his dream of building the Browning collection. He donated his personal library of Browning books to the university in 1918, and the Baylor graduating class of 1919, as its parting gift to the school, purchased and donated a life-sized portrait of Robert Browning painted by his son. Using the annotated catalogue from the 1913 Sotheby's auction, Armstrong began acquiring items from the former Browning estate with the funds he raised. He also appealed to friends, former students, colleagues, and the public for donations of Browning items when they became available through various auctions and galleries. Katharine Cornell bought and donated a pair of miniature portraits of the poets. In 1920, on the occasion of Baylor University's Diamond Jubilee, journalist and Browning scholar Lilian Whiting presented to the collection one of its more unique items, a bronze sculpture of the Brownings' clasped hands created in 1853 by their friend and neighbor in Florence, American artist Harriet Hosmer. The Browning collection's first home was a corner in Baylor's Carroll Library, which suffered a devastating fire in 1922. Thanks to the quick actions of concerned students and bystanders, the collection survived as several people rushed into the building and passed the priceless items, including the clasped hands sculpture, out the window to a gathered crowd of onlookers. When the university rebuilt and rededicated the library in 1924, it included a special Browning Room, complete with three stained-glass windows depicting Browning poems.

By 1925, *The Times* of London declared Baylor University had "the best collection of Browningiana in the world."[7] As the reputations of both Dr. Armstrong and the Browning collection grew and attracted attention in the press and in academic circles, support came from all corners of the world. Armstrong's connections to Browning societies and scholars in England and Italy, as well as other locations, generated interest in and donations to the collection. In 1942, university president Pat M. Neff pledged $100,000 of university funds toward construction of a separate Browning Library if Armstrong could raise a matching sum. Undaunted by the challenge, the professor and his wife undertook a renewed fundraising campaign, and in the next several years their efforts far exceeded the requested match. According to one writer, Dr. Armstrong "realized that much more than $100,000 would be required to create the building of his dreams, and no one who was his friend, student, or acquaintance escaped his pleas for assistance." Indeed, one of his telegrams reached a former student, a soldier stationed in Europe during World War II. Even while serving near the front lines in a global war, he could not refuse a request from "Dr. A" for a financial contribution to the building fund.[8]

On May 7, 1948, the 136th anniversary of Robert Browning's birth and four years after President Neff's initial fundraising challenge, Dr. Armstrong presided over a ceremonial groundbreaking for the new library. Designed by prominent Texas architect Wyatt C. Hedrick, with the New York City firm of Eggers and Higgins as associate architects, the three-story Italian Renaissance–style building was completed in December 1951 at a cost of $1.75 million,

*Designed by renowned Texas architect Wyatt C. Hedrick, the Italian
Renaissance–style Armstrong Browning Library opened in December 1951.*
Photograph by Cynthia J. Beeman.

more than seventeen times the original fundraising goal. According to Lois Smith Douglas, "Every detail of the exquisite building, with its beautiful stained-glass windows, soft grey Texas granite, and handsomely carved mahogany furnishings, all illustrative of Browning motifs, is the harvest of the devoted heart and brain of A. J. Armstrong."[9]

With both Dr. and Mrs. Armstrong intimately involved with design decisions, the library immediately became a monument on the Baylor campus, showcasing not only the world-renowned collection of Browning books, manuscripts, and artifacts, but also the spectacular details of the building itself. Solid bronze entry doors, modeled on the fifteenth-century doors of the Baptistery building in Florence, Italy, feature bas relief panels that depict themes from Robert Browning's poems. Sixty-two stained glass windows

Hankamer Treasure Room, Armstrong Browning Library. Oak parquet floors, an elaborate hand-painted ceiling, and striking stained glass windows are among the elegant features of this room on the library's main floor. Paintings and other artwork date to the fourteenth century. Photograph by Cynthia J. Beeman.

(including the three previously installed at the Carroll Library), their brilliant colors and artistry beautifully illustrating the poetry of the Brownings, dramatically illuminate soaring interior spaces. A meditation foyer, topped by a dome finished in gold leaf, features a two-ton bronze chandelier. The famous Hosmer sculpture rests in a specially designed alcove called the Cloister of the Clasped Hands, flanked by walls illustrated with words from the poets' most romantic verses written for each other: Elizabeth Barrett Browning's "How do I love thee? Let me count the ways," from *Sonnets from the Portuguese,* and Robert Browning's "O lyric love, half-angel and half-bird, and all a wonder and a wild desire" from *The Ring and the Book.* Other interior features include black walnut-

Stained glass window detail, Hankamer Treasure Room. Stained glass windows throughout the library illustrate the poems of Robert Browning and Elizabeth Barrett Browning and include verses such as this one from Elizabeth Barrett Browning's Sonnets from the Portuguese, *published in 1850.* Photograph by Cynthia J. Beeman

paneled walls, Italian marble columns, gleaming terrazzo and oak parquet floors, elaborately decorated ceilings, and elegantly appointed bookcases and furniture, including many pieces once owned by the Brownings.

The highlight of the third floor is the Elizabeth Barrett Browning Salon, which Mary Maxwell Armstrong insisted on including in the library's plan and which features the poet's writing table and other personal items. Artwork displayed throughout the building includes portraits of both poets and their son; paintings executed by Pen Browning; paintings and sculptures owned by the Brownings; family heirlooms such as a clock, a prayer bench, jewelry, and furniture; and various paintings and drawings depicting scenes from the writers' poems. In addition to its incomparable Browning collection, the library's literary treasures include a growing archive

Detail of stained glass window by Jacoby Studios, 1950, John Leddy-Jones Research Hall, Armstrong Browning Library. This verse, which appears in numerous locations throughout the library, is from the invocation to Robert Browning's The Ring and the Book. *Published in 1868–69, the collection is considered his masterwork.* Photograph by Cynthia J. Beeman.

(opposite) Dr. A. J. Armstrong seated in the Foyer of Meditation. With its Classical references that include soaring arched windows, marble columns, gold-leaf domed ceiling, and bronze chandelier, the Foyer of Meditation is the most dramatic room in the library. Courtesy Armstrong Browning Library, Baylor University, Waco.

of works by nineteenth-century writers, including the Minor English Poets Collection and Women Poets Collection.[10]

Although ill health prompted Dr. Armstrong to retire in 1952, just one year after the dedication of the new library, the university continued to covey the title of director of the Armstrong Browning Library upon him until his death in May 1954 at age eighty-one. Mary Maxwell Armstrong served as director from 1954 to 1959 and continued to work with the Guardian Angels library support group until 1966, when she moved to Pennsylvania to live with her son. She died in September 1971 and was interred next to her husband

Portrait of Dr. A. J. Armstrong by Wayman Adams, 1952. Commissioned to paint portraits of Dr. A. J. and Mary Maxwell Armstrong for the new library, artist Adams depicted Dr. Armstrong reading a book of poems and wearing Robert Browning's signet ring on his right hand. The portraits hang in specially designed alcoves in the Foyer of Meditation. Courtesy Armstrong Browning Library, Baylor University, Waco.

Mary Maxell Armstrong (foreground), *circa 1950s.*
Courtesy Armstrong Browning Library, Baylor University, Waco.

in Waco's Oakwood Cemetery. The Texas Historical Commission placed historical markers for the Armstrong Browning Library and for Dr. Andrew Joseph Armstrong and Mary Maxwell Armstrong at the library on the Baylor University campus in 2006.

MARKER LOCATION: 710 Speight Ave. on the campus of Baylor University, Waco

Pomegranate detail, stained glass window, John Leddy-Jones Research Hall. Inspired by an early series of poems by Robert Browning and symbolizing the music and meaning of poetry, an artistic motif of bells and pomegranates recurs throughout the library in decorative architectural details. Photograph by Dan K. Utley.

WYATT C. HEDRICK

Baylor University hired Wyatt Cephas Hedrick (1888–1964), one of the most prolific architects practicing in Texas during the first half of the twentieth century, to design the Armstrong Browning Library. A native of Pittsylvania County, Virginia, Hedrick attended Roanoke College and Washington and Lee University, where he earned a degree in engineering in 1910. He began his career as an engineer in Virginia and then moved to Texas in 1913 to take a job as a construction engineer in Dallas. Within a year he opened his own construction firm in Fort Worth, and by 1921 he was practicing architecture, joining the established firm of Sanguinet and Staats. He opened his own architectural office in 1925, and the following year he bought the Sanguinet and Staats firm when the two senior partners retired. With offices in Fort Worth, Dallas, and Houston, Hedrick designed numerous landmark buildings in Texas, many in the Art Deco or Art Moderne styles. Although some of his most prominent buildings are no longer extant (such as the legendary Shamrock Hotel in Houston, razed in 1987), many others remain and have national, state, and local historical designations. Some of the most impressive examples of Hedrick's architecture, in chronological order, are:

West Texas Utilities Power Plant, 1922, 100 N. Second St., Abilene

Snider Hall and Virginia Hall, 1927, 3305 and 3325 Dyer St., Southern Methodist University campus, Dallas

Houston Yacht Club, 1927, 3620 Miramar, Houston

Dairy Barn, 1927, Texas Tech University campus, Lubbock

Fort Worth Elks Lodge No. 124, 1927–28, 512 W. 4th St., Fort Worth

Fort Worth and Denver South Plains Railway Depot (now Buddy Holly Center), 1928, 1801 Crickets Ave. (formerly Ave. G), Lubbock

Baker Hotel, 1929, 200 E. Hubbard, Mineral Wells

Petroleum Building, 1929, 214 W. Texas Ave., Midland
Yucca Theater, 1929, 208 N. Colorado St., Midland
Texas and Pacific Railway Terminal and Warehouse, 1930,
    Lancaster and Throckmorton streets, Fort Worth
Fort Worth Power and Light (Electric Building), 1930,
    410 W. 7th St., Fort Worth
Main Post Office, 1933, 300 W. Lancaster St., Fort Worth
Will Rogers Auditorium, Coliseum, and Pioneer Tower, 1936,
    3301 W. Lancaster St., Fort Worth
Main Post Office and U.S. Courthouse, 1939, 205 E. 5th St.,
    Amarillo

Sources: THC marker files and THC NR files; Christopher Long, "Wyatt Cephas Hedrick," *New Handbook of Texas,* vol. 3, pp. 540–41; *Sanguinet, Staats, and Hedrick: An Inventory of Their Drawings, Photographs, and Records,* Alexander Architectural Archive, University of Texas Libraries, University of Texas at Austin.

17 QUEEN OF THE AIR

Growing up in Texas, Bessie Coleman always wanted to "amount to something." Born January 26, 1892, in Atlanta, Cass County, she was the tenth of thirteen children born to George and Susan Coleman. George, who was three-fourths Native American, and Susan worked as day laborers and tenant farmers in the small East Texas town, as did most of their fellow African American neighbors. By the time Bessie was two years old, however, they had saved enough money to move to the bustling cotton town of Waxahachie, south of Dallas. They purchased a lot east of the railroad tracks and built a three-room frame house. Around 1901, George Coleman, hoping to escape the difficult life of a black man in Texas and find more opportunities as a Native American, moved to Indian Territory (Oklahoma).[1] Susan refused to uproot the family and remained in Waxahachie with her four youngest daughters, the older five of her surviving children having left home by that time. Working as a maid, she ensured her daughters attended school, and she purchased books as often as finances allowed. In all of her children, she instilled a strong sense of worth and an ambition to amount to something in life. Her daughter Elois recalled years later, "Even though Mother had to pinch pennies, she managed to get books from a wagon library that passed the house once or twice a year, telling of the accomplishments made by members of our race."[2] Despite the family's devotion to learning, the children suspended lessons for weeks or even months each year when school closed during harvest season and the entire family took to the fields to pick cotton.

In addition to her studies at school and the books she read at home, Bessie Coleman, an eager and enthusiastic student, also encountered the writings of the black press via the *Chicago Defender*, a weekly newspaper distributed in the South by African American Pullman porters traveling the nation's rail system. Founded by Robert S. Abbott in 1905, the influential publication addressed racial injustice with sensational headlines, fervent editorials, and articles relating stories of racial violence and discrimination throughout the United States. One of its most successful and aggressive campaigns called on African Americans— which the paper referred to as "the Race"—to flee the oppressive South and move north in what later became known as the Great Migration.[3]

In 1910, Coleman completed the six grades offered at the black school in Waxahachie and, with her mother's financial assistance and her own savings, enrolled in the Colored Agricultural and Normal University (now Langston University) in Langston, Oklahoma. The money did not go far, however, and she returned home after only one term, unable to afford another semester's tuition. Still determined to leave Texas and amount to something, she worked as a laundress to earn enough money to escape for good. It took several years, but finally in 1915 she boarded a northbound train and joined the Great Migration to Chicago.

Welcomed to her new home by her brothers Walter and John and their wives, Coleman moved into their crowded apartment on Chicago's South Side and began searching for work. She enrolled in a beauty school, became a manicurist, and found jobs in a series of barbershops along the Stroll, an area of State Street between 26th and 39th streets that had become the center of African American life and culture in Chicago. Her skill and good looks, along with her charm and growing talent for self-promotion, propelled her into relatively well-paying jobs in prominent shops, where she often worked at a table in the front window, her employers displaying her to the public in a calculated effort to draw more customers. The ploy worked, and she came in contact with many influential community leaders, including the *Chicago Defender*'s editor and publisher, Robert Abbott. He took notice of the young Texan and became a mentor of sorts, running stories about her, encouraging her success as well as his own in the process, knowing articles about the pretty young Bessie would increase newspaper sales and readership. He staged a citywide contest to find the "best and fastest manicurist in black Chicago," with a follow-up story about the winner—Coleman, of course.

Shortly after the story ran, World War I ended with the signing of the armistice on November 11, 1918. Many young African American men volunteered for military service during the war but continued to encounter racial discrimination despite their uniforms, relegated to segregated units such as the Eighth Illinois Infantry, in which Walter and John Coleman served. Regardless, many came home from overseas with an altered world view, having experienced more moderate treatment and acceptance as people of color in Europe than they knew at home. According to the family, it was John Coleman's drunken teasing of his sister, negatively comparing her to French women who he viewed as superior—particularly female aviators he saw or heard about during his service overseas—that spurred Bessie to pursue a career as a pilot.[4] Determined to learn to fly, she applied to a number of Chicago-area flight schools, but none accepted her as a student because of her gender and race. Abbott suggested she learn French and apply to an aviation school in France, so she enrolled in a language school and continued pursuing her goal. With her savings and sponsorships provided by Abbott and others, she sailed to France in November 1920. Turned down by the first school to which she applied, she went to Le Crotoy in the Picardie region, where the École d'Aviation des Frères Caudron accepted her as a student. After seven months of instruction, Bessie Coleman received an international pilot's license from the Fédération Aéronautique Internationale on June 15, 1921, becoming the first black woman in the world to earn a pilot's license.

Keen to capitalize on his investment with publicity for the *Defender,* Abbott arranged for massive press coverage of Coleman's return to the United States in September, and reporters for many of the country's black weekly newspapers met her as she arrived in port. She became a celebrity in the black community, heralded in front-page stories across the country. Recognizing the opportunity to promote herself as well as her dream of opening an avia-

Bessie Coleman, 1921. This image appeared on her international pilot's license.
Personal collection of the authors.

tion school for African Americans, she responded to reporters with charm, enthusiasm, and embellishment—tools she continued to use in pursuit of her personal and professional goals in the years to come. She returned to Chicago in October and continued to bask in her newfound fame, as noted in the *Defender*:

> Miss Bessie Coleman ... the only feminine aviatrix of the Race in the world, arrived in Chicago Saturday direct from France where she has just completed a ten months' course in aviating.... When asked why she took up the game of flying, she said:
>
> "Well, because I knew we had no aviators, neither men nor women, and I knew the Race needed to be represented along this most important line, so I thought it my duty to risk my life to learn aviating and to encourage flying among men and women of the Race who are so far behind the white men in this special line. I made up my mind to try; I tried and was successful."[5]

Despite the publicity and her hard-won international license, Coleman soon realized she needed more flight training in order to make a living as a pilot or instructor. While the ranks of fliers steadily grew in the United States as aviation became more popular, the only way to earn substantial money at the pursuit lay in the burgeoning barnstorming business. Performing aerial stunts, parachute jumps, and wing walks, aviators toured the country appearing at county and state fairs and other community gatherings, thrilling audiences with exhibition flying and offering airplane rides for fees. Coleman's flight instruction had not included stunt flying, so she returned to France for additional lessons to master the skills that would enable her to join the lucrative barnstorming circuit.

After six months in Europe—France, where she received further flight instruction; Holland, where she met famed airplane designer Anthony H. G. Fokker and toured his factory; and Germany, where the Pathé newsreel service filmed her flying over the former Kaiser's palace at Potsdam—Coleman once again returned to New

Bessie Coleman, circa 1925. Attired in the specially tailored flight suit made for her in France, Coleman is pictured standing on the wheel of an open-cockpit Curtiss JN-4 Jenny airplane, the type of aircraft she often flew in air shows. She fell to her death from a Jenny in a tragic accident in Florida in 1926. Courtesy Pacific Security Collection, Los Angeles Public Library.

York to great fanfare engineered by Robert Abbott, who arranged an air show at Curtiss Field on Long Island to show off the "Queen of the Air." The exhibition, which also featured a tribute to African American World War I veterans and the music of a jazz band, took place on September 3, 1922, and provided spectators with an opportunity to watch "the first public flight of a black woman in this country" as Coleman piloted a borrowed Curtiss JN-4 "Jenny" aircraft, launching her career as "Queen Bess, Daredevil Aviatrix."[6]

The following month, back in Chicago, Coleman performed for an adoring hometown crowd in a show that included a tribute to the veterans of the all-black unit her brothers served in during World War I. As reported in the *Defender,* "the hearts of the spectators stood still when . . . the daring girl made the figure 8 in honor of the Eighth Illinois Infantry. It looked as if she had lost control of her great plane and that it was turning and twisting, pilotless, back to earth. But thousands of hearts sighed with great relief when the machine was seen to right itself and soar straightaway though the air." The article went on to describe the thrill of passengers fortunate enough to ride in her plane and related her plans for upcoming flights: "She is constantly in demand and receives offers from different parts of the country. Already she has five engagements booked in five different cities. Yet with all her fame she is still the same unassuming, friendly Bessie Coleman."[7]

Friendly she may have been, but "unassuming" appears to have been an inaccurate description. As she attracted more attention and publicity, she engaged a series of managers and agents to book her performances, arrange for the use of airplanes since she had none of her own, promote her appearances, and coordinate endorsements and other money-making endeavors. A reporter for the entertainment magazine *Billboard* helped secure a deal for her to star in a feature-length film, but when she realized the opening scene called for her to appear dressed in rags with a pack on her back depicting a poor, ignorant black girl arriving in the big city from the South, she balked and refused to participate, reportedly storming off the New York film set with the parting comment, "No Uncle Tom stuff for me!"[8] Following that incident, Coleman gained a reputation as a somewhat difficult, temperamental, and eccentric celebrity, in part due to the film debacle but also because of her strident views and pronouncements regarding equal rights for women and blacks.

Still hoping to open a flight school for African Americans, Coleman met a California tire company advertising manager who hired her to airdrop promotional fliers. In January 1923, she took a train to California to begin her new venture. Publicizing the tire company as promised, she also used her fame in the black press to continue promoting herself and her planned flying school. By early February, she acquired sufficient funds to purchase a surplus U.S. Army Jenny, and she secured a sponsor for an exhibition flight at the opening of a new fairground. A few minutes into her flight, however, the engine stalled and her plane crashed to the ground. Seriously injured, she spent three months in a hospital but told a *Chicago Defender* reporter, "You tell the world I'm coming back."

When her family heard of the accident, her sister Elois thought she would give up flying, but their mother knew otherwise. According to Coleman's biographer, Doris Rich, "Susan, who once claimed she 'had thirteen children, raised up nine and one of them was crazy,' knew her Bessie. 'Oh, no,' she told Elois. 'That's only the beginning.'"⁹

Returning to Chicago in June, Coleman tried to resume her career, but it stalled. She performed in an exhibition flight in Ohio in September, but negative publicity concerning her trouble with managers—she had fired or otherwise parted ways with five of them in less than two years—helped spur her decision to take a break from flying and spend time with family. No longer seeing her as the crowd-pleasing "Queen Bess," Robert Abbott seemed to lose interest, and for a time the *Chicago Defender* ceased publishing articles about her. Not content to remain grounded for long, Coleman continued to seek opportunities to fly. Her chance came in the spring of 1925, and it took her back to Texas, where she gave a series of lectures and flying demonstrations sponsored by African American businessmen and community leaders.

Her first stop was Houston, where in a *Post-Dispatch* interview she said she wanted "to make Uncle Tom's cabin into a hangar by establishing a flying school."¹⁰ Speaking to audiences at civic clubs, churches, and schools, Coleman related her flying adventures, at times embellishing facts to make a better story, and showing film clips from Pathé newsreels of her flights. Her first Texas flight occurred on Juneteenth, June 19, 1925, the sixtieth anniversary of the date in 1865 when enslaved African Americans in Texas officially learned of the Emancipation Proclamation. The air show attracted a large audience of both black and white spectators who cheered as she flew a borrowed plane in a series of stunts. The following day, the city's black newspaper, the *Houston Informer*, reported "about 75 of our fearless citizens, most of whom were women" took advantage of the opportunity to ride in the plane with the famous aviator. The *Chicago Defender*, once again taking notice of her exploits, ran a small story with the headline "Aviatrix Performs for Texas Crowds." Coleman spent the rest of the summer performing for crowds or giving lectures in a number of Texas towns.

In Austin, in what was probably an arranged photo opportunity, she visited the Texas Governor's Mansion, where she met Gov. Miriam A. "Ma" Ferguson and her husband, former Gov. James E. "Pa" Ferguson.[11] While both Fergusons had many detractors due to a number of political controversies, including James Ferguson's impeachment, they were also known for their opposition to the Ku Klux Klan, a fact presumably appreciated by Coleman and her sponsors. In Dallas, Coleman shopped for a plane at Love Field, at that time a small airfield that doubled as a storage depot for used aircraft offered for sale by various companies. Unable to afford a new airplane, she settled on a used and somewhat dilapidated Jenny, and made a down payment to its seller. Once mechanics completed necessary engine repairs, and after Coleman made the final payment, she would finally own her own airplane. Still using a borrowed plane, she performed in a two-day air show in Wharton, hiring a pilot from Houston to fly the plane the second day so she could perform a parachute stunt. She also flew in Waxahachie, where local organizers arranged for a racially mixed audience but with separate entrances for whites and blacks. Coleman steadfastly refused to fly unless all spectators could enter by the same gates, and although she succeeded in that demand, the audience remained segregated once inside the arena. She did, however, take satisfaction in knowing she was the star attraction at the air show in her hometown, the place where as a small girl she picked cotton and lived in a three-room shack on the poor side of the railroad tracks.[12]

After her triumphant tour of Texas, Coleman returned to Chicago for a few months and spent Christmas with her family. In January 1926, her agent arranged for a lecture tour of black communities in Georgia and Florida. A popular speaker, especially among young people, Coleman renewed her dream of opening an aviation school, realizing it might be possible to earn the money she needed by continuing on the lecture circuit as well as flying in air shows whenever she could manage to borrow an airplane.

The one she had arranged to purchase remained in Dallas until she could raise funds to cover the final payment. Temporarily settling in Orlando, Florida, she lived with the Rev. Hezakiah and Viola Hill, who invited her into their home in the parsonage of Mount Zion Missionary Baptist Church. Viola Hill, recognizing Coleman would have a hard time raising enough money through lectures and stunt flying to establish her school, suggested she open a beauty shop to supplement her income. Coleman began working in the shop but also flew and performed parachute stunts whenever opportunities arose. Always on the lookout for sponsors, she found an enthusiastic one in the person of Edwin Beeman, heir to the Beemans Chewing Gum fortune, who lived at a family estate in an area of Orlando known as Beeman Park. Keenly interested in aviation, he arranged to make the final payment on Coleman's plane and have it delivered to Jacksonville, where she planned to perform in an air show sponsored by the Negro Welfare League on May 1, 1926.

Traveling to the North Florida town by train, Coleman gave a number of lectures in the days leading up to the event. Meanwhile, her plane, piloted by William D. Wills, a white mechanic who worked for the Dallas seller, was on its way to Jacksonville. Arriving at the airfield on April 28, Wills met some local pilots who later said they were amazed the plane had made it from Texas to Florida, remarking on its worn appearance and poor condition. In fact, Wills did encounter mechanical trouble on the flight that necessitated two unscheduled landings for repairs. Nonetheless, the Jenny arrived in Jacksonville, and Coleman, thrilled to have her own plane at last, arranged for Wills to fly it for part of her air show appearance so she could perform a parachute jump. She and Wills arrived at the airfield early on the morning of April 30 for a test flight.

With Wills at the controls in the front of the two-seat open cockpit and Coleman in the rear, they took off from the runway and circled the field at 2,000 feet. Coleman planned to scout potential landing sites for her parachute jump the next day. She left her seatbelt unfastened so she could lean up to peer over the edge of the plane for a better view of the field. Climbing to 3,500 feet, the plane suddenly accelerated and then went into a nosedive. When it reached an altitude of about 500 feet, it flipped upside down. As horrified spectators watched, Coleman, thrown from the rear seat, tumbled through the air and died instantly when her body hit the ground. Wills, still desperately trying to control the plane, died on impact when it crashed into a nearby field moments later.

News of the tragedy spread quickly throughout the country, although it received more notice in the black press than in the white press, which in some cases barely mentioned Coleman and instead focused on the fate of Wills. A *Dallas Morning News* headline read "Dallas Man is Killed in Plane," and while it included Coleman's name and a note that she was "said to be the only negro aviatrix in the world," the article failed to mention her connection to nearby Waxahachie or the fact she was a native Texan. Black newspapers reported more widely and prominently on the crash, and the story remained front-page news for several days. Within days of the accident, investigators determined the cause of the crash to be a loose wrench. Inadvertently left in the plane, possibly by Wills on one of his repair stops en route to Florida, it wedged in the gearbox, jamming the gears and triggering the sudden acceleration. Several pilots later noted the accident might have been prevented if Coleman had been able to buy a newer-model Jenny, one with a gearbox covered by a protective shell.[13]

African American communities in Jacksonville and Orlando galvanized to arrange funeral services for Coleman. The first occurred in Jacksonville on Sunday, May 2, at Bethel Baptist Church with an estimated crowd of five thousand in attendance. That evening, after a second service at St. Philip's Episcopal Church, Coleman's casket traveled by train to Orlando, where the Rev. Hezakiah Hill and Viola Hill presided over another funeral at Mount Zion Missionary Baptist Church on Monday morning. An elaborate service attended by the largest crowd in the church's history, it included choral tributes as well as speeches and eulogies from the ministers of every African American church in Orlando. The congregation of mourners then accompanied the coffin to the train station, where Viola Hill boarded the baggage car to ride with the body to Chicago. Several thousand people, including a military escort from the Eighth Illinois Infantry, met the train when it arrived on the morning of May 5. An estimated ten thousand mourners filed past the casket at a funeral home the rest of that day and the next. The final funeral, held on Friday, May 7, at Pilgrim Baptist Church, was an impressive service attended by Bessie's family and friends and a crowd of more than five thousand. Among the speakers and honorary pallbearers were veterans of the Eighth Illinois Infantry; local, state, and national political leaders; and Ida B. Wells-Barnett, the crusading civil rights and women's rights activist who, according to an account in the *Chicago Defender*, "acting as mistress of ceremonies, told of her meeting with Miss Coleman soon after her return from Europe."[14] Coleman's burial occurred later that day at Chicago's Lincoln Cemetery, and a year later her admirers placed a memorial stone on her grave.

Commemorative tributes continued in the years after Coleman's death. In 1931, a group of African American pilots in Chicago began a tradition of annual flyovers above Lincoln Cemetery, dropping flowers on her grave. Although they ceased when the original group of flyers began to age and retire, the tributes resumed in the 1980s under the auspices of another group of pilots. Memorial aviation groups included Bessie Coleman Aero Clubs in California and the Chicago-based Bessie Coleman Aviators Club. In 1990, the city of Chicago renamed a road at O'Hare International Airport in her honor, and five years later, the U.S. Postal Service issued a Bessie Coleman stamp as part of its Black Heritage series. In 2000, a ceremony in Galveston marked her induction into the Texas Aviation Hall of Fame. The Smithsonian Institution's National Air and Space Museum featured her in its "Black Wings: African American Pioneer Aviators" exhibit, and she is the subject of several biographies and numerous children's books.[15]

Bessie Coleman's life and accomplishments are commemorated with two Official Texas Historical Markers—one in Atlanta, where a street leading to the city airport also bears her name, and one in a downtown park in Waxahachie near the site of the Coleman family home. Her greatest legacies, however, are her intelligence, talent, determination, perseverance, and unrelenting quest for women's rights and racial equality that continue to inspire generations of Americans. True to her own dreams throughout her remarkable life, she showed the world she could amount to something.

MARKER LOCATIONS: 101 N. East St., Atlanta; 430 E. MLK, Waxahachie.

Stinson Airport, the primary general aviation airport in San Antonio, has a colorful history involving a fascinating family of early-twentieth-century aviation pioneers. Spanning the history of flight from barnstormers to jets, the site's significance is tied to its association with two of the earliest women aviators in the United States—sisters Katherine and Marjorie Stinson—as well as their mother, Emma, and brothers Eddie and Jack.

A serious student of music, Alabama native Katherine Stinson (1891–1977) decided to take flying lessons when she read a newspaper article about stunt pilots, hoping to earn enough money for a trip to Europe to further her musical education. She convinced famed aviator Max Lillie of Chicago to take her on as a student, and in 1912 she became the fourth licensed woman pilot in the nation. A skilled aviatrix, she soon forgot about her musical training and concentrated on aviation instead, setting new records for stunt and distance flying. Her siblings Marjorie and Eddie took lessons at the Wright Flying School in Ohio—Marjorie became the ninth licensed woman pilot in the United States—and together with their mother and other brother, Jack, the Stinsons operated the Stinson Aviation Company in Hot Springs, Arkansas. Lillie, who relocated to San Antonio to take advantage of better winter flying conditions afforded by the temperate South Texas weather, encouraged the Stinsons to move to Texas, as well. They heeded his advice, and by 1914 both Katherine and Marjorie worked as flight instructors for American and Canadian military pilots at Fort Sam Houston. Within a few years, Marjorie negotiated a deal with the City of San Antonio to lease five hundred acres on which the family established the Stinson School of Flying. While Marjorie and Eddie offered both flight and mechanical instruction, Katherine flew in air shows and exhibitions; toured the United States, Europe, China, and Japan; and set new endurance and distance records, all the while raising money and generating publicity for the aviation school. During World War I, Eddie Stinson worked as a civilian flight instructor at Kelly Field in San Antonio. Katherine and Marjorie volunteered for flying service during the war, were turned down because of their gender, and instead performed in exhibition flights to raise money for the American Red Cross. Katherine later served as a Red Cross ambulance driver in France during the war. While overseas, she contracted tuberculosis, the lasting effects of which caused the end of her flying career in the

Katherine Stinson, circa 1918.
Courtesy Texas Historical Commission resource files.

1920s. She moved to Santa Fe, New Mexico, where she married former World War I fighter pilot Miguel Otero and became an architect. She died at age 86 in 1977.

Marjorie Stinson (1895–1975) continued flying after the war and toured the country as a barnstormer. She later moved to Washington and worked for the U.S. Navy as an aeronautical draftsman. She retired in 1945 and spent years researching aviation history. Upon her death in 1975, her family scattered her ashes over Stinson Airport. Jack Stinson (1900–76), who began his career in aviation working as a mechanic with his sisters in San Antonio, held a number of aviation jobs and eventually founded the Stinson School of Aviation in Long Island, New York, where he trained pilots for World War II. He died in 1976, a year after his sister Marjorie, and his ashes, like hers, were scattered over Stinson Airport. Eddie Stinson (1893–1932) became an aircraft designer and established the Stinson Aircraft Corporation in 1926. Tragically, he died in a plane crash in 1932.

In recognition of the Stinson family legacy and the importance of their airfield to the history of aviation in Texas, the Texas Historical Commission placed an Official Texas Historical Marker at Stinson Airport in 2001.

MARKER LOCATION
8535 Mission Rd., San Antonio

Sources: Stinson Airport, Bexar County, THC marker files; Christine A. Keffeler, "Katherine Stinson," New Handbook of Texas, vol. 6, p. 105.

18 "HELLOOO, BABY!"

[Ring! Ring!] Hellooo, Baby!

Thus begins one of the most recognized song openings from the early years of rock and roll. Written at the last minute to fill the "B" side of a record, the song, "Chantilly Lace," was an instant hit in 1958. Its composer, a radio disc jockey from Beaumont, Texas, named J. P. Richardson, was better known by his on-air persona, the Big Bopper. Sadly, the Big Bopper is remembered primarily for the tragic manner in which he died—in a plane crash in a snowy field in rural Iowa along with fellow musicians Buddy Holly and Ritchie Valens. Don McLean's 1971 song "American Pie" later immortalized the event as "the day the music died." Prior to that fateful flight in 1959, however, the Big Bopper led a colorful life in Beaumont.

Jiles Perry Richardson Jr. was born in Sabine Pass on October 24, 1930, to oilfield roughneck Jiles Perry Richardson Sr. and his wife, Elsie Stalsby Richardson. His family and friends called him J. P. or Jape. When he was six years old and about to enter first grade, the family moved to nearby Beaumont. Eventually, after growing to a family of five with the addition of two more sons, the Richardsons lived in the working-class neighborhood of Multimax Village, a World War II–era federal housing project built for Beaumont's wartime shipyard workers. Developing an appreciation of music from his mother, an accomplished amateur musician who played guitar and piano to entertain her family, young J. P. began playing on a toy guitar purchased from Sears and listened to the radio to learn popular songs of the time. As a teenager, he wrote songs, sang in the high school choir, and performed individually for school assemblies. He also played football for the Beaumont High School

Royal Purples. His nickname, "Killer," was a tongue-in-cheek moniker given to the soft-spoken, good-natured J. P. by his teammates. After graduating in 1947, Richardson enrolled in Lamar College as a pre-law student and, wanting to continue his involvement with music, played cymbals in the college marching band.[1]

Richardson soon got a part-time job as an announcer at a new Beaumont radio station, KTRM (990 AM; now KZZB). At that time, the city had a professional minor league baseball team, the Beaumont Exporters of the Texas League, and the station manager assigned him to perform sound effects for broadcasts of the team's games. Popular with the KTRM staff as well as the listening public, Richardson quit college by 1949 to work full-time at the radio station. In one of his early gigs, he hosted the "Club 990 Show" from 9:00 P.M. to midnight, playing easy listening songs and dubbing himself the "Head Waiter of Club 990." His smooth on-air personality and music selection made him a local celebrity. Before long he also hosted an afternoon show on which his sidekick, a rubber squeeze-toy frog named Aloysious that "talked," provided humor along with the music. By the early 1950s, J. P. Richardson was the most popular disc jockey in the Golden Triangle (Beaumont, Orange, Port Arthur) of Southeast Texas. By all accounts, his energetic and outgoing on-air persona contrasted sharply with his naturally quiet, almost shy demeanor.

In early 1952, Richardson met Adrianne "Teetsie" Fryou on a blind date, and his life changed. The daughter of a sugarcane farmer from Montegut, Louisiana, Teetsie moved to Beaumont to help out when her sister had a baby. Her sister and brother-in-law asked a family friend to introduce Teetsie to a nice young man, and he brought J. P. Richardson to their house. Both Teetsie and J. P. reportedly told friends and family it was love at first sight; they married at St. Anthony's Catholic Church just over two months later on April 18, 1952.[2]

Rising to a supervisory position at the radio station by early 1953, Richardson worked with a colorful cast of announcers and disc jockeys. KTRM on-air staff often played pranks on each other, and the station was a lively place to work. One of his colleagues, Gordon Baxter, known for storytelling and early talk radio, became a close friend. Future country and western singing star George Jones, who worked as a KTRM announcer for a short time, later had a hit record with one of Richardson's songs. During this time radio was the primary source of news and entertainment for most people, particularly in Southeast Texas, before television became widely available. Radio station personalities were in great demand as hosts of local events and commercial activities such as business openings and sales promotions. J. P. Richardson's popularity soon caught the attention of a number of the station's sponsors who wanted him to promote their interests on KTRM. Whenever Richardson made personal appearances around the region, playing music and performing commercials for the sponsors, business improved.

Advertising gimmicks became popular in the 1950s, as well, around the same time rhythm and blues, bebop, and rockabilly music began to take hold. Challenged to come up with a new gimmick to attract listeners to the station, Richardson said he liked bebop music, and he was a big man, so he would become the Big Bopper. The character he created was boisterous, slightly outrageous, and very cool, spinning the latest rhythm and blues records and giving the advertisers and station executives exactly what they wanted—a high-energy personality who effectively sold products and brought thousands of listeners to KTRM. Richardson had fun with the Big Bopper character, chattering along with the records and building up a large fan base of listeners. The character differed so much from the real J. P. that many people had no idea Richardson and the Big Bopper were one and the same, and he liked it that way. Archie P. McDonald, a professor of history at Stephen F. Austin State University who grew up in Beaumont, remembered decades later the surprise he felt in learning J. P. Richardson was the Big Bopper. McDonald often kept the radio on in his bedroom, listening to the mellow sounds of the "Club 990 Show" even though, as he said, "I was not supposed to be up that late at night."[3] Richardson began writing songs for himself and other artists, and a friend, Bill Hall, became the Big Bopper's manager. By this time J. P. and Teetsie were the parents of a daughter, Debra, and he was mindful of the need to earn a good salary to support his family. But just as his fame began to spread throughout the region, bringing with it the possibility of recording contracts and career advancement, he received greetings from the U.S. government.

After Richardson's draft notice arrived in March 1955, his buddies at the radio station sent him off with a farewell party and gifts, and he spent the next two years in the U.S. Army, stationed at Fort Bliss in El Paso. While he worked as a radar instructor, Teetsie supplemented his meager military pay by starching uniforms for other soldiers. Discharged as a corporal in the spring of 1957, Richardson eagerly returned to Beaumont to resume his radio career at KTRM. He pitched an idea to station owner Jack Neil, hoping to make a splash with his return to the station. He wanted to stage a Disc-a-thon in which he would stay on the air continuously and try to beat the standing record of 122 hours set by an El Paso disc jockey. Neil eventually agreed to the plan, and Richardson lined up sponsors. In addition to the publicity value for the station, he also intended to make some extra money and promote the Big Bopper.

The Disc-a-thon began at noon on April 29, 1957. The lobby of Beaumont's downtown Jefferson Theatre served as a temporary studio where the public could gather on the sidewalk outside and watch the action through the large front windows. In the crowd was a teenaged Archie McDonald, who remembered his astonishment at seeing Richardson's crew cut hair style—a clean-cut image that did not mesh with his idea of how a rock and roll deejay should look. He also remembered an ambulance and medical crew standing by outside the theater.[4] Richardson received a complete physical exam before beginning the stunt, and a doctor remained on call to monitor him until the end. He took cold showers during five-minute news breaks ten times a day, chain-smoked cigarettes, drank gallons of coffee, at times breathed pure oxygen administered by his wife, and received continuous encouragement from family, friends, colleagues, and fans who came by the theater to watch him spin records and to cheer him on to victory. When it was all over on May 4, he had broken the record by staying on the air for 122 hours and 8 minutes. He played a total of 1,821 songs, culminating triumphantly and appropriately with Elvis Presley's "All Shook Up."

The Disc-a-thon took a heavy toll on the disc jockey, however. Friends reported he suffered hallucinations toward the end, and his brother Cecil later told a reporter he had almost given up and "actually cried for his mother over the air." His friend and fellow announcer Gordon Baxter told of a conversation he had with J. P. near the end of the marathon: "Bax, I've died. Honest to God, I've died, been across and back. They talked to me. It's okay, Bax, don't be afraid to die. It was light over there, and warm. I didn't want to come back."[5] Richardson left the studio on a stretcher, taken by ambulance to a local hospital to recover, and reportedly slept for 24 hours. But the Disc-a-thon was a rousing promotional success, earning money for the station, local charities, and Richardson, who received about $750 in overtime pay. More importantly, it cemented the Big Bopper's fame. He went on to take part in additional promotional stunts for the station, and while none rivaled the Disc-a-thon in physical endurance, all remained popular with local fans.

While working as the most famous disc jockey in Southeast Texas, Richardson also pursued songwriting. Personally a fan of country music, he had some success in selling tunes recorded by a number of artists in Texas and Louisiana. At the same time, rock and roll novelty songs began to hit the charts, and Richardson often played a couple of those songs—"Witch Doctor" by David Seville and "The Purple People Eater" by Sheb Wooley—on his radio shows. Capitalizing on the novelty fad, the Big Bopper collaborated with his friend Gordon Ritter to write "The Purple People Eater Meets the Witch Doctor" in 1958. Houston recording studio executive Pappy Daily agreed to record it with the Big Bopper on vocals, but he wanted a second song for the "B" side. Traveling with his friend and fellow KTRM announcer Jerry Boynton from Beaumont to Houston for the recording session, Richardson worked on a new song that soon eclipsed anything he had done before. According to his brother Cecil, "He started writing the song in Liberty, Texas, and had it done by the time they arrived in Houston"—a distance of forty-three miles.[6] The song was "Chantilly Lace." With its opening telephone ring, catchy tune, and amusing lyrics relating a boy's conversation with his girlfriend, it became an instant hit.

The Big Bopper, Mercury Records promotional photo. With the phenomenal success of his record Chantilly Lace *propelling him to the top of the charts, J. P. Richardson appeared in concert in the persona of his alter-ego, the Big Bopper, complete with flashy wardrobe and lace and telephone props.* Courtesy Museum of the Gulf Coast, Port Arthur.

Almost immediately after the record's release, Richardson was in demand as a stage performer. Appearing as the jive-talking Big Bopper, clad in a flashy leopard-print or striped coat and using a prop phone as he sang "Chantilly Lace," he charmed audiences everywhere he went. By early fall, he made his national television debut on Dick Clark's *Saturday Night Beechnut Show* (a precursor to Clark's long-running *American Bandstand* show). "Chantilly Lace" made *Billboard* magazine's Top 100 within days of the television

broadcast and by the end of the year sold a million copies. Richardson embarked on an East Coast concert tour later that year, and
although he disliked touring because it took him away from his
family, it was a boon to his career and helped sell records. Almost
overnight, the Big Bopper was a national star.

With rock and roll music taking the country by storm, record
producers and concert promoters arranged for the genre's stars
to make personal appearances at everything from supermarket
openings and local high school dances to events at large concert
venues. Dances for teenagers, billed as wholesome entertainment
and often including invitations for their parents to attend, as well,
became particularly popular in small-town America. One such
promotional tour began its sojourn through the upper Midwest in
January 1959. Planned as a three-week extravaganza and booked
to play mostly in ballrooms and armories in Wisconsin, Minnesota, and Iowa, the Winter Dance Party tour boasted some of rock
and roll's hottest rising stars, including Dion and the Belmonts,
Buddy Holly and the Crickets, Ritchie Valens, and the Big Bopper.
The musicians all had different reasons for joining the tour. Some,
including seventeen-year-old Ritchie Valens of Pacoima, California,
and J. P. Richardson, both riding a wave of newfound fame with
hit songs, hoped for major advancements in their nascent careers.
Others, including the acknowledged star of the tour, Buddy Holly
of Lubbock, Texas, already enjoyed wide success. But Holly, in the
midst of a financial tug-of-war with his manager, signed on as
much for the money as for the public exposure.

The Million Dollar Ballroom in Milwaukee, Wisconsin, hosted
the opening night performance of the tour on January 23, 1959. A
Milwaukee Sentinel reporter wrote in the following day's paper: "It
was crazy, daddy—the goings-on Friday night at George Devine's
Million Dollar Ballroom. Nearly 6,000 young people turned out to
hear such rock 'n' roll stars as Buddy Holly and the Crickets, Big
Bopper, Dion and the Belmonts and Ritchie Valens. If you haven't
heard them, you haven't lived, man." The effusive reviewer praised
not only the show's performers but rock and roll music in general.
He went on to say, "The liveliest performance was Big Bopper, a
chubby crewcut cat, who sported a leopard skin coat and white

Winter Dance Party poster, Surf Ballroom, Clear Lake, Iowa. Joining a marathon tour of the upper Midwest to promote his burgeoning singing career, J. P. Richardson appeared with some of the most popular rock and roll musicians in the country. Courtesy Museum of the Gulf Coast, Port Arthur.

bucks. He stomped and shuffled his weight around with ease and—surprisingly enough—he had the voice to match his bulk. Everybody demanded and got his hit version of 'Chantilly Lace.'"[7]

Despite an auspicious opening night, and although enthusiastically received by audiences wherever they played, the musicians suffered through a tour plagued with logistical problems from the outset. Tour managers arranged for the troupe to travel by bus from town to town during a time when the region experienced one of the coldest winters in recent memory. Bouncing back and forth on a poorly planned itinerary from state to state and town to town, with temperatures often falling below zero, the converted school bus carrying the bands had constant mechanical and heating problems. On at least one occasion, the group ended up stranded on the side of the road in subfreezing weather when it broke down. The worst problem proved to be a lack of heat on the bus, to the extent that the Crickets' drummer, Carl Bunch, ended up in a hospital with frostbitten feet. He remained hospitalized when the musicians played to a sold-out crowd at the Surf Ballroom in Clear Lake, Iowa, on the night of February 2. By that time, fed up with the abominable traveling conditions, they dreaded getting back on the tour bus. Richardson bought a sleeping bag from a local sporting goods store, hoping it would help him get some sleep on the freezing bus as it traveled through the night to the next gig. As it turned out, however, he would never use that new sleeping bag.[8]

Visiting backstage with the owner of the Surf Ballroom, Buddy Holly asked about the possibility of chartering a plane to take him and the remaining two Crickets, Tommy Allsup and Waylon Jennings, to the tour's next gig. He hoped to get some sleep and have his laundry done, then meet the rest of the group in time for the show the following night. The club owner called a friend at the nearby Mason City airport and arranged for a local pilot, Roger Peterson, to fly Holly and his friends to Fargo, North Dakota, the airport nearest to Moorhead, Minnesota, the next stop on the tour. As word of the air travel plan spread among the musicians, destiny changed for Allsup and Jennings. J. P. Richardson, feeling miserable because of a bad cold, asked Jennings for his seat on the plane,

The Big Bopper, Winter Dance Party tour, 1959. A reporter for the Milwaukee Sentinel *singled out the Big Bopper in his review of the show, praising the singer's rollicking performance of "Chantilly Lace" and other tunes.* Courtesy Museum of the Gulf Coast, Port Arthur.

offering his new sleeping bag in trade. Jennings, feeling sorry for his ailing friend, agreed. Meanwhile, Ritchie Valens tried to get Allsup to give up his seat, as well. Allsup initially refused, but ultimately Valens talked him into flipping a coin for the plane ride. It came up heads, and Valens won the seat.[9]

The three musicians reached the airport just after midnight. Peterson, who arrived shortly before them, warmed up the plane as snow started to fall. Each passenger paid a $36 fare and then boarded the plane, which took off at approximately 12:50 A.M. All appeared normal to the flight service owner, observing from the airport tower, until he saw the plane's taillight descend and then disappear. Efforts to reach the pilot by radio failed, and checks with airports along the route to Fargo revealed no contact with the plane. Several families living on farms near the Mason City airport later reported hearing a low-flying plane during the night, and one woman said it barely missed hitting her house. By midmorning on February 3 an air search revealed the wreckage of the plane, which crashed in a farm field about five miles north of the airport. There were no survivors. Musicians Buddy Holly, age twenty-two; J. P. Richardson, age twenty-eight; Ritchie Valens, age seventeen; and pilot Roger Peterson, age twenty-one, all died instantly upon impact. A Civil Aeronautics Board investigation later blamed the crash on a combination of the pilot's inexperience with instrument flying and an unreliable weather briefing that underestimated the severity of an approaching storm. It was rock and roll's first major celebrity tragedy.[10]

News of the crash spread quickly. The families of Buddy Holly and Ritchie Valens heard about it on the radio, as did the Big Bopper's brother-in-law, who rushed to tell his sister before she heard the news of her husband's death in such a shocking and impersonal way. J. P.'s colleagues at KTRM were not as lucky; they learned of the loss of their friend through a radio news bulletin. Teetsie Richardson, pregnant with her second child and staying with her family in Louisiana while J. P. was on tour, returned to Beaumont to prepare for his funeral. An overwhelming outpouring of grief and sympathy followed the Big Bopper's death. Elvis Presley, serving in the army in Germany, sent a floral arrangement in the shape of a guitar. Buddy Holly's mother sent a heartfelt letter to Teetsie, sharing in the young widow's grief even as she buried her own son. Crowds of mourners in Beaumont lined the route of the Big Bopper's funeral procession and people across the region tuned their radios to KTRM as Gordon Baxter played a Dixieland jazz tribute for his departed friend.[11]

Although "Chantilly Lace" earned a gold record, Richardson never got to see it or enjoy its success. The gold record instead went to his widow, who gave birth to a son, Jay Perry Richardson, in late April, three months after his father's death. Years later, in 2007, Jay P. Richardson arranged to have his father's body exhumed and examined by a forensic pathologist to set to rest rumors that the musicians on that fateful flight died from causes other than the crash itself. Months after the tragedy, when the snow melted, the farmer on whose land the wreck occurred came across the pistol that Buddy Holly carried in his luggage. Although friends confirmed Holly traveled with the gun because he often carried large amounts of cash to pay expenses, news of its discovery eventually gave rise to conspiracy theories. After the pathologist's investigation concurred with the original cause of death cited in the coroner's report—brain damage sustained by sudden trauma in the crash—the family reinterred the Big Bopper's remains in a more prominent location in Forest Lawn Memorial Park, on the northeast side of Beaumont, where an Official Texas Historical Marker now commemorates his life.[12] A number of J. P. Richardson's personal effects found at the crash site are displayed at the Museum of the Gulf Coast in Port Arthur, as part of an extensive exhibit on music legends of Southeast Texas. They include a pair of dice, a bottle of aspirin, a hairbrush, a mirror, and his watch, inscribed on the back: "KTRM Champion Disc-a-thon, 122 hrs 8 min, J P Richardson, 5–4–57."

Who can say what J. P. Richardson's ultimate impact on the music world would have been had he not died in that snowy field in Iowa? Many of his songs are still recognizable to rock and roll fans, including those he recorded like "Chantilly Lace," as well as others made popular by contemporary artists such as George Jones ("White Lightning") and Johnny Preston ("Running Bear").

Grave marker for Jiles Perry Richardson Jr. (the Big Bopper), Forest Lawn Memorial Park, Beaumont. Decorated with images of a guitar, a record, musical notes, and a radio microphone, the bronze plaque that marks his grave is a simple monument to a Southeast Texas music legend. Photograph by Cynthia J. Beeman.

He clearly was more than a "one-hit wonder," the dubious label attached to many early rock and roll stars. Some of his friends and family said his real goal was to have some fun, make some money, and then buy his own radio station someday. But with his life cut short after a mere twenty-eight years, the world will never know his ultimate potential.

MARKER LOCATION: 4955 Pine St., Beaumont

JEFFERSON THEATRE

The site of J. P. Richardson's record-breaking Disc-a-thon in 1957, the Jefferson Theatre in downtown Beaumont is one of the city's most revered landmarks. The opulent structure owes its existence, as do many of Southeast Texas' historic public buildings, to the phenomenal oil discoveries that shook the world in the early twentieth century. When the famed Spindletop oil well blew in on January 10, 1901, Beaumont changed literally overnight from a small, sleepy village to a wild, bustling boomtown. The modern oil era began with Spindletop, giving rise to numerous international oil companies and generating a new class of millionaires. A second major discovery at Spindletop in 1925 ushered in another wave of prosperity, resulting in the construction of many civic and cultural facilities in Jefferson County.

Designed by New Orleans architect Emile Weil and financed by the Jefferson Amusement Company, the Jefferson Theatre became a landmark virtually from the day of its completion. A feature article in the November 15, 1927, edition of the *Beaumont Journal* gushed, "Surpassing the most exquisite structure yet attempted in Beaumont, equal in beauty to the elaborate show places of ancient Greece, replete with architectural and engineering ingenuity, the million dollar Jefferson Theatre is ready to swing open its doors to patrons of Southeast Texas." The theatre boasted an intricately designed interior with Italian marble stairs and floors, crystal chandeliers, ornate painting and tile work, plush carpets, leather-covered seats, and an elaborate proscenium arch. The crown jewel, though, was the Robert Morton Wonder Organ, powered by a ten-horsepower motor and featuring 778 pipes. The "wonder" in the instrument's name referred to its capability to mimic sounds as varied as birdcalls and other animal noises, automobile and fog horns, cathedral chimes, and brass and stringed instruments. Hosting live theatre and musical performances as well as films, the Jefferson remained a popular gathering place until

Jefferson Theatre, Beaumont. The site of J. P. Richardson's 1957 Disc-a-thon, the 1927 Jefferson Theatre is a treasured landmark in Beaumont's downtown historic district. Courtesy Texas Historical Commission historic survey files.

the early 1970s, when downtown Beaumont fell on hard times. Briefly leased to an evangelist, it eventually closed and remained empty until the Jefferson Theatre Preservation Society, formed by the Beaumont Junior Forum and the Junior League of Beaumont, purchased it in 1975 and began raising funds for its restoration. The society, joined by numerous entities including the Beaumont Main Street Project, successfully spearheaded a massive restoration project that returned the grand building to its original glory and refurbished its most cherished features, including the wonder organ. A cornerstone in the redevelopment and preservation of Beaumont's downtown historic district, the Jefferson Theatre reclaimed its role as the town's premier cultural arts venue.

MARKER LOCATION

345 Fannin St., Beaumont

Sources: Jefferson Theatre, Jefferson County, THC marker files and THC NR files; East Texas Historical Association, Terry Preservation Award nomination.

CITY OF LUBBOCK CEMETERY

While Buddy Holly is fondly remembered and celebrated in his hometown of Lubbock, most prominently at the Buddy Holly Center in the restored Fort Worth and Denver South Plains Railway Depot downtown, there is as yet no Official Texas Historical Marker dedicated specifically to him. He is, however, mentioned in the marker for the City of Lubbock Cemetery, where his final resting place still draws tourists and fans a half-century after his death. Originally platted on five acres of pastureland in 1892, the cemetery began with the burial of Henry Jenkins, a cowboy from nearby Cochran County who died of pneumonia while staying in a Lubbock hotel in March of that year. Now encompassing more than 160 acres and containing some sixty thousand burials, the cemetery provides a capsule history of the town on the Texas High Plains. Until the late 1960s, the graveyard remained segregated along racial, ethnic, religious, and economic lines, and several cemetery associations cared for different sections. One group, Los Socios del Sementerio, also provided for burials of migrant farm workers in the area. Now unified as one large burial ground, the City of Lubbock Cemetery is one of the largest in Texas and contains a number of impressive monuments. An eleven-foot stone angel, the work of noted sculptor Charles Umlauf commissioned by the cemetery board in 1958, stands not far from Buddy Holly's burial site. The unassuming tombstone that marks the rock and roll musician's grave features a bas relief carving of his electric guitar and a simple epitaph—with the family spelling of his surname—that reads: "In loving memory of our own Buddy Holley, September 7, 1936–February 3, 1959."

MARKER LOCATION

Just south of the main entrance to Lubbock City Cemetery at 2011 E. 31st St., on road marked "Azalea," Lubbock

Sources: City of Lubbock Cemetery THC marker and HTC files; City of Lubbock Cemetery brochure, Lubbock.

19
THE THEATER
OF TOMORROW
TODAY

As a child in the small East Texas town of Livingston, Margo Jones often walked to the Polk County Courthouse on the town square, climbed the stairs to the balcony, and watched as her attorney father tried cases in the courtroom below. Captivated by his impassioned arguments before the court, she thought of becoming a lawyer until one day she suddenly realized her true fascination lay not in the legal arguments she observed but in the drama of the courtroom. Staging performances in the family barn with her brothers and sister, Margo Jones preferred not to act in plays—she wanted to produce and direct them. "It wasn't until I was eleven that I decided positively to be a play director," she later told a reporter. "By this time I had learned that my father's law practice was interesting to me primarily because it dealt with the dramatics of human nature—the very drama of life fascinated me and I knew that I must direct plays in order to satisfy myself."[1]

Born December 12, 1911, in Livingston, Margaret Virginia Jones—known simply as Margo—grew up in a two-story frame house with an older sister and two younger brothers. Her sister's death from influenza on New Year's Day 1925 devastated Margo, and, determined to leave Polk County, she took extra classes and graduated from high school early at age fifteen. In the fall of 1927, she enrolled in the College of Industrial Arts (later Texas Woman's University) in Denton. Although the school did not offer a degree in theater, it had a drama club. Jones joined it and performed as an actor, but directing remained her chief interest. As often as her class schedule and finances allowed, she traveled to nearby Dallas to attend theater performances, studying details of staging as she watched the plays. Working part-time at the college library, she pored over old issues of *Theatre Arts Monthly* magazine, avidly reading about U.S. and European theater history and current trends in the dramatic arts. She read the Greek classics as well as works by William Shakespeare, Anton Chekhov, Henrik Ibsen, and contemporary playwrights such as Eugene O'Neill. She earned a bachelor's degree in speech in 1932, followed by a master's degree in educational psychology in 1933. Her thesis explored the psychology of female characters in three of Ibsen's plays.[2]

Diploma in hand, Jones boldly set out for Dallas and talked her way into a scholarship at the Southwestern School of the Theatre. She attended classes in all aspects of theatrics and impressed her teachers with her eagerness to learn and her boundless enthusiasm. John Rosenfield, the influential theater and arts critic for the *Dallas Morning News* whom she had met while publicizing college productions from Denton, observed her progress with interest and served as a mentor. Within a year, she applied for and won a place at the summer school of the prestigious Pasadena Playhouse in California. An acclaimed community theater and workshop, the Playhouse attracted talented young actors, directors, and playwrights, including fellow Texan Horton Foote of Wharton.

Gaining valuable experience and working with people who would remain a part of her professional life, Jones completed the summer school and then took advantage of an opportunity to direct a play at the nearby Ojai Community Theatre. When a wealthy Ojai arts patron invited her on a trip around the world, Jones spent the spring and summer of 1935 experiencing theater in Asia, Africa, and Europe. She returned to the United States via New York in September and briefly spent time in the city, where she attended a performance of the Group Theatre, an ensemble company formed by the famed Lee Strasberg and others, and renewed her determination to make the theater her life's work. Although excited by New York theater, she embraced the small but growing idea of decentralization—the establishment of professional resident theaters throughout the country, away from an exclusive New York center. Thinking she should begin in her own backyard, she returned to Texas to work with the Houston Federal Theatre Project. One of Pres. Franklin D. Roosevelt's Depression-era New

Deal relief efforts, the Federal Theatre Project, under auspices of the Works Progress Administration, began in May 1935 with the goal of providing jobs for unemployed theater professionals. Its director, Hallie Flanagan, inspired Jones with her dream of establishing a national theater network. Operating within the city's recreation department, the Houston project provided significant leadership experience for the aspiring director.

Determined to return to Europe, and particularly to travel to Russia for the renowned Moscow Art Theatre Festival, Jones finagled an appointment as a delegate to the festival from the Texas Centennial Commission and, in order to pay for the trip, convinced the editor of the *Houston Chronicle* to hire her as a correspondent. Amazed by the enthusiasm of the diverse Russian theater audiences, which ranged from wealthy aristocrats to poor farmers and peasants, she became more convinced of her belief that culture lay at the heart of a country's soul. Brooks Atkinson, theatre critic for the *New York Times,* also attended the Moscow festival, and Jones used the opportunity to meet him. According to biographer Helen Sheehy, Jones waited for Atkinson in a Moscow hotel lobby and, upon seeing him, walked up and said, "Mr. Atkinson, my name is Margo Jones. You don't know me, but someday you will."[3] Her words proved prophetic, for Atkinson became one of her greatest supporters in subsequent years, writing often about her career in his newspaper column. Her larger-than-life personality became a sort of trademark, with her ebullient greetings—always in her exaggerated Texas drawl, beginning with "Baby," "Darling," or "Honey"—captivating her listeners and more often than not getting her exactly what she wanted.

Jones returned to Houston in the fall of 1936 and convinced the city recreation department to fund a resident amateur theater, the Houston Community Players, which she directed for the next seven years. The company of actors, writers, and technical workers included Nina Vance, later founder and artistic director of Houston's famed Alley Theater; actor Ray Walston, later a star in Broadway productions, television, and motion pictures; and writer William Goyen—like Jones, a native of East Texas (born in Trinity, thirty-five miles from Livingston)—who became a successful playwright, screenwriter, and novelist.[4] The Houston Community Players mounted a variety of theatrical plays and musicals, and in addition to her duties as director and promoter, Jones became actively involved in the national scene by serving on the board of the National Theatre Conference (NTC), an organization that published educational materials and encouraged the growth of regional theater throughout the country. In 1939, on a trip to Washington, D.C., for an NTC meeting, Jones saw a play presented "in-the-round" by a company from Portland, Oregon.

Impressed by the production and enthralled by the possibilities of presenting plays on a center stage surrounded by the audience, rather than in a more formal and traditional proscenium stage arrangement, Jones determined to try the approach in Houston. The innovative production design, known as arena theater or theater-in-the-round, gradually gained supporters within the nation's theater community, and its widespread popularity is largely credited to the enthusiastic promotion of Margo Jones. According to an account written years later by William Goyen, she convinced the Houston City Council to fund her plan to stage the 1939 summer season of the Houston Community Players in a ballroom in the downtown Lamar Hotel, where she could use the theater-in-the-round approach. Goyen remembered her impassioned appeal at a council meeting, quoting her famously earthy mode of speech: "Honey, I don't care *what* it costs, you got the money. Houston's got the money. Give me the Grand Ballroom in the Lamar Hotel. What the hell's a *ballroom* when you haven't got a damn *ball?* When you can have *theatah,* when you can have *plays?* Wonderful, magical plays. Honey, we got to have some magic, some *wonder.* Give me that *ballroom.*"[5] Her legendary powers of persuasion worked, and the company produced a successful season in the hotel ballroom. Jones continued to direct the Houston Community Players for the next three years, staging plays in ballrooms at several downtown hotels. Always on the lookout for new works to produce, she traveled to New York in the summer of 1942 and met with a theatrical agent who gave her a script by a young writer named Tennessee Williams. Entranced with the play and identifying strongly with its southern themes, Margo wanted to know more about the playwright. "In a few months," Sheehy wrote, "Margo would meet Mr. Williams, a fellow 'cottonchopper.' She'd call him 'baby' and would buy the beers."[6]

Resigning from her position in Houston in September 1942, Jones moved to Austin where, funded by a Rockefeller Foundation grant, she taught drama at the University of Texas (UT). A feature article in the arts section of the *Austin Tribune* heralded her arrival, relating her views on theater-in-the-round and praising her recent distinction as "the only woman selected by *Stage Magazine* as one of the 10 outstanding young directors in America."[7] In the same issue of the *Tribune*, a small article announced a speech by Dr. E. William Doty, Dean of Fine Arts at UT and Jones's new boss, at the upcoming meeting of the Woman's Culture Club of Llano, some seventy miles west of Austin.

Jones approached her new position from the perspective of a theater professional, rather than as an academic, and inevitably ruffled a few feathers at the university, including those of the dean. When Doty insisted she use a full grading scale in evaluating her students, rather than giving each one either an A or an F, she told him, "Oh no, oh no, darling, you either belong in the theatre or you don't."[8] Tremendously popular among the students—if not the faculty—the hard-charging, chain-smoking, heavy-drinking, freely cussing Jones guided productions of the classics as well as newer experimental pieces at the university theater. On a trip to New York City in November 1942, she met Tennessee Williams, and the encounter marked the beginning of their longtime professional association and personal friendship. She brought copies of several of his plays back to Austin, and the following summer she returned to California to direct the Pasadena Playhouse summer school. All the while, she used her growing theater contacts in New York and around the country to promote Tennessee Williams as a brilliant, up-and-coming playwright. Williams, also living in California that summer, spent countless hours with Jones discussing *You Touched Me*, a new play co-written with Donald Windham that she wanted to produce.

In the fall she took a leave of absence from UT to stage *You Touched Me* at the Cleveland Playhouse in Ohio, a prestigious regional amateur theater similar to the Pasadena Playhouse. Never one to pass up a golden opportunity, she used the press attention the Cleveland production afforded to begin earnestly promoting her plan for a national network of professional theaters, decentralized from New York, that would produce new works in addition to reviving the classics and hosting touring companies of Broadway productions. Williams, also basking in the press attention showered on his play, told a friend Margo Jones was the "most vital accident of my life," calling her a combination of "Joan of Arc and Gene Autry—and nitroglycerine!"[9]

Following the successful Cleveland production, Jones returned to Austin and her students but continued to bristle under the university's academic requirements. By 1944, ready for another challenge and encouraged by her friend John Rosenfield in Dallas, she applied to the Rockefeller Foundation for another grant to begin her long-held dream of establishing a national theater network. Asking for travel funds to tour amateur theaters around the country to gather information for her plan, she wrote in her application, "I believe in decentralized theatre. I believe there is no reason why good theatre should be bottle-necked in New York. . . . I believe in a dramatic map for America that will include great native play-houses in every town large enough to want one."[10] With Rosenfield's support and his pledge to help her establish a professional theater in Dallas at the culmination of the project, she received the grant and toured the country, reading new plays by a variety of playwrights as she traveled. She read Tennessee Williams's *The Glass Menagerie* and immediately knew it was a masterpiece. When presented with the opportunity to serve as assistant director of the play's Chicago tryout in advance of its debut on Broadway, she interrupted her Rockefeller fellowship to accept the offer. At one point during rehearsals, she successfully defended the integrity of the play when a producer wanted Williams to rewrite it to have a happy ending.

Having gained the cachet of association with a Broadway production, and with the continued advocacy of Rosenfield, Jones caught the attention of influential arts patrons in Dallas who requested she return to Texas and launch the professional theater

Now there didn't seem to be any limits."[15] Seeking to relieve tension by taking on another form of artistic expression, she asked Joe Glasco, an artist friend of Goyen, to teach her to paint. He gave her a set of oil paints and canvases and a few lessons.

On July 11, the three friends returned to Jones's apartment in the Stoneleigh Hotel after a night at the theater. Glasco left after a short time, but Goyen remained with Margo until her behavior became erratic. Writing about that night years later, he described a desperate scene. Jones, smoking, drinking vodka from a bottle, and dancing naked around the room as music blared from a record player, grabbed her oil paints and began flinging the bright colors onto the walls, carpet, and furniture. Goyen fled the apartment and returned to New York the next day.[16]

Despite a hangover, Jones went to work at the theater the following morning. When her assistant arrived at the apartment and found it covered in paint, she arranged for a hotel housekeeper to clean the mess. Unable to remove all the stains from the carpet, the hotel staff called in a professional cleaning service whose workers used chemical solvents to dissolve the last of the paint and finish cleaning the apartment. Returning home that evening, Jones sat on the floor reading scripts until she fell asleep. Feeling ill the next morning, she grew sicker through the day and overnight with a mysterious rash and a fever, until finally a doctor admitted her to a hospital. Her physicians called in a specialist to diagnose her ailment, which turned out to be toxic poisoning caused by carbon tetrachloride, the solvent used to clean the carpet. Her condition worsened, and on Sunday, July 24, 1955, she lapsed into a coma and died. The official cause of death was listed as kidney failure.

Newspapers across the country announced the death of the forty-three-year-old director and heralded her contributions to the theater. An editorial in the *Dallas Morning News* said, "Margo Jones loved to talk, loved to laugh, and loved the theater . . . she loved it completely, without question and without reservation. . . . Margo was a theater person inside and out, down to her toes." William Goyen sent a letter to the *Morning News* two days later, writing, "We all know what Margo has done for all of us, and for so many more. She provided that rare 'surround' of magic and WON-DERMENT, as she called it, which brightened life. She was always one to call in support of any project, and she gave her 'Margo-ness' to it. That is irreplaceable, and all our loss." Condolences poured into Theatre '55 from all over the country, and friends, colleagues, and family attended a funeral service in Dallas before the return of Jones's body to her hometown of Livingston for burial. Two months later, in response to the publicity surrounding her death, the National Institute of Rug Cleaning trade association issued a nationwide press release warning against the use of carbon tetra-chloride "for any sort of home cleaning."[17]

Theatre '55, renamed the Margo Jones Theatre, continued in operation with the support of its board and Dallas arts patrons for a few years, but loss of revenue and prestige following Jones's death led to its closing at the end of 1959. Her legacy continues, however. Her dream of decentralized professional theater in the United States became a reality, with hundreds of nonprofit resident theaters across the country showcasing new productions and providing stepping stones to Broadway, film, and television for writers, actors, and others in the theater profession. Dallas philanthropists Eugene and Margaret McDermott—major supporters of Jones's theater from its inception—donated funds to establish the Margo Jones Theatre at Southern Methodist University, and a theater at Texas Woman's University also bears her name. In 1961, *Inherit the Wind* playwrights Jerome Lawrence and Robert E. Lee inaugurated an annual Margo Jones Award for "the producer or theatre executive who best carries out the spirit of the late Margo Jones in encouraging new plays and new playwrights." Two Official Texas Historical Markers commemorate her life and accomplishments—one at her family's former home in Livingston, and the other at her gravesite in the town's Forest Hill Cemetery. Her philosophy, which she detailed in her book, provides a fitting epitaph: "I believe that, as a result of theatre, life can be better. . . . I want for other people what I want for myself: to live life to its fullest, to see good plays, to read good books, to see great paintings, to hear fine music and so on with all the fine experiences the world offers. I believe that children in every community should grow up with the opportunity to see the great plays of the past and the present because it will make life more exciting for them. . . . With more great theatre, great art, great music throughout the world, life is bound to be better."[18]

MARKER LOCATIONS: 517 S. Washington St., Livingston (birthplace); Forest Hill Cemetery, 1700 S. Washington St., Livingston (grave)

STONELEIGH HOTEL

Designed by Dallas architect Frank J. Woerner and built in 1923, the Stoneleigh Hotel on Maple Avenue offered Dallasites a new kind of residence—the apartment hotel. Apartment hotels, already in widespread use in larger cities of the Northeast and based on "flats" or efficiency hotels popular in Paris as early as the seventeenth century, offered city dwellers convenient homes close to downtown offices. Marketed to an upscale clientele as "the ideal home where all housekeeping problems have been solved for you," the Stoneleigh quickly became an elegant address for the city's elite. Residents chose from a wide array of amenities, including linen service, maid service, full kitchens or compact kitchenettes, and grocery delivery from a market in the basement. Separate kitchen entrances leading off the hallways allowed hotel cleaning staff to access the apartments without disturbing the residents, and smaller units included such innovative touches as Murphy beds and foldaway ironing boards. An on-site refrigeration plant provided each room with chilled water and air conditioning, and interior furnishings, including carpets, bedding, furniture, curtains, light fixtures, and kitchen appliances came from the Sanger Brothers Department Store in downtown Dallas. An elegantly appointed lobby greeted guests, who could also take advantage of comfortable lounges (one for men and another for women), a children's play area, a barbershop, a parking garage capable of housing forty automobiles, a dining room, and a ballroom.

In 1934, businessman Harry E. Stewart bought the operation, and during his ownership it became known as the Stoneleigh Court Hotel. Among the changes he ordered in a $100,000 renovation project were an Art Deco redesign of the lobby and the conversion of the entire eleventh floor into a luxury penthouse suite complete with marble floors, ornate tile work, elegant oak paneling imported from London, and antique furnishings. Located near the Dallas Little Theater on Maple Avenue, the hotel became a popular destination for visiting artists and celebrities and served

A Distinctive Address

Make your permanent home at the
Stoneleigh. You will find comfort and
sumptuous hospitality. Rooms, Suites
and Apartments by lease or by the
month.

....

The Stoneleigh

DON E. STEWART, Manager

Advertisement for the Stoneleigh Hotel, Dallas, 1936. Billed as an elegant home for the city's elite, the Stoneleigh offered apartment hotel living in downtown Dallas. Residents, including Margo Jones, enjoyed the convenience of a concierge service as well as numerous other amenities. Courtesy Texas Historical Commission, National Register of Historic Places files.

Historic photo, Stoneleigh Hotel, Dallas. An elegant building located on fashionable Maple Avenue, the Stoneleigh Hotel retains its historic appearance and remains a popular destination for visitors. Courtesy Texas Historical Commission, National Register of Historic Places files.

as a social center for the city's arts community in the early and mid-twentieth century. Writers, actors, and other theater professionals who came to town to attend productions or work at Theatre '47 often stayed at the hotel, and its director, Margo Jones, lived in a Stoneleigh apartment. Renovated several times over the years, the hotel remains a popular destination. In recognition of its architectural and historical significance, the owners listed it in the National Register of Historic Places in 2007.

LOCATION: 2927 Maple Ave., Dallas

Sources: Stoneleigh Court Hotel, Dallas County, THC NR files; Helen Sheehy, *Margo: The Life and Theatre of Margo Jones* (Dallas: Southern Methodist University Press, 1989).

SHERMAN LITTLE THEATER

The Little Theater movement, which popularized the establishment of small amateur community theaters, began in earnest in Texas in 1919 with a group known as the Green Mask Players in Houston. The Dallas Little Theater, established in 1920 and considered the most successful venture of its type in the state, built its own theater building in 1927 on stylish Maple Avenue not far from the Stoneleigh Hotel. By the 1930s, almost seventy little theaters staged plays in towns large and small across Texas. The citizens of Sherman, sixty-five miles north of Dallas in Grayson County, organized the Sherman Little Theater in 1925. With support from community groups, businesses, and professors and students at Austin College, the little theater debuted its first production, *Old Man Minick,* based on a short story by Edna Ferber, in 1926. Little theaters in Texas held annual festivals and competitions, and the same year it opened the Sherman Little Theater took first place in the play competition held in Dallas. With local citizens cast as actors, the Sherman Little Theater produced several plays each year, and widespread community support led to the group's incorporation as Sherman Community Players in 1950. A new performance hall, Finley Playhouse, opened in 1954, providing a per-

manent venue for plays, children's programs, and community events. The Texas Historical Commission awarded an Official Texas Historical Marker to the Sherman Little Theater (Sherman Community Players) in 2001 in recognition of its contributions to the cultural history of Grayson County.

MARKER LOCATION: 500 N. Elm St., Sherman

Sources: Sherman Little Theater (Sherman Community Players), Grayson County, THC marker files; Helen B. Frantz and Gynter Quill, "Little Theater Movement," *New Handbook of Texas,* vol. 4, p. 238.

Notes

CHAPTER 1. SAVING ELMER'S WOODS

1. Kleb Family House, Harris County, Official Texas Historical Marker files, Texas Historical Commission, Austin (hereafter cited as THC marker files). Additional sources for chapter 1 are from Kleb Woods Nature Preserve, Nature Center, and Heritage Farm, 20301 Mueschke Road, Tomball, Texas.

2. Kleb Family House marker file; Peter Applebome, "Rural Recluse Collides with an Unnatural World," *New York Times*, Nov. 9, 1988.

3. Kleb Family House marker file; Rob Meckel, "Fellow Dreamers Join Man's Quest," *Houston Post*, Nov. 21, 1988, section A, p. 1.

4. Kleb Family House marker file; Applebome, "Rural Recluse Collides."

5. John L. Tveten, "Recluse Wants Land to be Sanctuary," *Houston Chronicle*, Feb. 25, 1989, section E, p. 4.

6. Kleb Family House marker file; obituary, Elmer Kleb, *Houston Chronicle*, July 8, 1999, section A, p. 22.

7. Kleb Family House marker file.

8. Kim Jackson, "Kleb Nature Center, Farm Opens: Preservation of Property Keeps Northwest History from Disappearing," *Houston Chronicle*, Oct. 5, 2006, "This Week" section, p. 7; Betty L. Martin, "Nature Preserves Plan to Spread Wings in '07: Area Planning Bird Count on New Year's Day," *Houston Chronicle*, Dec. 28, 2006, "This Week" section, p. 1.

9. Thom Marshall, "Former Farm Becomes One with Nature: Family Land Turns into Preserve, as Last Resident Wished," *Houston Chronicle*, June 5, 2004, section A, p. 31.

CHAPTER 2. "WHILE YOU ARE HESITATING OTHERS ARE BUYING—ACT TO-DAY!"

1. Barbara Rozek, *Come to Texas: Attracting Immigrants, 1865–1915* (College Station: Texas A&M University Press, 2003), p. 141.

2. Rozek, *Come to Texas*, p. 145; Colorado County Historical Commission, *Colorado County Chronicles: From the Beginning to 1923*, vol. 1 (Austin: Nortex Press/Eakin Publications, 1986), p. 284.

3. *Colorado County Chronicles*, p. 295; F. B. Largent Jr., "Rock Island, Texas," *The New Handbook of Texas*, vol. 5 (Austin: The Texas State Historical Association, 1996), p. 636 (hereafter cited as *New Handbook of Texas*).

4. *Colorado County Chronicles*, pp. 296–98; Mark Odintz, "Cheetham, Texas," *New Handbook of Texas*, vol. 2, p. 55.

5. *Colorado County Chronicles*, pp. 296–98; Jeff Carroll, "Sheridan, Texas," *New Handbook of Texas*, vol. 5, p. 1019.

6. Ruby Ethel Tardiff, "One Woman's World," *El Campo Citizen*, Nov. 15, 1966.

7. *Pen and Sunlight Sketches of Greater Kansas City* (American Illustrating Company, 1911), p. 141.

8. *Colorado County Chronicles*, p. 291; Provident City plat maps, book 1, pages 1, 11, 13, Colorado County Clerk's Office, Columbus, Texas.

9. Provident City, Colorado County, marker file, Texas Historical Commission, Austin; *The Homefinder Monthly Magazine*, vol. 3, no. 6, Sept. 1, 1911, p. 5 (Kansas City: Provident Land Company).

10. *The Homefinder Monthly Magazine*, vol. 3, no. 6, Sept. 1, 1911, pp. 1–16.

11. *Colorado Citizen*, Columbus, Texas, May 19, 1911; and *Weimar Mercury*, Weimar, Texas, July 18, 1913 (quoting from the *Hallettsville New Era*.)

12. *Eagle Lake Headlight*, Eagle Lake, Texas, May 29, 1915.

13. Tardiff, "One Woman's World," *El Campo Citizen*, Nov. 15, 1966.

14. James G. Hopkins to Frances Rickard, June 16, 1986, in Provident City marker file.

CHAPTER 3. A PLAN FOR THE COMING SEASON

1. Keith J. Volanto, *Texas, Cotton, and the New Deal* (College Station: Texas A&M University Press, 2005), p. 4; Karen Gerhardt Britton, *Bale o' Cotton: The Mechanical Art of Cotton Ginning* (College Station: Texas A&M University Press, 1992), pp. 22–23. Additional sources for chapter 3 are the Texas Collection, Baylor University (see finding aids for oral history interviews related to cotton farming in Washington County); Thad Sitton and Dan K. Utley, *From Can See to Can't: Texas Cotton Farmers on the Southern Prairies* (Austin: University of Texas Press, 1997); and Raymond E. White, "The History of the Texas Cotton Ginning Industry, 1822–1957," Master of Arts thesis, the University of Texas, 1957.

2. Britton, *Bale o' Cotton*, p. 82; James Ricky Lewis, "Texas Cotton Gin House Architecture: A Survey and Case Study of the Cotton Gin as a Historic Building Type," Master of Architecture thesis, the University of Texas at Austin, 1977, p. 19.

3. James L. Hailey, "Burton, Texas," *New Handbook of Texas*, vol. 1, p. 862; Burton Farmers Gin, Washington County, marker file.

4. Britton, *Bale o' Cotton*, p. 85; Minutes, Burton Farmers Gin Association, vol. 1, pp. 2–5, Burton Cotton Gin Museum, Burton.

5. Minutes, vol. 1, pp. 2–5.

6. Britton, *Bale o' Cotton*, pp. 85–87; Lewis, "Texas Cotton Gin House Architecture," pp. 70–72.

7. Britton, *Bale o' Cotton*, p. 85.

8. Ora Nell Wehring Moseley, quoted in Dan K. Utley, "Voices of the Cotton Culture: An Oral History of the Burton Farmers Gin," *Heritage Magazine* (Texas Historical Foundation), winter 1993, p. 10.

9. Britton, *Bale o' Cotton*, p. 86.

10. The American Society of Mechanical Engineers (ASME), "Burton Farmers Gin: A National Historic Mechanical Engineering Landmark," commemorative program dated April 15, 1994, in the possession of Dan K. Utley.

11. Historical narrative, Burton Farmers Gin marker application, p. 4.

12. ASME program.

13. Eddie Wegner, quoted in Utley, "Voices of the Cotton Culture," pp. 8–9.

14. Grover Williams, quoted in ibid., p. 8.

CHAPTER 4. THE HEALER OF LOS OLMOS

1. Paul Rosenfield, "Don Pedrito: Truth or Legend?" *Dallas Times Herald Sunday Magazine*, Dec. 3, 1967, pp. 53–55. Additional sources for chapter 4 are Brooks County Historical Survey Committee, *The Faith Healer of Los Olmos: Biography of Don Pedrito Jaramillo* (Falfurrias: Brooks County Historical Survey Committee, 1972); John DePue, "In the Name of Don Pedrito, They Invoke Prayers," *Corpus Christi Caller-Times*, Aug. 17, 1969; Joe S. Graham, "The Role of the *Curandero* in the Folk Medicine System of West Texas," in *American Folk Medicine*, ed. Wayland D. Hand (Berkeley: University of California Press, 1976); and Lael Moore, "Ruth Dodson, South Texas Folklorist," *Texas Historian*, May 1971.

2. Los Olmos, Brooks County, marker file.

3. Rosenfield, "Don Pedrito," pp. 53–55.

4. Ruth Dodson, "Don Pedrito Jaramillo: The Curandero of Los Olmos," *The Healer of Los Olmos and Other Mexican Lore*, Publications of the Texas Folklore Society, no. 24, ed. Wilson M. Hudson (Dallas: Southern Methodist University Press, 1951), p. 10; Agnes G. Grimm, "Viola Ruth Dodson," *New Handbook of Texas*, vol. 2, p. 668.

5. Dodson, "Don Pedrito Jaramillo," pp. 9–10.

6. Ibid., p. 10.

7. Ibid., pp. 9–10; Grimm, "Viola Ruth Dodson," p. 668; Francis E. Abernethy, "James Frank Dobie," *New Handbook of Texas*, vol. 2, pp. 662–63.

8. Dodson, "Don Pedrito Jaramillo," pp. 12, 14.

9. Ibid., p. 11.

10. Don Pedro Jaramillo, Brooks County, marker file.

11. Letter from Florence Schuetz, chair, Brooks County Historical Survey Committee, to Bob Watson, Texas State Historical Survey Committee, July 9, 1971, Don Pedro Jaramillo marker file.

12. Letter from Rosine (Mrs. Will E.) Wilson to Bob Watson, Texas State Historical Survey Committee, July 23, 1971, Don Pedro Jaramillo marker file.

13. Letter from Herbert Gambrell to Bob Watson, Texas State Historical Survey Committee, July 14, 1971, Don Pedro Jaramillo marker file.

14. Faye Bartula, "Large Turnout Sees Don Pedro Historical Marker Dedication," *Alice Echo News*, Alice, Texas, Mar. 27, 1972; "Fire Ruins Don Pedro Gravesite," *Falfurrias Facts*, Falfurrias, Texas, Mar. 15, 1972.

CHAPTER 5. TOO MANY BARRELS OF OIL

1. Roger M. Olien, "Oil and Gas Industry," *New Handbook of Texas*, vol. 4, pp. 1119–28. Additional sources for chapter 5 are N. Ethie Eagleton, *On the Last Frontier: A History of Upton County, Texas* (El Paso: Texas Western Press, 1971); Diana Davids Olien and Roger M. Olien, *Oil in Texas: The Gusher Age, 1895–1945* (Austin: University of Texas Press, 2002); Carl Coke Rister, *Oil! Titan of the Southwest* (Norman: University of Oklahoma Press, 1949); Walter Rundell Jr., *Early Texas Oil* (College Station: Texas A&M University Press, 1977); Walter Rundell Jr., *Oil in West Texas and New Mexico: A Pictorial History of the Permian Basin* (College Station: Texas A&M University Press [for Permian Basin Petroleum Museum, Library and Hall of Fame, Midland], 1982); and Daniel Yergin, *The Prize: The Epic Quest for Oil, Money, and Power* (New York: Simon and Schuster, 1991).

2. James Collett, "McCamey, Texas," *New Handbook of Texas*, vol. 4, p. 370; *McCamey, Texas: Child of Black Gold* (McCamey: McCamey History Committee, 1975), p. 14; Deolece Parmelee, "Monahans and Wickett: These Towns Were Inevitable," *Water, Oil, Sand and Sky: A History of Ward County, Texas* (Monahans: Monahans Junior Chamber of Commerce, 1962), pp. 39–41; Glenn Justice, "Monahans, Texas," *New Handbook of Texas*, vol. 4, p. 791.

3. Samuel D. Myres, *The Permian Basin, Petroleum Empire of the Southwest: Era of Discovery, from the Beginning to the Depression* (El Paso: Permian Press, 1973), p. 391.

4. "Ruins of Storage Tank in Monahans Monument to West Texas' Lush Era," *Drill Bit* magazine, June 1955, pp. 9–11 (Odessa: Drill Bit Publishing Company); Prissy Neill, "McCamey's Million Barrel White Elephant," *Texas Historian* 37, no. 1 (Sept. 1976): 6–9; *McCamey, Texas: Child of Black Gold*, p. 16; Parmelee, "Monahans and Wickett," p. 41.

5. Myres, *Permian Basin*, p. 391.

6. "Ruins of Storage Tank in Monahans Monument to West Texas' Lush Era," *Drill Bit*, pp. 9–11; *McCamey, Texas*, p. 17; Neill, "McCamey's Million Barrel White Elephant," p. 7.

7. *McCamey, Texas*, p. 17; Neill, "McCamey's Million Barrel White Elephant," pp. 7–9.

8. "One Killed, 4 Injured," *Monahans News*, Aug. 2, 1935, p. 1.

9. "Ruins of Storage Tank in Monahans Monument to West Texas' Lush Era," *Drill Bit*, p. 10; Neill, "McCamey's Million Barrel White Elephant," p. 9.

10. U.S. Geological Service aerial photographs; Google Earth satellite images.

11. "The Tank's Not Working," *Monahans News*, Feb. 27, 1997.

12. "Prospects Are Good for Baseball in Monahans," *Monahans News,* Feb. 26, 1937; "No Tank for Baseball," *Monahans News,* Mar. 19, 1937; Linda Stephens, "Oil Tank Makes Great Dance Hall," *Monahans News,* Mar. 6, 1997.

13. Steve Patterson, "Wayne's (and Amalie's) World," *Monahans News,* Mar. 13, 1997; Steve Patterson, "Wayne's World II," *Monahans News,* Mar. 20, 1997; Jeanna Cuny, "Museum a Remnant of Oil Heyday," *Odessa American,* Apr. 1, 1999, pp. 1B–2B.

14. "Parmelee Joins Wayne in Dream for Tank," *Monahans News,* Mar. 27, 1997; Cuny, "Museum a Remnant of Oil Heyday," p. 2B.

15. Old Holman Hotel, Ward County, marker file; J. Conrad Dunagan, "Eugene Holman," *New Handbook of Texas,* vol. 3, pp. 671–72.

16. Elizabeth Heath, "Million Barrel Museum" brochure (Monahans: Specialty Printing Company, 1987).

17. Mike Wheeler, "Million Gallon [*sic*] Oil Tank Gets Recognition: West Texas Town Erects Historical Marker," *Odessa American,* Mar. 12, 1989.

18. Ibid.

CHAPTER 6. "WE SHALL COME REJOICING"

1. Elise Waerenskjold, quoted in Darwin Payne, "Early Norwegians in Northeast Texas," *Southwestern Historical Quarterly* 65, no. 2 (Oct. 1961): 199–200. Additional sources for chapter 6 are Dickson D. Bruce Jr., *And They All Sang Hallelujah: Plain-Folk Camp-Meeting Religion, 1800–1845* (Knoxville: University of Tennessee Press, 1974); Ellen Eslinger, *Citizens of Zion: The Social Origins of Camp Meeting Revivalism* (Knoxville: University of Tennessee Press, 1999); Charles A. Johnson, *The Frontier Camp Meeting: Religion's Harvest Time* (Dallas: Southern Methodist University Press, 1955); Lois E. Myers and Rebecca Sharpless, *Rock beneath the Sand: Country Churches in Texas* (College Station: Texas A&M University Press, 2003); and Joyce Gibson Roach, "Let Angels Prostrate Fall: Camp Meetings in Texas," an online article accessed through the Institute of Texan Cultures website: www.texancultures.utsa.edu.

2. Louis Fairchild, *The Lonesome Plains: Death and Revival on an American Frontier* (College Station: Texas A&M University Press, 2002), p. 137.

3. Ibid., p. 136.

4. William A. Owens, "Anglo-Texan Spirituals," *Southwestern Historical Quarterly* 86, no. 1 (July 1982): 31.

5. Ibid., p. 34.

6. Knowles Shaw, "Bringing in the Sheaves," *Baptist Hymnal,* ed. Walter Hines Sims (Nashville: Convention Press, 1956), p. 432.

7. Bluff Dale Tabernacle, Erath County, marker file; Cathey Yarbrough Sims, "Bluff Dale, Texas," *New Handbook of Texas,* vol. 1, pp. 610–11.

8. Lingleville Tabernacle, Erath County, marker file; "Lingleville, Texas," *New Handbook of Texas,* vol. 4, p. 206.

9. Morgan Mill Tabernacle, Erath County, marker file; William R. Hunt, "Morgan Mill, Texas," *New Handbook of Texas,* vol. 4, p. 839.

10. Pecan Cemetery and Pecan Cemetery Tabernacle, Erath County, marker file; William R. Hunt, "Purves, Texas," *New Handbook of Texas,* vol. 5, p. 373.

11. Will L. Thompson, "Softly and Tenderly," *Baptist Hymnal,* ed. Walter Hines Sims (Nashville: Convention Press, 1956), p. 236.

CHAPTER 7. THE MUSIC MAN OF SCHULENBURG

1. "A true 'Shorthorn Forever,'" *Schulenburg Sticker,* June 17, 2004; inscription, Carl T. Morene tombstone, Schulenburg City Cemetery; "A Sad Death," *Shiner Gazette,* Feb. 13, 1896; untitled article on death of A. F. Morene, *Shiner Gazette,* Oct. 24, 1900.

2. Archie W. Scott, oral history interview with Dan K. Utley, July 8, 2008. Tape in possession of the interviewer. Mr. Scott was a friend and co-worker of Carl Morene; "Carl T. Morene Prominent Schulenburg Citizen Dies," *Schulenburg Sticker,* Jan. 23, 1948; U.S. Census, 1930, Schulenburg, Texas.

3. Carl T. Morene: A Shorthorn Forever, Fayette County, marker file.

4. "A true 'Shorthorn Forever,'" *Schulenburg Sticker,* June 17, 2004.

5. "Baker Tells about Morene's Influence," *Schulenburg Sticker,* n.d., 2004. Part of a series of articles published by the newspaper in support of the Morene commemoration project; copy provided by Mildred Klesel Bohlmann.

6. "Koehler Tells of His Experiences in SHS Orchestra," *Schulenburg Sticker,* 2004. Moravia is located south of Schulenburg in northern Lavaca County.

7. "Testimonial about Carl T. Morene," *Schulenburg Sticker,* 2004; "A true 'Shorthorn Forever,'" *Schulenburg Sticker,* June 17, 2004.

8. "Morene Buys Harp for SHS Orchestra," *Schulenburg Sticker,* 2004.

9. "A true 'Shorthorn Forever,'" *Schulenburg Sticker,* June 17, 2004.

10. "Schulenburg Orchestra Wins Honors at Kingsville Music Meet," *Schulenburg Sticker,* Apr. 12, 1935; "High School Wins Honor," *Schulenburg Sticker,* May 3, 1935; "Schulenburg Orchestra Makes Successful Concert Tour," *Schulenburg Sticker,* May 10, 1935; "High School Orchestra to Give Free Concert Monday Night," *Schulenburg Sticker,* May 13, 1935; "School Orchestra Renders Splendid Program Monday," *Schulenburg Sticker,* May 27, 1938; "Schulenburg High School Orchestra to Broadcast Sunday," *Schulenburg Sticker,* Apr. 22, 1938.

11. "Carl Morene Writes School Song; Adopted," *Schulenburg Sticker,* Mar. 4, 1938.

12. Archie W. Scott oral history; "Scott Writes about Morene as Campaign Winds Down," *Schulenburg Sticker,* Dec. 23, 2004.

13. "Morene Started SHS Drum and Bugle Corps," *Schulenburg Sticker,* 2004.

14. "Anniversary of Morene's Death Commemorated," *Schulenburg Sticker,* Jan. 20, 2005; "A True 'Shorthorn Forever,'" *Schulenburg Sticker,* June 17, 2004; "Carl T. Morene Prominent Schulenburg Citizen Dies," *Schulenburg Sticker,* Jan. 23, 1948; "Stanzel Tells about Dec. 1947 Football Game," *Schulenburg Sticker,* Oct. 21, 2004.

15. "'Angels at Work in Schulenburg,'" *Schulenburg Sticker,* July 29, 2004; "Schulenburg's 'Music Man' Remembered with Marker," *Victoria Advocate,* Nov. 18, 2005; fundraising materials, Carl T. Morene marker file.

16. Personal recollection of Dan K. Utley; dedication ceremonies program, Carl T. Morene marker file.

CHAPTER 8. LINDBERGH LANDED HERE

1. Letter from Bob Watson, Texas Historical Commission, to Mrs. Frank D. Arthur, Leakey, Texas, July 16, 1975, and staff evaluation form, Charles A. Lindbergh in Texas, Real County, marker file. Additional sources for chapter 8 are Von Hardesty, *Lindbergh: Flight's Enigmatic Hero* (New York: Tenabi Books, 2002); Anne Morrow Lindbergh, *Bring Me a Unicorn: Diaries and Letters of Anne Morrow Lindbergh, 1922–1928* (New York: Harcourt Brace Jovanovich, 1972); Anne Morrow Lindbergh, *Flower and the Nettle: Diaries and Letters of Anne Morrow Lindbergh, 1936–1939* (New York: Harcourt Brace Jovanovich, 1976); Anne Morrow Lindbergh, *Hour of Gold, Hour of Lead: Diaries and Letters of Anne Morrow Lindbergh, 1929–1932* (New York: Harcourt Brace Jovanovich, 1973); Anne Morrow Lindbergh, *North to the Orient* (New York: Harcourt Brace and Company, 1935); Anne Morrow Lindbergh, *War Within and War Without: Diaries and Letters of Anne Morrow Lindbergh, 1939–1944* (New York: Harcourt, 1980).

2. A. Scott Berg, *Lindbergh* (New York: G. P. Putnam's Sons, 1998), pp. 70–73; Charles A. Lindbergh, *"We"* (New York: G. P. Putnam's Sons, 1927), pp. 63–83.

3. Lindbergh, *"We,"* pp. 41–44.

4. Ibid., p. 87.

5. Charles A. Lindbergh in Texas marker file.

6. Lindbergh, *"We,"* p. 98.

7. Charles A. Lindbergh, *The Spirit of St. Louis* (New York: Charles Scribner's Sons, 1955), pp. 412–13; *Uvalde Leader-News,* Mar. 7, 1924.

8. Lindbergh, *"We,"* pp. 99–103; Lindbergh, *The Spirit of St. Louis,* pp. 413–16; Jack Keasler, "Tracking the 'Lost' Barnstorming Pal of 'Slim' Lindbergh," *Smithsonian Magazine,* May 1976, pp. 59–65.

9. Lindbergh, *The Spirit of St. Louis,* pp. 418–19; Lindbergh, *"We,"* pp. 144–48; Berg, *Lindbergh,* p. 79.

10. Lindbergh, *The Spirit of St. Louis,* pp. 506–10.

11. *Abilene Reporter-News,* Sept. 26, 1927; Lindbergh in West Texas, Taylor County, marker file.

12. *New York Times,* May 8, 1933; Berg, *Lindbergh,* p. 284; Anne Morrow

Lindbergh, *Locked Rooms and Open Doors: Diaries and Letters of Anne Morrow Lindbergh, 1933–1935* (New York: Harcourt Brace Jovanovich, 1974), pp. 34–37.

13. *Spearman Press,* Sept. 26, 1934; Lindberghs Land at Spearman, Hansford County, marker file.

14. Berg, *Lindbergh,* pp. 554–60; *New York Times,* Feb. 8, 2001.

CHAPTER 9. PYRAMIDS ON THE ROAD TO MONTE NE

1. Jeannette P. Nichols, "Bryan's Benefactor: Coin Harvey and His World," *Ohio Historical Quarterly* 67, no. 4 (Oct. 1958): 299. Additional sources for chapter 9 are Monte Ne, National Register of Historic Places file, Arkansas Historic Preservation Program, Little Rock; Harry A. Stokes, "William Hope Harvey: Promoter and Agitator," master's thesis, Northern Illinois University, 1965; William H. "Coin" Harvey and Monte Ne Collection, Rogers Historical Museum, Rogers, Arkansas.

2. Nichols, "Bryan's Benefactor," pp. 299–310; Nan Marie Lawler, "The Ozark Trails Association," master's thesis, University of Arkansas, 1991, p. 8; Nancy A. Williams, ed., *Arkansas Biography: A Collection of Notable Lives* (Fayetteville: University of Arkansas Press, 2000), p. 133.

3. William Hope Harvey, *Coin's Financial School* (Chicago: Coin Publishing Company, 1894), vol. 1, no. 3, n.p.

4. Nichols, "Bryan's Benefactor," p. 323.

5. Lawler, "Ozark Trails Association," p. 9.

6. Ibid., pp. 1–7.

7. Clara B. Kennan, "The Ozark Trails and Arkansas's Pathfinder, Coin Harvey," *Arkansas Historical Quarterly* 7, no. 4 (winter 1948): 300.

8. Ibid., pp. 304–306.

9. Ibid., pp. 304–308; Lawler, "Ozark Trails Association," p. 25.

10. Lawler, "Ozark Trails Association," p. 36.

11. Ibid., pp. 38–40; Kennan, "Ozark Trails and Arkansas's Pathfinder," p. 308.

12. Lawler, "Ozark Trails Association," pp. 40–45.

13. Ibid., pp. 46–54.

14. Ibid., p. 52; Clara B. Kennan, "Coin Harvey's Pyramid," *Arkansas Historical Quarterly* 6, no. 2 (summer 1947): 134–38.

15. Lawler, "Ozark Trails Association," p. 62; "James E. Swepston Funeral Set Today," *Amarillo Daily News,* Feb. 10, 1949, p. 1; "J. E. Swepston Died Wednesday as Result of Heart Ailment," *Tulia Herald,* Feb. 10, 1949, n.p.; Nancy Dunn, Museum Manager, Artesia Historical Museum and Art Museum, email correspondence with Dan K. Utley, June 24, 2008.

16. Lawler, "Ozark Trails Association," pp. 66–70; Although the Ozark Trails Association survived minimally, at least as a legal entity, until 1926 or 1927, it effectively reached the end following the Duncan, Oklahoma, meeting in 1924.

17. Michael Wallis, *Route 66: The Mother Road* (New York: St. Martin's Press, 1990), pp. 5–9.

18. The Ozark Trail at Tampico, Hall County, and the Ozark Trails Association, Swisher County, THC marker files.

CHAPTER 10. A GATHERING IN THE WOODS

1. Robert S. Maxwell and Robert D. Baker, *Sawdust Empire: The Texas Lumber Industry, 1830–1940* (College Station: Texas A&M University Press, 1983), p. 3.

2. Ibid., p. 5.

3. Ibid., p. 170.

4. Char Miller, *Gifford Pinchot and the Making of Modern Environmentalism* (Washington: Island Press/Shearwater Books, 2001), p. 150.

5. Gifford Pinchot, *Breaking New Ground* (Seattle: University of Washington Press, 1947), p. 324.

6. Yale Forest School, *Biographical Record of the Graduates and Former Students of the Yale Forest School, with Introductory Papers on Yale in the Forestry Movement and the History of the Yale Forest School* (New Haven: Yale Forest School, 1913), pp. 10–13.

7. Ibid., pp. 13–25; Lou Ella Moseley, *Pioneer Days of Tyler County* (Fort Worth: Miran Publishers, 1975), pp. 193–94.

8. "The House of Thompson," reprint from *American Lumberman*, Sept. 26, 1908, pp. 68–76.

9. Yale Forest School, *Biographical Record*, pp. 214–39; German POWs in the East Texas Timber Industry, Angelina County, marker file.

10. Curt Meine, *Aldo Leopold: His Life and Work* (Madison: University of Wisconsin Press, 1988), pp. 83, 503.

11. Ibid., p. 82.

12. The Yale Forestry Summer Camp and Gifford Pinchot, Tyler County, marker file. The documentation Folweiler referenced for individuals present at the 1909 gathering at Mooney's Lake was *Southern Industrial and Lumber Review*, May 1909, p. 60. Unfortunately, the file did not contain a copy of the article, and efforts to locate the source proved unsuccessful.

13. Pinchot, *Breaking New Ground*, p. 351.

14. "Conservation of Timber Resources Is Discussed: Gifford Pinchot Meets with Lumbermen in East Texas," *Dallas Morning News*, May 12, 1909.

15. Maxwell and Baker, *Sawdust Empire*, 171–76.

CHAPTER 11. GHOSTS AT MITCHELL FLAT

1. Elton Miles, *Tales of the Big Bend* (College Station: Texas A&M University Press, 1976), pp. 150, 156–58; Thomas E. Alexander, *The Stars Were Big and Bright: The United States Army Air Forces and Texas During World War II,* vol. 2 (Austin: Eakin Press, 2001), p. 123; "Marfa's in the Dark about

Those Lights, but That Doesn't Stop the Party," *Fort Worth Star-Telegram,* Oct. 4, 1987, section 1, p. 32. Additional sources for chapter 11 are Lana Cunningham, "Marfa Man Tells of Encounter with Lights," *Midland Reporter-Telegram,* June 14, 1984, section C, pp. 1–2; Dennis Stacy, "Ghost Lights and Flying Saucers," Southwest Airlines *Spirit Magazine,* Oct. 1985, pp. 70–74 and 130–33; and David Stipp, "Marfa, Texas, Finds a Flickering Fame in Mystery Lights," *Wall Street Journal,* Mar. 21, 1984, n.p.

2. Miles, *Tales of the Big Bend,* pp. 150, 159–60, 165.

3. Ibid., p. 165.

4. Ibid., p. 165.

5. Bryan Woolley, "Bright Lights and the BBC," *Dallas Morning News,* Sept. 15, 1999, p. 8C.

6. Kirby Warnock, "Ghost Lights," Southwest Airlines *Spirit Magazine,* Apr. 1982, p. 73.

7. Historical Officer, Marfa Army Air Field, "Station History to 1 January, 1943," Dec. 28, 1943, p. 1 (hereafter noted as AAF Report).

8. AAF Report, pp. 1–4; William A. McWhorter, "Marfa Army Air Field," a paper delivered to the West Texas Historical Association, Abilene, Texas, Mar. 30, 2007.

9. AAF Report, pp. 10 and 63; Alexander, *Stars Were Big and Bright,* p. 125.

10. AAF Report, pp. 64–67.

11. Alexander, *Stars Were Big and Bright,* pp. 125 and 127; AAF Report, pp. 17–18.

12. Alexander, *Stars Were Big and Bright,* pp. 129–30.

13. Ibid., pp. 131–32. Some sources show Lanza's original name as Coccozza.

14. Warnock, "Ghost Lights," p. 70; Miles, *Tales of the Big Bend,* p. 154.

15. Miles, *Tales of the Big Bend,* p. 150.

16. Ibid., pp. 151–52, 153–54.

17. Alexander, *Stars Were Big and Bright,* pp. 132–35.

CHAPTER 12. CHASING THE NEXT FRONTIER

1. Richard J. Maturi and Mary Buckingham Maturi, *Will Rogers, Performer: An Illustrated Biography with a Filmography* (Jefferson, N.C.: McFarland, 1999), p. 81. Additional sources for chapter 12 are Ray Robinson, *American Original: A Life of Will Rogers* (New York: Oxford University Press, 1996) and Bryan B. Sterling and Frances N. Sterling, *Will Rogers and Wiley Post: Death at Barrow* (New York: M. Evans and Company, 1993).

2. Richard M. Ketchum, *Will Rogers: His Life and Times* (New York: American Heritage Publishing Company, 1973), pp. 9, 21–33.

3. Ibid., pp. 37–38, 41–43; Arthur Frank Wertheim and Barbara Bair, eds., *The Papers of Will Rogers: The Early Years,* vol. 1, November 1879–April 1904 (Norman: University of Oklahoma Press, 1996), p. 154.

4. Wertheim and Bair, *Papers of Will Rogers*, p. 79.

5. Ibid., p. 79, 132 fn. Sources differ on the exact name of the school Rogers attended. At the time he was there it was known as Kemper School, and in 1899 it became Kemper Military School.

6. Ibid., pp. 147, 160–61. The Johnson House became known as the Hotel Higgins not long after Rogers stayed there.

7. Ibid., p. 147; Ben Yagoda, *Will Rogers: A Biography* (New York: Alfred A. Knopf, 1993), p. 30.

8. Wertheim and Bair, *Papers of Will Rogers*, p. 147.

9. Ibid., pp. 182–83 and 193–94.

10. Ketchum, *Will Rogers*, pp. 75–78; Wertheim and Bair, *Papers of Will Rogers*, p. 323.

11. Yagoda, *Will Rogers*, pp. 57–60; Ketchum, *Will Rogers*, pp. 75–78.

12. Herschel C. Logan, *Buckskin and Lace: The Life of Texas Jack, Buckskin clad Scout, Indian Fighter, Plainsman, Cowboy, Hunter, Guide and Actor, and his wife. . Mlle. Morlacchi, Premiere Danseuse in Satin Slippers* (Harrisburg, Pa.: Stackpole Company, 1954), pp. 9–22.

13. Ibid., pp. 22–24, 31–32, and 65–108.

14. Ibid., pp. 186–203.

15. Wertheim and Bair, *Papers of Will Rogers*, 328–29.

16. Donald Day, ed., *The Autobiography of Will Rogers* (Boston: Houghton Mifflin Company, 1949), pp. 22–23.

17. Ketchum, *Will Rogers*, p. 83; Day, p. 23; Wertheim and Bair, *Papers of Will Rogers*, pp. 384–85.

18. Wertheim and Bair, *Papers of Will Rogers*, pp. 404–405.

19. Ibid., p. 560.

20. Maturi and Maturi, *Will Rogers, Performer*, p. 205.

21. Carol Morris Little, *A Comprehensive Guide to Outdoor Sculpture in Texas* (Austin: University of Texas Press, 1996), p. 320.

22. Script of a speech in April 1930 introducing Jimmy Rolph at dinner in San Francisco, California, Speech #006-A-94, Will Rogers Memorial Museums archives, Claremore, Oklahoma. Punctuation and capitalization are Will Rogers's own.

CHAPTER 13. ALIEN CITY IN A STRANGE LAND

1. C. Harvey Gardiner, *Pawns in a Triangle of Hate: The Peruvian Japanese and the United States* (Seattle: University of Washington Press, 1981), pp. 8–24; Arnold Krammer, *Undue Process: The Untold Story of America's German Alien Internees* (Lanham, Md.: Rowman and Littlefield Publishers, 1997), pp. 10–11; Emily Brosveen, "World War II Internment Camps," *New Handbook of Texas*, vol. 6, pp. 1082–83. Additional sources for chapter 13 are Michi Weglyn, *Years of Infamy: The Untold Story of America's Concentration Camps* (New York: Morrow Quill Paperbacks, 1976); *Japanese Americans in World War II: A National Historic Landmark Theme Study* (Washington,

D.C.: U.S. Department of the Interior, National Park Service, 2005); Karen Lea Riley, *Schools behind Barbed Wire: The Untold Story of Wartime Internment and the Children of Arrested Enemy Aliens* (Lanham, Md.: Rowman and Littlefield Publishers, 2002); and Robert H. Thonhoff, *Camp Kenedy, Texas* (Austin: Eakin Press, 2003).

2. Thomas K. Walls, *The Japanese Texans* (San Antonio: University of Texas Institute of Texan Cultures at San Antonio, 1996), pp. 178–83; Brosveen, "World War II Internment Camps"; Robert H. Thonhoff, "Kenedy Alien Detention Camp," *New Handbook of Texas*, vol. 3, pp. 1066–67; Gardiner, *Pawns in a Triangle of Hate*, pp. 29–34; Krammer, *Undue Process*, pp. 131–35; Jeffery Burton, Mary M. Farrell, Florence B. Lord, and Richard W. Lord, *Confinement and Ethnicity: An Overview of World War II Japanese American Relocation Sites* (Seattle: University of Washington Press, 2002), pp. 386–87.

3. Gardiner, *Pawns in a Triangle of Hate*, pp. 36–39; Walls, *Japanese Texans*, pp. 185–87; Brosveen, "World War II Internment Camps"; Krammer, *Undue Process*, pp. 101–105; Burton, et al., *Confinement and Ethnicity*, pp. 398–99.

4. "Dallas Firms Get Contracts for Two Camps," *Dallas Morning News*, June 28, 1940; "Dallas Firm Gets Migratory Camp Job," *Dallas Morning News*, June 30, 1940.

5. Krammer, *Undue Process*, p. 110; Gardiner, *Pawns in a Triangle of Hate*, pp. 59–61; Walls, *Japanese Texans*, pp. 187–89, 197; Brosveen, "World War II Internment Camps."

6. Brosveen, "World War II Internment Camps"; Krammer, *Undue Process*, p. 115.

7. Walls, *Japanese Texans*, pp. 196–97; Gardiner, *Pawns in a Triangle of Hate*, pp. 60–61; Brosveen, "World War II Internment Camps"; Krammer, *Undue Process*, pp. 110–11; Burton, et al., *Confinement and Ethnicity*, pp. 381–86.

8. Walls, *Japanese Texans*, pp. 195–96; Gardiner, *Pawns in a Triangle of Hate*, p. 60; Krammer, *Undue Process*, 111–13; "Alien Enemy Detention Facility, Crystal City, Texas," film, Immigration and Naturalization Service, U.S. Department of Justice, 1945, Washington, D.C.: National Archives, Record Group 85.4.2, Records of World War II Internment Camps (hereafter cited as INS film.)

9. Walls, *Japanese Texans*, pp. 189–93; Krammer, *Undue Process*, 114–15; Brosveen, "World War II Internment Camps"; INS film.

10. Brosveen, "World War II Internment Camps"; Krammer, *Undue Process*, p. 115; Walls, *Japanese Texans*, pp. 191–97; INS film.

11. INS film; Brosveen, "World War II Internment Camps"; Walls, *Japanese Texans*, p. 197.

12. Walls, *Japanese Texans*, 197–98; Krammer, *Undue Process*, 112–14; Brosveen, "World War II Internment Camps."

13. "Enemy Aliens Interned at Seagoville Slated for Other U.S. Camps,"

Dallas Morning News, May 9, 1945, section 2, p. 1; Brosveen, "World War II Internment Camps"; Walls, *Japanese Texans,* pp. 200–203; Gardiner, *Pawns in a Triangle of Hate,* p. 160.

14. Craig Gima, "In a Small Town in Texas . . ." *Honolulu Star-Bulletin,* Nov. 8, 2002.

15. Walls, *Japanese Texans,* pp. 209–10; Crystal City Family Internment Camp, World War II, Zavala County, marker file.

CHAPTER 14. FIGHTING EVERY STEP OF THE WAY

1. Jacquelyn Dowd Hall, *Revolt against Chivalry: Jessie Daniel Ames and the Women's Campaign against Lynching* (New York: Columbia University Press, 1979), p. 13. Additional sources for chapter 14 are Jessie Daniel Ames, papers, Texas State Archives and Library Commission, Austin, Texas; Lulu Daniel Ames, papers, Austin History Center, Austin, Texas; Henry E. Barber, "The Association of Southern Women for the Prevention of Lynching, 1930–1942," *Phylon* (Dec. 1973): 378–89; and Donald L. Grant, *The Anti-Lynching Movement, 1883–1932* (San Francisco: R and E Research Associates, 1975).

2. The Woman's Club of Georgetown, Williamson County, marker file.

3. Hall, *Revolt against Chivalry,* p. 18.

4. "Woman Suffrage," *New Handbook of Texas,* vol. 6, pp. 1039–41.

5. Hall, *Revolt against Chivalry,* p. 31.

6. *Williamson County Sun* (Georgetown, Texas), Feb. 24, 1972, section 2, p. 5.

7. Judith N. McArthur and Harold L. Smith, *Minnie Fisher Cunningham: A Suffragist's Life in Politics* (New York: Oxford University Press, 2003), p. 92.

8. Ibid., p. 92.

9. Wilma Dykeman and James Stokely, *Seeds of Change: The Life of Will Alexander* (Chicago: University of Chicago Press, 1962), p. 135.

10. Ibid., p. 144; Julius Wayne Dudley, "A History of the Association of Southern Women for the Prevention of Lynching, 1930–1942," Ph.D. dissertation, University of Cincinnati, 1979, p. 299.

11. Dudley, "History of the Association of Southern Women," p. 235.

12. Hall, Revolt Against Chivalry, pp. 260–66, 296.

CHAPTER 15. CROSSING THE GREAT DIVIDE

1. Steve Waksman, *The Electric Guitar and the Shaping of Musical Experience* (Cambridge: Harvard University Press, 1999), p. 34. Additional sources for chapter 15 are John Hammond, *John Hammond on Record: An Autobiography with Irving Townsend* (New York: Ridge Press, 1977); Dave Oliphant, *Texan Jazz* (Austin: University of Texas Press, 1996); and Maurice J. Summerfield, *The Jazz Guitar: Its Evolution, Players and Personalities since 1900* (Blaydon on Tyne, UK: Ashley Mark Publishing Company, 1998).

2. Waksman, *Electric Guitar*, p. 7.

3. Peter Broadbent, *Charlie Christian, Solo Flight: The Seminal Electric Guitarist* (Blaydon on Tyne, UK: Ashley Mark Publishing Company, 2003), pp. 13–17, 19; Wayne E. Goins and Craig R. McKinney, *A Biography of Charlie Christian, Jazz Guitar's King of Swing* (Lewiston, NY: The Edwin Mellen Press, 2005), pp. 1–5.

4. Goins and McKinney, *Biography of Charlie Christian*, pp. 11 and 52.

5. Broadbent, *Charlie Christian*, pp. 31–38.

6. Goins and McKinney, *Biography of Charlie Christian*, pp. 28–31.

7. Ibid., p. 20.

8. Ibid., pp. 17–23 and 38–39.

9. Waksman, *Electric Guitar*, p. 20.

10. Goins and McKinney, *Biography of Charlie Christian*, p. 74; Bradley Shreve, "Alphonso E. Trent," *Handbook of Texas Online*, http://www.tshaonline.org/handbook/online/articles/TT/ftrsh.html (accessed May 11, 2008).

11. James Lincoln Collier, *Benny Goodman and the Swing Era* (New York: Oxford University Press, 1989), p. 19.

12. Ibid., p. 25.

13. Ibid., p. 215.

14. Ross Firestone, *Swing, Swing, Swing: The Life and Times of Benny Goodman* (New York: W.W. Norton, 1993), pp. 77–81.

15. Goins and McKinney, *Biography of Charlie Christian*, pp. 176–77.

16. Ibid., p. 175; Rudi Blesh, *Combo: U.S.A.: Eight Lives in Jazz* (Philadelphia: Chilton Book Company, 1971), p. 175.

17. Goins and McKinney, *Biography of Charlie Christian*, pp. 176–77.

18. James Sallis, *The Guitar Players: One Instrument and Its Masters in American Music* (New York: William Morrow, 1982), p. 102; Firestone, *Swing, Swing, Swing*, p. 267.

19. Waksman, *Electric Guitar*, p. 34; Sallis, *Guitar Players*, pp. 114–15.

20. Goins and McKinney, *Biography of Charlie Christian*, pp. 328–31.

21. Ibid., pp. 329–30.

22. Telephone conversation with Tom Scott, Fannin County Museum of History, Bonham, Texas, May 9, 2008; Goins and McKinney, *Biography of Charlie Christian*, p. 346.

23. Collier, *Benny Goodman*, p. 289.

CHAPTER 16. HARVEST OF THE DEVOTED HEART

1. Lois Smith Douglas, *Through Heaven's Back Door: A Biography of A. Joseph Armstrong* (Waco: Baylor University Press, 1951), p. 13. Additional sources for chapter 16 are Margaret Royalty Edwards, "A. Joseph Armstrong," *New Handbook of Texas*, vol. 1, p. 242; Betty A. Coley, "Mary Maxwell Armstrong," *New Handbook of Texas*, vol. 1, p. 244; Jack W. Herring, "Armstrong Browning Library," *New Handbook of Texas*, vol. 1, p. 245;

and Avery T. Sharp and Larry E. Fink, *The Armstrong Browning Library* (Waco: Baylor University/Armstrong Browning Library, 2007).

2. Cynthia A. Burgess, "The Armstrong Browning Library Observes Its Golden Jubilee by Honouring the Past and Embracing the Future," *Antiquarian Book Monthly,* Oct. 2001, p. 17.

3. Ibid., pp. 17–18; Douglas, *Through Heaven's Back Door,* pp. 77–83; Dr. Andrew Joseph Armstrong and Mary Maxwell Armstrong, McLennan County, marker file.

4. Douglas, *Through Heaven's Back Door,* p. 181; Burgess, "Armstrong Browning Library," p. 18; "Professor with a Passion," *Time* magazine, May 17, 1948.

5. Douglas, *Through Heaven's Back Door,* pp. 181 and 232.

6. Ibid., p. 135.

7. *The Times* (London), Mar. 31, 1925, Texas supplement, p. 38.

8. Burgess, "Armstrong Browning Library," p. 20.

9. Douglas, *Through Heaven's Back Door,* p. 4.

10. Burgess, "Armstrong Browning Library," pp. 20–21; Armstrong marker file; Armstrong Browning Library website, Baylor University, http://www.browninglibrary.org/ (accessed Aug. 30, 2008).

CHAPTER 17. QUEEN OF THE AIR

1. Doris L. Rich, *Queen Bess: Daredevil Aviator* (Washington: Smithsonian Institution Press, 1993), pp. 3–8; 1900 U.S. Census, Ellis County, Texas, Enumeration District 12, page 5. Additional sources for chapter 17 are Von Hardesty, *Black Wings: Courageous Stories of African Americans in Aviation and Space History* (Washington: Smithsonian Institution, 2008); Elizabeth Amelia Hadley Freydberg, *Bessie Coleman: The Brownskin Lady Bird* (New York: Garland Publishing, Studies in African American History and Culture Series, 1994); Ann Hodgman and Rudy Djabbaroff, *Skystars: The History of Women in Aviation* (New York: Atheneum Press, 1981); and Ruthe Winegarten, *Black Texas Women: 150 Years of Trial and Triumph* (Austin: University of Texas Press, 1995).

2. Rich, *Queen Bess,* p. 9.

3. Wallace Best, "Chicago Defender," *The Electronic Encyclopedia of Chicago* (Chicago: Chicago Historical Society, 2005); James Grossman, "Great Migration," *The Electronic Encyclopedia of Chicago* (Chicago: Chicago Historical Society, 2005); Rich, *Queen Bess,* pp. 13–14.

4. Rich, *Queen Bess,* pp. 26–27.

5. "Aviatrix Must Sign Away Life to Learn Trade," *Chicago Defender,* Oct. 8, 1921, p. 2.

6. "Bessie to Fly Over Gotham; Queen Bess to Ride Air Next Sunday," *Chicago Defender,* Aug. 26, 1922, p. 1; Rich, *Queen Bess,* pp. 48–49.

7. J. Blaine Poindexter, "Bessie Coleman Makes Initial Aerial Flight; Chicagoans See Girl Who Flew over Berlin in Series of Stunts," *Chicago Defender,* Oct. 21, 1922, p. 3.

8. Rich, *Queen Bess,* p. 57.

9. Ralph Eliot, "Bessie Coleman Says Good Will Come from Hurt, Wants World to Know She Is Going to Fly Again; Says Escape Proves It's Tame," *Chicago Defender,* Mar. 10, 1923, p. 3; Rich, *Queen Bess,* pp. 68–71.

10. *Houston Post-Dispatch,* May 7, 1925, p. 4, quoted in Rich, *Queen Bess,* p. 85.

11. Rich, *Queen Bess,* pp. 88–89; "Aviatrix Performs for Texas Crowds; Miss Bessie Coleman Main Attraction at Houston Flying Circus," *Chicago Defender,* July 25, 1925, p. 1; "Governor 'Ma' Ferguson Greets Bessie Coleman," *Chicago Defender,* Aug. 15, 1925, p. 1.

12. Rich, *Queen Bess,* pp. 94–95.

13. Ibid., pp. 109–11 and 118–19; E. B. Jourdain Jr., "Bessie Coleman, Aviatrix, Killed," *Chicago Defender,* May 8, 1926, p. 1; "Dallas Man Is Killed in Plane," *Dallas Morning News,* May 1, 1926, p. 1.

14. Evangeline Roberts, "Pioneer Aviatrix Starts Last Journey; Chicago Pays Parting Tribute to 'Brave Bessie' Coleman," *Chicago Defender,* May 15, 1926.

15. Roni Morales, "Bessie Coleman," *New Handbook of Texas,* vol. 2, pp. 199–200.

CHAPTER 18. "HELLOOO, BABY!"

1. Tim Knight, *Chantilly Lace: The Life and Times of J. P. Richardson* (Port Arthur: Port Arthur Historical Society, 1989), pp. 1–2; Larry Lehmer, *The Day the Music Died: The Last Tour of Buddy Holly, the "Big Bopper," and Ritchie Valens* (New York: Schimer Books, 1997), p. 26–27. Additional sources for chapter 18 are John Goldrosen and John Beecher, *Remembering Buddy: The Definitive Biography of Buddy Holly* (New York: Penguin Books, 1986); Rick Koster, *Texas Music* (New York: St. Martin's Press, 1998); Ron Franscell, "'They Didn't Bury the Big Bopper' Says His Son," *Beaumont Enterprise,* Mar. 11, 2007; "Autopsy of 'Big Bopper' to Address Rumors about 1959 Plane Crash," *Washington Post*/Associated Press, Jan. 18, 2007.

2. Lehmer, *Day the Music Died,* p. 27.

3. Knight, *Chantilly Lace,* p. 4; Archie P. McDonald, oral interview, Feb. 15, 2007, notes only, in possession of Cynthia J. Beeman.

4. McDonald interview.

5. Lehmer, *Day the Music Died,* p. 30; Ron Franscell, "Lost Songs of the Big Bopper," *Beaumont Enterprise,* Feb. 2, 2002.

6. Lehmer, *Day the Music Died,* p. 34.

7. Joe Botsford, *Milwaukee Sentinel,* Jan. 24, 1959, quoted in ibid., pp. 62–63.

8. Lehmer, *Day the Music Died,* pp. 89–90, 92–93.

9. Ibid., pp. 96–97.

10. Ibid., pp. 103–105.

11. Ibid., pp. 108–10; Knight, *Chantilly Lace,* pp. 41–42.

12. Ron Franscell, "What Killed the Big Bopper? Autopsy 48 Years Later Reveals New Clues," *Beaumont Enterprise*, Mar. 8, 2007.

CHAPTER 19. THE THEATRE OF TOMORROW TODAY

1. Ida Belle Hicks, "Margo Jones Finds Her Cherished Texas Background Key to a Career," *Fort Worth Star-Telegram*, Dec. 1, 1946. Additional sources for chapter 19 are Kay Cattarulla, *Sweet Tornado: Margo Jones and the American Theater*, a documentary film by North Texas Public Broadcasting, Inc., Dallas, 2006, and Margo Jones Collection, Texas/Dallas History and Archives, Dallas Public Library.

2. Margo Jones, *Theatre-in-the-Round* (New York: Rinehart and Company, 1951), pp. 40–42.

3. Helen Sheehy, *Margo: The Life and Theatre of Margo Jones* (Dallas: Southern Methodist University Press, 1989), p. 27.

4. Ibid., pp. 29–30; Reginald Gibbons, "Charles William Goyen," *New Handbook of Texas*, vol. 3, pp. 268–69.

5. William Goyen, "Margo," in *Goyen: Autobiographical Essays, Notebooks, Evocations, Interviews*, ed. Reginald Gibbons (Austin: University of Texas Press, 2007), p. 25.

6. Sheehy, *Margo*, p. 47.

7. "New Star in the Theatrical Heaven: Margo Jones, Famed American Director, at University on Rockefeller Fellowship," *Austin Tribune*, Oct. 11, 1942.

8. Sheehy, *Margo*, p. 48.

9. Ibid., p. 59.

10. Ibid., p. 65.

11. "Theater '47 to Open June 1 with Theater-in-the-Round," *Dallas Morning News*, Mar. 21, 1947, section 1, p. 8; Jones, *Theatre-in-the-Round*, p. 60; Sheehy, *Margo*, pp. 128–29.

12. Murray Schumach, "A Texas Tornado Hits Broadway: Margo Jones, Director of 'Summer and Smoke,' Makes the Stage Her World," *New York Times*, Oct. 17, 1948.

13. Jones, *Theatre-in-the-Round*, pp. 3–4.

14. Sheehy, *Margo*, pp. 252–55.

15. Ibid., p. 261.

16. Goyen, "Margo," pp. 24–25; Sheehy, *Margo*, pp. 261–62.

17. "Point of View—Margo," *Dallas Morning News*, July 29, 1955; "William Goyen: For Margo Jones," *Dallas Morning News*, July 31, 1955; "Margo Jones' Death Brings Poison Warning," *Dallas Morning News*, Sept. 19, 1955.

18. Lewis Funke, "News of the Rialto, Annual Margo Jones Award is Set Up," *New York Times*, Mar. 12, 1961; Jones, *Theatre-in-the-Round*, pp. 92–93.

Index

Page numbers in *italics* denote photographs.

READY-TO-USE
ACTIVITIES AND MATERIALS ON
PLAINS
INDIANS

A Complete Sourcebook
for Teachers K-8